# Practical Reading

# Practical Reading:

# Processing Information

## Jossie A. Moore
Southwest Tennessee Community College

Upper Saddle River, NJ 07458

**Library of Congress Cataloging-in-Publication Data**

Moore, Jossie A.
   Practical reading : processing information / Jossie A. Moore.
     p. cm.
   Includes index.
   ISBN 0-13-026246-3
    1. Reading (Higher education) 2. Reading comprehension. 3. College readers.  I. Title.

   LB2395.3 .M66 2002
   428.4'071'1—dc21

                                   2002031269

VP/Editor in Chief: Leah Jewell
Sr. Acquisitions Editor: Craig Campanella
Editorial Assistant: Joan Polk
Prepress and Manufacturing Buyer: Ben Smith
Cover Design: Kiwi Design
Cover Art: Sara Hollander
Director, Image Resource Center: Melinda Reo
Manager, Rights & Permissions: Zina Arabia
Interior Image Specialist: Beth Boyd-Brenzel
Cover Image Specialist: Karen Sanatar
Production/Formatting/Art Manager: Guy Ruggiero
Electronic Art Creation: Mirella Signoretto and Interactive Composition Corp.
Marketing Manager: Rachel Falk
Marketing Assistant: Anne Marie Fritzky
Copyeditor: Kathryn Graehl

Credits appear on pp. 289–291, which constitute a continuation of the copyright page.

This book was set in 10/12 Palatino by Interactive Composition Corp. and was printed and bound by Hamilton Printing Company. The cover was printed by Coral Graphics.

 © 2003 by Pearson Education, Inc.
Upper Saddle River, New Jersey 07458

Printed in the United States of America

10 9 8 7 6 5 4 3 2 1

ISBN 0-13-026246-3

Pearson Education LTD., London
Pearson Education Australia PTY, Limited, Sydney
Pearson Education Singapore, Pte. Ltd
Pearson Education North Asia Ltd, Hong Kong
Pearson Education Canada, Ltd., Toronto
Pearson Educación de Mexico, S. A. de C. V.
Pearson Education–Japan, Tokyo
Pearson Education Malaysia, Pte. Ltd
Pearson Education, Upper Saddle River, New Jersey

To my sons,
Juan and Jerry

# CONTENTS

# PREFACE

*Practical Reading* is more than simply a collection of readings for the adult student in a reading course; it focuses on reading as a process that students can learn by developing and applying active reading strategies and critical thinking skills. Its primary goal is to teach students the major reading skills along with practical strategies they can use to help them gain confidence in their reading ability and become informed, lifelong learners.

This text uses an experiential, holistic learning method that emphasizes doing as well as reading through information processing. By receiving extensive practice in combining basic reading concepts with information-processing techniques, the learner acquires mastery of the essential reading skills in a natural, meaningful context. This active participation in the learning process enables students to become better, more proficient readers who not only can understand what they read but also can analyze it, store it, remember it, and retrieve it as needed. This is what information processing is all about—being able to read and turn what is read into something meaningful to the reader.

*Practical Reading* begins with a pretest that allows students to identify their strengths and weaknesses prior to beginning their studies. They will know which specific areas will require most of their time and effort. The posttest at the end of the text also allows them to assess their performance after the completion of their studies. The text is divided into two major parts.

## PART I: PROCESSING THE WRITTEN WORD

This four-chapter section contains not only a description with examples of information-processing techniques, reading aids, and vocabulary development strategies but also an overview of the basic reading skills. Also included are reading concepts that are defined and illustrated in an easy-to-understand and memorable step-by-step format. Moreover, short practice exercises are available to check understanding and the need for follow-up work. In addition, a mastery test closes out each chapter. Finally, this handy reference guide is coded for ease of use. Students may refer to it often until they master the concepts.

## PART II: APPLIED READING

Part II begins with an introduction that includes notes on listening and reading rate flexibility. Fifteen reading selections are included: ten general-interest articles, four subject area excerpts, and one novel excerpt. Each selection, which may be from 200 to 1,360 words in length, is followed by postreading activities and practice exercises. These practice exercises encourage information processing along with comprehension and vocabulary development.

### General-Interest Selections

The general-interest selections are drawn from a variety of current magazine and newspaper publications. Related practice exercises accompanying the readings reinforce skills presented in Part I and provide a structure for students to check their comprehension and to think critically about the selection. These exercises consist of seven parts: prereading, postreading, comprehension, reflecting, collaborating, Web Watch, and vocabulary review.

- **Prereading** is a warm-up activity that helps students establish a context for reading, assess prior knowledge of the subject, and make predictions about the selection contents. Included in this section are the selection title, the first paragraph, the vocabulary review, and, sometimes, the major headings.
- **Postreading,** a two-part activity that follows the selection, allows the student to tie loose ends together and assess understanding of the reading.
- **Comprehension exercises** give students an opportunity to further assess their understanding of the selection. This activity usually includes twenty items, mostly multiple-choice, divided into three major categories: Skimming for Facts, Relating the Facts, and Connecting with the Author.

  In **Skimming for Facts,** the learner practices literal reading skills by searching for directly stated answers to five multiple-choice questions.

  In **Relating the Facts,** the reader looks for relationships among ideas and observes the organization of these ideas in the writing. Activities include those related to main ideas, relationships, signal words, major and minor details, sequencing, and mapping. Of the items presented in this section, most are multiple-choice questions, but many involve application.

In **Connecting with the Author,** students practice their critical thinking skills by focusing on how the author thinks and uses special
writing techniques to present ideas. In this section, students function on a higher level: interpretation and evaluation. Activities include making inferences, drawing conclusions, predicting outcomes, and analyzing the author's use of language. This section
consists of ten multiple-choice questions that are often arranged
like this:

| QUESTION(S) | READING CONCEPT(S) |
|---|---|
| 1–4 | Inferences |
| 5 | Conclusions, generalizations, or predictions |
| 6–7 | Style, figurative language, or propaganda |
| 8 | Fact and opinion |
| 9 | Mood or tone |
| 10 | Audience or purpose |

- **Reflecting** is an independent practical application that allows learners
  to think deeply about what they have read and relate it to what they
  already know. Students make real-life connections by thinking and
  writing about ideas from the selection and attempting to apply these
  ideas in other work, school, or life situations. Through reflecting,
  students verify that learning has taken place and that it has merit
  in situations other than those presented in the reading.
- **Collaborating** provides opportunities for productive discussion in
  small-group activities that involve communication, problem solving,
  and teamwork. A finished product is the end result of collaboration,
  an activity that prepares students for the world of work.
- **Web Watch** consists of an Internet activity that provides further readings on a related topic, additional practice on a skill or technique, or
  just informative fun and games.
- **Vocabulary** includes difficult words highlighted in each selection.
  Syllabic divisions and brief definitions are provided for each word
  to make the readings more meaningful. Vocabulary practice consists
  mainly of solving crossword puzzles. The net effect is increased
  lifelong learning and growth in vocabulary development and
  word usage.

## SUBJECT AREA SELECTIONS

These reading selections consist of five subject area excerpts from four
textbooks and one novel. Subject areas include those most likely encoun-
tered in college studies, such as psychology, biology, sociology, literature,
and computer technology. Except for vocabulary, information-processing,

and review questions, most features for these excerpts are the same as those in the general-interest selections. The differences are described briefly below.

- **Vocabulary** contains mostly technical jargon or specialized terms. Practice remains in the crossword puzzle format.
- **Information processing** includes highlighting, annotating, mapping, and summarizing information. These activities help prepare students for meaningful reading in the content areas.
- **Review questions** make up the comprehension exercises because of their similarity to those found in most subject area textbooks. Question types vary from multiple-choice to open-ended items and allow practice in critical thinking and problem solving.

## ACKNOWLEDGMENTS

I am deeply grateful to many people who have contributed ideas, time, and effort in the preparation of this text. I give heartfelt thanks and appreciation to the following people for their outstanding contributions:

Lynn Q. Troyka, The City University of New York, and Joseph W. Thweatt, Southwest Tennessee Community College, for giving me the opportunity to energize my creativity during the preparation of the instructor's resource manual for their textbook *Structured Reading, Fifth Edition.*

Anonymous and known reviewers from around the country for their thoughtful ideas and advice: Elizabeth Semtner Edwards, Rose State College; Sue McGowan Hightower, Tallahassee Community College; Jessica Carroll, Miami-Dade Community College; Karen J. Patty-Graham, Southern Illinois University, Edwardsville; Donald Brotherton, DeVry Institute of Technology; Ted Walkup, Clayton State University.

My reading colleagues and associates, including Dr. Ada Shotwell, and Dr. Lana Smith, The University of Memphis, for their continuing support.

The staff at Prentice Hall: Craig Campanella, senior acquisitions editor; Karen Schulz, assistant editor; Joan Polk, editorial assistant, and everyone else involved in the design and production of this book, for their leadership, dedication to excellence, patience, and encouragement.

And, last, I thank my husband Jimmy, my mother Mrs. America, and other family members who are always here for me.

# PRETEST

PREREADING EXERCISE

Study the title, the Vocabulary Review, and the first paragraph of the selection. Then write a sentence expressing what you believe this selection is about.

_____

_____

## Top-Drawer Desk Cleaning

_Mukul Pandya_

---

**VOCABULARY REVIEW**
**clutter (clut-ter):** things scattered in disorder
**cold call (cold call):** unplanned, random sales call
**dramatically (dra-mat-i-cal-ly):** vividly, strikingly
**efficiency (ef-fi-cien-cy):** capable of producing desired results
**expandable (ex-pand-a-ble):** able to be stretched out
**looms (looms):** comes into sight in large form
**modest (mod-est):** reasonable, not extreme
**mounds (mounds):** large heaps
**referrals (re-fer-rals):** recommendations made by others
**solicited (so-li-cit-ed):** enticed or lured
**stints (stints):** periods of work
**suburban (su-bur-ban):** near the outskirts of a city
**viable (vi-a-ble):** workable

---

The desk **looms** in the corner office, a **viable** symbol of corporate    1
power. It is, however, so buried under **mounds** of paper that you can
hardly see the Very Important Person who sits behind it. There is a stack
of printouts, memos, and reminders. Somewhere beneath it all, there's a
diary. Somewhere else, there's a telephone. In short, this is a desk that's
ready for the services of Jeffrey Mayer, power desk cleaner to corporate
America.

Mayer, who calls himself an executive **efficiency** expert, cleans off    2
the desks of CEO's too busy or disorganized to do it themselves. And for
Mayer, neatness not only counts, it adds up. He gets $250 an hour.

For that price, the executives get more than just a clean desk. If they    3
pay attention to Mayer's teachings, they also learn how to keep it clean.
Wherever he goes on an office desk cleaning, he carries a stack of folders
and **expandable** file pockets—the better to hold all that **clutter.** "People

think keeping piles of papers out on their desks will serve as reminders of what they need to do," says Mayer, 39. "But piles only bury things." His solution is simple: Make a list instead. "Then put all the papers in folders by category and put them away," he advises.

4      Mayer, who owns a consulting company in Chicago, came to his life's career early, growing up in **suburban** Highland Park, Illinois. He was the son of an insurance executive and a housewife. "My mother told me, 'If you get your work done, you can go out to play,'" he remembers.

5      "I liked orderliness," says Mayer. In 1985, after **stints** running the family insurance business and as an estate planner, Mayer decided to bring his gift for orderliness to the business world. His first client, **solicited** by a **cold call** on the telephone, was a stockbroker. At the time, Mayer charged a mere $300 for six hours.

6      From that **modest** beginning, Mayer's business grew **dramatically.** Now he sees as many as 100 clients a year at $1000 a session. If the fee seems high, well, Mayer has an explanation: "My clients are able to make more money with less effort after I've worked with them."

7      Mayer still gets clients from cold calls, but most now come from **referrals.** Some people even give a session with the dean of the desk cleaners as a birthday gift for the CEO in their lives.

8      Neat, huh?

*(400 words)*

## POSTREADING EXERCISE

Now that you have read the selection, revise the sentence you wrote in the prereading exercise.

_____

_____

_____

## COMPREHENSION EXERCISE
*Circle the letter of the best answer.*

### SKIMMING FOR FACTS

1. What is Mayer's business title?
    a. executive office cleaner
    b. executive efficiency expert
    c. executive custodian
    d. executive insurance broker

2. Before starting his business, Mayer worked in the family's
    a. insurance business.
    b. garage.

    c. department store.
    d. stock market.

3. Mayer now bills his clients at
    a. $50 per hour.
    b. $600 per hour.
    c. $300 per six hours.
    d. $1000 per session.

4. Although Mayer's first customer came from a _____,
    most of his business today comes from _____.
    a. referral, friends
    b. newspaper ad, television commercials
    c. cold call, referrals
    d. radio ad, television commercials

5. Many executives do not have a neat desk because they are
    a. too lazy or too busy.
    b. disorganized or busy.
    c. afraid of missing something.
    d. satisfied with clutter.

## RELATING THE FACTS

6. Which sentence best represents the main idea of paragraph 3?
    a. Executives get more than just a clean desk; they also learn how to keep it that way.
    b. His solution is simple: Make a list instead.
    c. File papers in folders and put them away.
    d. Executives get more than what they want.

7. What is the primary pattern of development for paragraph 3?
    a. cause-effect
    b. classification
    c. example
    d. comparison-contrast

8. The last sentence in paragraph 5 is a
    a. major detail.
    b. minor detail.
    c. topic sentence.
    d. key idea.

9. The last sentence in paragraph 6 is a(n)
    a. major detail.
    b. minor detail.
    c. example.
    d. key idea.

10. Which type of relationship does the first sentence in paragraph 7 signal?
    a. contrast
    b. comparison
    c. cause-effect
    d. process

CONNECTING WITH THE AUTHOR

11. In paragraph 7, the author suggests that
    a. Mayer's clients have no self-respect.
    b. Mayer's business is open only six months a year.
    c. Mayer's clients are satisfied customers.
    d. Mayer's business is for men only.

12. You can infer from paragraph 1 that
    a. communication is an important part of an executive's job.
    b. desks say nothing about the person behind them.
    c. demanding people use desks to hide from the public.
    d. Jeff Mayer is clumsy.

13. Which of the following can you infer from paragraph 3?
    a. Mayer is married with children.
    b. Mayer sees his work as boring.
    c. Mayer appears to be a student.
    d. Mayer has good alphabetizing skills.

14. In paragraph 4, it appears that
    a. Mayer's brother is brave, too.
    b. Mayer's family is too religious.
    c. Mayer's mother is too strict.
    d. Mayer's father earns a good living.

15. In paragraph 5, you can conclude all of the following *except*
    a. Mayer's starting price was too low.
    b. Mayer wanted more than the family business.
    c. Mayer's sales experience helped him start his own business.
    d. Mayer was jealous of his father's business.

16. What valid generalization can you make from paragraph 5?
    a. An interest may lead to success in business.
    b. Children who work in family businesses earn good pay.
    c. Parents ought to push children into family businesses.
    d. Unhappy workers should start their own businesses.

17. In paragraph 1, the author's focus on the desk
    a. paints a clear picture of clutter.
    b. describes the situation Mayer faces on his jobs.
    c. shows its importance in the corporate setting.
    d. all of the above.

18. Which of the following sentences taken from the selection is an opinion?
    a. "There is a stack of printouts, memos, and reminders."
    b. "His solution is simple: Make a list instead."
    c. "I liked orderliness."
    d. "He was the son of an insurance executive and a housewife."

19. The author's use of the pun (a play on words) in the last two words ("Neat, huh?") of the selection
    a. expresses happiness.
    b. captures movement.
    c. shows doubt.
    d. sends a double meaning.

20. The author's purpose in writing this selection is to
    a. inspire.
    b. persuade.
    c. entertain.
    d. frighten.

## VOCABULARY EXERCISE

*Complete the following sentences with words from the list.*

| | | | | |
|---|---|---|---|---|
| clutter | cold call | dramatically | efficiency | expandable |
| looms | modest | mounds | referrals | |
| solicited | stints | suburban | viable | |

21. The instructor kept _____ of papers to be graded stacked on her desk.

22. Building more new houses could be a(n) _____ solution to the problem of homelessness in America.

23. Sam did several _____ in the military and in college before finally settling down on the farm.

24. My doctor thinks he can do everything; he refuses to make _____ to other medical experts.

25. The clerk _____ donations for her favorite charity from everyone who entered the store.

26. All eyes were on Sheila as she _____ dumped the tray on the floor and walked quickly out the door.

27. It is often impossible to find a bus going to most _____ areas after dark.

28. Any person who is highly skilled in his or her craft may be known as a(n) _____ expert.

29. Although Sue is rich, she is _____ when it comes to spending money for clothes.

30. I keep all of my important papers in _____ file folders.

31. The teacher's red ink on a graded paragraph _____ out at the student who makes many errors.

32. By Friday, there is just too much _____ on my desk.

33. Many small businesses depend on the _____ to get clients.

Name: _____ , Course/Section: _____ , Date: _____

# PRETEST SCORE AND COMPREHENSION ERROR REVIEW CHART

## PRETEST SCORE
*Record the number of correct answers and perform operations in the box.*

| | |
|---|---|
| Central Idea _____ (out of 1) $\times$ 9 = _____ | |
| Vocabulary _____ (out of 13) $\times$ 7 = _____ | |
| Comprehension _____ (out of 20) $\times$ 5 = _____ | |
| Total | = _____ divided by 2 = _____ |

**Pretest score:** _____ **(out of 100)**

## COMPREHENSION ERROR REVIEW
*To identify strengths and weaknesses, circle the number of any incorrect answer in numbers 1–20 of the pretest.*

*The numbers circled indicate your weaknesses. Read across the line to identify chapter sections and topics that will require most of your attention.*

| Item # | Chapter Section(s) and Reading Skill |
|---|---|
| | ***Skimming for Facts*** |
| 1 | (3b.2) Major Detail (3b.3) Minor Detail |
| 2 | (3b.2) Major Detail (3b.3) Minor Detail |
| 3 | (3b.2) Major Detail (3b.3) Minor Detail |
| 4 | (3b.2) Major Detail (3b.3) Minor Detail |
| 5 | (3b.2) Major Detail (3b.3) Minor Detail |
| | ***Relating the Facts*** |
| 6 | (3a.4) Stated Main Idea (3a.5) Implied Main Idea |
| 7 | (3b.1) Signal Words (3b.4) Paragraph Patterns |
| 8 | (3a.1) General and Specific Ideas (3a.2) Topic |
| | (3a.3) Key Idea (3a.4) Stated Main Ideas |
| | (3b.2) Major Detail (3b.3) Minor Detail |
| 9 | (3a.3) Key Idea (3b.1) Signal Words |
| | (3b.2) Major Detail (3b.3) Minor Detail |
| 10 | (3b.1) Signal Words (3b.4) Paragraph Patterns |
| | ***Connecting with the Author*** |
| 11 | (4a.1) Inferences |
| 12 | (4a.1) Inferences |

| 13 | (4a.1) Inferences |
| 14 | (4a.1) Inferences |
| 15 | (4a.2) Conclusions (4a.3) Making Predictions |
| 16 | (4a.4) Generalizations |
| 17 | (4b.2) Style (4b.3) Figurative Language (4b.4) Propaganda |
| 18 | (4b.1) Fact-Opinion |
| 19 | (4b.2) Tone (4b.2) Mood |
| 20 | (4b.2) Audience (4b.2) Purpose |

## GOAL STATEMENT

*Considering your pretest score and the error review above, write a paragraph describing your strengths and weaknesses in reading. End with a statement of the goals you would like to achieve in your reading course this semester.*

# PART I

# Processing the Written Word

# Keys to Processing:
## *Identifying the Main Ingredients*

**1**

Good readers are active readers who become involved in the reading process. This process involves a three-step sequence: reading, understanding, and remembering. Therefore, in this section you will first learn to recognize and use the reading essentials. These are key reading tools, such as prereading, monitoring your reading, developing a flexible reading rate, and use of visual aids. Second, you will learn and practice different ways to process information. Doing this will strengthen your understanding and remembering. Here you will focus on highlighting or underlining, mapping and outlining, charting, diagramming, paraphrasing, summarizing, and annotating. By learning and practicing these skills, as explained below, you will become an active, skillful reader.

## 1A THE ESSENTIALS OF READING

Four important tools for improving reading include prereading, monitoring, reading rate flexibility, and visual aids.

### 1a.1 Prereading

Prereading is an activity to perform before you read

- to put you in the mood for reading,
- to help you establish a purpose for reading,
- to ready your mind for what's to come,
- to assess your background knowledge of the topic, and
- to organize your background knowledge as an aid to understanding.

Follow these steps for prereading a passage:

**Step 1:** Read the title and first and last paragraphs. Though not always on a conscious level, you will prepare your mind for what's to come.

**Step 2:** Brainstorm the topic for five to ten minutes. Write down everything that comes to your mind. Don't stop to make corrections or worry about spelling. If you can't think of anything to say, just write, "I can't think of anything to say" and continue writing. Your goal is to keep your pen moving and to bring in your background knowledge.

**Step 3:** Ask questions you want answered about the topic. This arouses your curiosity and helps to establish your purpose for reading. (For example, ask, *What questions do I have about the topic? Why is this topic important? How can knowing about this topic benefit me?*)

**Step 4:** Make a written prediction about the selection. Write what you think the selection is all about. At this point, there are no right or wrong answers, so write what you think. (To arrive at a more informed prediction, try reading the title and the first paragraph.)

**Step 5:** Create a cluster of ideas. (See Figure 1.1.) Clustering is a visual form of brainstorming that can help you activate your background knowledge. Draw a wheel, with your subject at the hub and related details on the spokes. Write down details as you think of them and make connections among them. Enclose items in circles or squares, and use lines and arrows to show relationships.

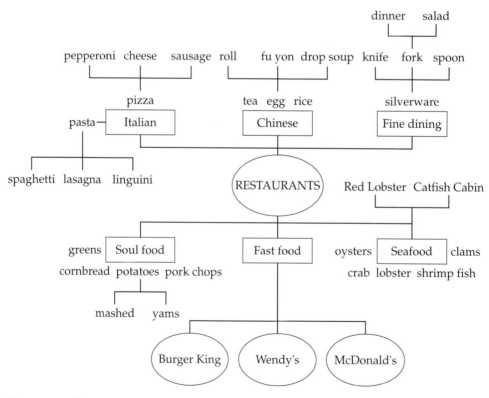

**Figure 1.1** Clustering

**Step 6:** Discuss the topic with a study partner. This often gives you another viewpoint and access to someone else's background knowledge.

## 1a.2 Monitoring

Monitoring puts you in charge as you read. It allows you to give yourself constant feedback on your progress or lack of progress during reading. This strategy is crucial to your reading success because no one knows you better than you know yourself. You know better than anyone else when what you are reading is too difficult and you are not understanding, when the words are confusing and you need to look them up, or when you are reading too fast and need to slow down. This is what monitoring is all about. To monitor your reading, follow these steps:

**Step 1:** Glance through the reading for checkpoints, places to stop and check for comprehension. Look at the paragraphs, pages, and sections, paying close attention to how the material is organized. *Ask: Where are my checkpoints: at the end of each paragraph, each page, or each section?*

**Step 2:** Stop at each checkpoint and ask thoughtful questions in the margin of your text. *Ask: What questions do I have about the reading? Are these questions answered by rereading certain parts? How is this information related? What does it all mean? How can I use this information?*

**Step 3:** Observe the difficulty of the vocabulary. Try to use the surrounding words to figure out word meanings. Break words down into any familiar parts (prefixes, roots, and suffixes). If these strategies do not work, highlight any unfamiliar words and look them up in a dictionary.

**Step 4:** Turn headings and/or the first sentences of paragraphs into questions. These questions are often called guide questions because they give you a purpose for reading, lead you to specific answers, and help you to focus on the important ideas. Use words such as *who, what, when, where, how,* and *why* to make up questions.

**Step 5:** Break down each difficult sentence into manageable parts. (See Figure 1.2.) Remove all modifiers, phrases, and clauses, and leave only the subject and verb.

**Step 6:** Turn the author's ideas into your own words. Write a one-sentence summary of important ideas at each checkpoint. Pack this sentence with key information. Find major or repeated ideas and fit them into a sentence using connecting words, such as *and, however, for example, but,* and *moreover.*

## 1a.3 Developing a Flexible Reading Rate

Your reading rate is determined by two major factors: your purpose for reading and the difficulty of the material being read. The following

**Original Sentence:**

Before Al could take pictures of the animal lovers at the pet zoo, where tame animals roam freely among the guests, he fainted from the strong fumes that rose from a forgotten underground gas line that had sprung a leak.

**Labeled Sentence:**

|  clause  |  phrase  |  phrase  |
| Before Al could take pictures | / | of the animal lovers | / | at the pet |

|  clause  |  phrase  |
| zoo, | / | where tame animals roam freely | / | among the guests, | / |

|  phrase  |  clause  |  phrase  |
| **he fainted** | / | from the strong fumes | / | that had risen | / | from a |

|  clause  |
| forgotten underground gas line | / | that had sprung a leak. |

**Figure 1.2**  Breaking Down a Difficult Sentence

chart shows the suggested rate and *purposes* for reading various types of - materials.

| READING TYPES | MATERIAL AND PURPOSE |
| --- | --- |
| **Study Reading** | Textbook or technical material |
| | *To understand thoroughly and to memorize* |
| **Rapid Reading** | Newspapers, magazines, nonfiction, some fiction |
| | *To get a general idea of the material* |
| **Skimming** | Any type—textbook chapter, novel |
| | *To survey, to get a general overview, to review* |
| **Scanning** | Any type—telephone directory, dictionary |
| | *To locate specific information (names, places, dates)* |

*Source: College Reading*, Janet Maker and Minnette Lenier, Wadsworth Publishing Co., Belmont, California.

To get the most from your reading, first establish your purpose for reading, and then survey the material to determine the level of difficulty. Next, decide how much time it should take you to complete the reading assignment. Of course, if you are reading to prepare for a test, you will read much more slowly than if you are reading a magazine or newspaper article for pleasure. In other words, do not expect to read everything at the same rate. The following strategies will guide you in increasing your reading rate. Experiment to see which strategy works best for you.

*Strategy 1: Survey the material.* There are several reasons why survey-ing is important. Some of the purposes are (1) to introduce you to the sub-ject and main ideas, (2) to see how the parts are related to the whole, (3) to become acquainted with the difficulty of the material, (4) to review for class discussion and exams, and (5) to determine whether this is what you want to read. Follow these steps to survey a selection or chapter:

**Step 1:** Read the title.
**Step 2:** Look at the illustrations and emphasis in the text (boldface, italics, underlining).
**Step 3:** Read the headings and subheadings, the first sentence of each paragraph, the first paragraph and/or introduction, and the summary or conclusion.
**Step 4:** Review any questions.

*Strategy 2: Cluster ideas in thought groups.* Your natural rhythm in reading should enable you to cluster ideas quite easily. Instead / of / fixating / on / each / word / like / this / or / reading / word for word, / group words / and phrases together / into meaningful clusters. / Force your eyes / to stop, / or fixate, / in the center / of each word grouping. / Use the area of vision / lying just outside / the line of / direct sight / to view words / to the left and right / of the fixation. / The decreased number / of fixations / results in faster reading / and more understanding. /

*Strategy 3: Use a pacer.* Use an index card or your hand to pace yourself as you read. Place the card or your hand under each line and move it down the page at a rate that forces you to read ahead of it. This helps to focus your attention and decreases the number of regressions, or repeat readings, that you make while reading.

*Strategy 4: Set time limits.* First survey the reading content to determine its level of difficulty. Next, depending on your purpose for reading, determine a suitable start and finish time. (Refer to the reading rate chart in the Appendix.) Use a stopwatch or another timer to check your progress at the end of the first fifteen minutes. Make adjustments as needed, and then read for another fifteen minutes. When you meet your target rate, push yourself to read even faster by adding another page to the total number of pages to be read in fifteen-minute intervals.

*Strategy 5: Practice reading easy material.* During your free time, make a conscious effort to practice reading about thirty minutes to an hour each day. During this practice, read for pleasure, choosing materials that are easy and interesting. Novels or magazine articles are great sources for pleasure reading, and you don't have to worry about trying to remember the contents for a test. With these types of materials, push yourself to read rapidly. Over time, your reading skill and speed will transfer to your other, more challenging reading.

*Strategy 6: Practice skim reading.* Instead of reading every word, read selected parts, depending on your purpose. Three of the most common reasons for skimming are to find specific information, to get a general picture of the contents, and to review. A word of warning: *Skim reading is not a substitute for reading the material.* In other words, never skim your class assignments, for these are to be studied and, in many instances, learned.

To skim read, first determine your purpose, and then follow the steps related to your purpose below.

If your purpose is **to find specific information:**

**Step 1:** Identify clues from key words, or make up questions to help focus your search.

**Step 2:** Look through the material rapidly, going from line to line looking for clues.

**Step 3:** Stop when you find what you are looking for, and read the information carefully.

If your purpose is **to get an overview:**

**Step 1:** Survey the contents. Read the title, headings, subheadings, notes on visuals, introduction, first and last paragraphs, and summary.

**Step 2:** Look for signals: definitions, examples, enumerated points, main ideas, bulleted ideas, steps, guide words (*first, next, also, finally*), and changes in print (italics or boldface or color).

**Step 3:** Look rapidly through all other information.

**Step 4:** Stop and carefully read the information given in or introduced by the signals above.

If your purpose is **to review:**

**Step 1:** First, read to get an overview of the material.

**Step 2:** Read all highlighted information.

**Step 3:** Use the major headings to make up questions; then read selectively to find the answers.

**Step 4:** Look through the material until you find one of the key areas above.

**Step 5:** Stop and read the material carefully.

## 1a.4  Using Visual Aids

Visual aids are pictures, maps, charts, diagrams, graphs, and special textbook type. Authors use pictures, maps, charts, diagrams, and graphs as "information stuffers" to limit the number of words needed. In this case, the old saying "A picture is worth a thousand words" is true. Special type points out what's important to learn and remember. Follow these steps to understand visual aids:

**Step 1:** Determine the purpose of the visual. *Ask: Why does the author include this visual?*

**Step 2:** Identify the type of visual; then read the title, footnotes, and captions. This gives you a general overview of the visual.

**Step 3:** Identify parts and their relationship to the whole. *Ask: What are the key parts: variables (e.g., years, dates, amounts) and overall contents? How are these parts related? What does it all mean?*

**Step 4:** Summarize the contents of the visual, paying close attention to the special parts noted in step 3. *Ask: What comparisons can be made? Then look for higher or lower, larger or smaller, and increases and decreases.*

**Step 5:** Observe the varied type signals: color, **boldface,** *italics*, and other special features (bullets, asterisks, CAPITALS, and <u>underlining</u>).

**Step 6:** Relate the visual to the text. *Ask: How does this visual add to my overall understanding of the text information? What's the point?*

**Pictures** may be cartoons, drawings, illustrations, photos, and so on.

**Charts and tables** present condensed information in an organized format (vertical and horizontal rows, columns with headings and features).

| Time from Start of Reaction | Rate of Forward Reaction Rate of Reverse Reaction | Reaction Mixture ● Reactants ○ Products | Concentration | |
|---|---|---|---|---|
| | | | Reactamts | Products |
| 0 | | | 20 | 0 |
| 10 | | | 12 | 8 |
| 20 | | | 8 | 12 |
| 30 | | | 6 | 14 |
| 40 | | | 6 | 14 |
| 50 | | | 6 | 14 |

| Personal Budget | | |
|---|---|---|
| Date: July 11, 2002 | | |
| This worksheet can help you analyze your personal budget. Enter values into the yellow boxes, replacing sample data. Results will be shown in the green boxes. | | |
| Income | Monthly Amount | Percent |
| Net pay | $3,750 | 94.89% |
| Investments | $150 | 3.80% |
| Interest | $52 | 1.32% |
| Other | $0 | |
| **Total income** | **$3,952** | 100.00% |
| Income | Monthly Amount | Percent |
| Rent or mortgage | $1,200 | 42.11% |
| Car payments | $275 | 9.65% |
| Credit card payments | $50 | 1.75% |
| Telephone | $50 | 1.75% |
| Utilities | $75 | 2.63% |
| Taxes | $1,050 | 36.84% |
| Child care | $0 | |
| Cable TV | $25 | 0.88% |
| Insurance (personal and property) | $125 | 4.39% |
| Other | $0 | |
| **Total fixed expenses** | **$2,850** | 100.00% |

**Graphs** are pictures showing changes in data and in the relationship between two variables: *circle* or *pie* (part to whole), *line* (action or trends), and *bar* (separate amounts).

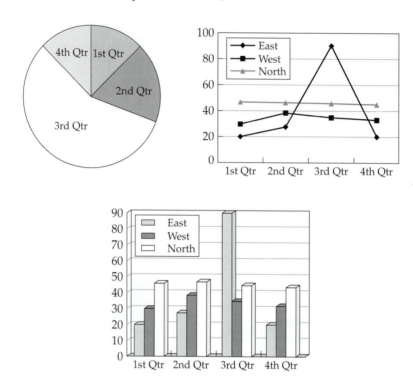

**Diagrams** are pictures with labeled parts.

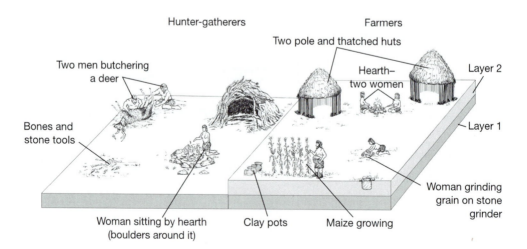

**Maps** are pictures of geographic locations.

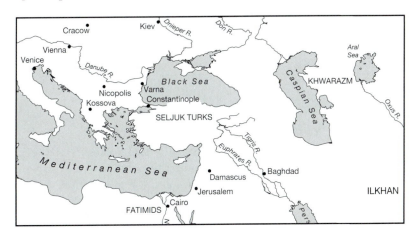

## EXERCISE 1.1  PREREADING A SELECTION

*To preread the selection "Yin, Yang, and the Cosmic Egg—A Chinese Tale,"
complete the following exercises.*

1. Brainstorm about the title of the selection.

   _____

   _____

   _____

   _____

   _____

   _____

   _____

   _____

   _____

2. Ask two questions that you believe will be answered in the selection.

   Question 1: _____

   Question 2: _____

3. Write a sentence expressing what you believe the selection is about.

   _____

   _____

   _____

4. For a more informed prediction, read the title and first paragraph of the selection below. Then write another sentence expressing what you believe the selection is about.

_____

_____

_____

*Yin, Yang, and the Cosmic Egg—A Chinese Tale*

The creation of the world began with two forces: Yin, the power of darkness and shadow, and Yang, the power of sunshine and light. Yin and Yang had a child, a god named Pan Gu, and it was he who formed the world as we know it.

5. After reading the title and first paragraph above, fill in the circles below. Then create a cluster of ideas that might be covered in the selection. Allow your mind to roam freely.

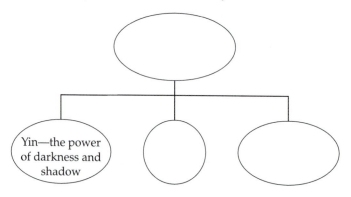

## EXERCISE 1.2   MONITORING YOUR READING

*Read the selection "Yin, Yang, and the Cosmic Egg—A Chinese Tale" on page 22 and complete the activities below.*

1. Identify one logical checkpoint for this selection.

_____

2. Ask two thoughtful questions.

   Question 1: _____

   Question 2: _____

3. Check your vocabulary: Write two difficult words from the selection and a definition of each.

   Word 1: _____    Definition: _____

   Word 2: _____    Definition: _____

4. Turn the first sentence of each paragraph into a question.

   Question 1: —————————————————————————

   Question 2: —————————————————————————

   Question 3: —————————————————————————

5. Find a difficult sentence and break it down into its key idea(s).

   —————————————————————————————————

6. Write a one-sentence summary for the end of one checkpoint.

   —————————————————————————————————

   —————————————————————————————————

## EXERCISE 1.3   SKIMMING

*Skim the selection and complete the following exercises.*

1. Find answers to the following questions.

   a. What is Yin? ————————————————————

   b. What is Yang? ———————————————————

   c. Who was Pan Gu? ————————————————

   d. What did Pan Gu's voice become? ——————————

   e. What finally happened to Pan Gu? ————————

2. Give an overview of the contents. Write the gist, or main point, of the selection.

   —————————————————————————————————

   —————————————————————————————————

   —————————————————————————————————

3. Review the contents, looking for key information.

   a. What information do you consider important, and why?

      —————————————————————————————————

      —————————————————————————————————

   b. Write two questions, and read to find the answers.

      Question 1: ————————————————————

      Answer: ———————————————————————

      Question 2: ————————————————————

      Answer: ———————————————————————

# Yin, Yang, and the Cosmic Egg—
# A Chinese Tale

*Anita Ganeri*

1    The creation of the world began with two forces: Yin, the power of darkness and shadow, and Yang, the power of sunshine and light. Yin and Yang had a child, a god named Pan Gu, and it was he who formed the world as we know it.

2    Pan Gu was formed inside a gigantic egg. Inside the egg, everything was dark. For 18,000 years, Pan Gu lived in the darkness of the egg, growing steadily bigger. Finally he grew so big that the egg could not hold him. Cracks appeared in its shell, wider and wider until the egg split open. The clear, light parts of the egg floated upward to form the heavens; the dark, heavy parts of the egg sank downward to form the Earth.

3    Then Pan Gu broke free of the egg and stood up straight and tall. To keep the heavens and Earth from merging into one again, he grew taller still and, each day, pushed them farther apart. Another 18,000 years passed in this way. Then Pan Gu, wearied by his great work, lay down and died. His breath formed the clouds and wind; his rumbling voice became the thunder. His right eye became the Moon and his left eye the Sun. His hair and whiskers became the stars in the sky. The rain and dew formed from his sweat, and the rivers, mountains, plants and trees, rocks and precious gems were also created from his body.

## EXERCISE 1.4    DEVELOPING A FLEXIBLE READING RATE
*Using one of your textbooks, follow the directions below.*

1.  Survey a chapter.

2.  Draw a cluster map of the ideas in a paragraph as you read.

3.  Read a couple of pages, using your hand or an index card as a pacer.

4.  Read a chapter and time yourself in fifteen-minute intervals.

## EXERCISE 1.5    INCREASING YOUR READING RATE
*Read an interesting magazine article. Push yourself to read it rapidly. Then answer the following questions.*

1.  What is the title of the article? _____

2.  Who wrote the article? _____

3.  What was the article about? _____

_____

4. What did you like best about the article? _____

_____

_____

5. Would you recommend the article to a friend? ___ Yes ___ No

## EXERCISE 1.6   USING VISUAL AIDS

*Locate a graph in one of your textbooks and answer the questions below.*

1. What is the purpose of the visual? _____

_____

2. Give an overview of the visual.

   Title: _____

   Footnote: _____

   Caption: _____

   _____

   _____

3. Identify the contents of the graph.

   Variables: _____

   Percentages: _____

   Other information: _____

   _____

4. How are the parts related to the whole?

   Comparisons: _____

   _____

   _____

5. Write a summary of the contents. _____

_____

_____

_____

6. How does the graph help you understand the text? _____

_____

_____

_____

## 1B READING PROCESSES

The strategies in this section encourage you to be actively involved in the reading process. They include highlighting or underlining, outlining and mapping, charting and diagramming, and paraphrasing, summarizing, and annotating. Here is how these strategies work: First, they force you to think about what you are reading. Second, they make you use a pen or pencil. Third, they help you turn the writer's ideas into your own. Through your use of these strategies, a powerful combination is formed: thinking, writing, and reasoning. Together, this combination leads you to understand, remember, and recall what you read.

### 1b.1  Highlighting and Underlining

To become an active reader, underline or highlight text information with a pen or highlighter. However, before you mark anything, read the material and determine what is important. Follow these steps to highlight or underline key information:

**Step 1:**  Read the passage closely.
**Step 2:**  Underline or highlight the important parts:

> **The topic**, a word or phrase identifying the subject
>
> **The topic sentence**, a sentence summarizing the major details in a paragraph
>
> **The major ideas** that give direct support or evidence for the topic sentence
>
> **Enumerated points**—any numbered or lettered details
>
> **Key information**—repeated words, definitions, and examples.
>
> *Ask: What is the most important information?*

**Step 3:**  Be extremely selective. Do not underline or highlight too much—just the crucial points noted above.

Here is an example of underlining to highlight key information in a paragraph:

> <u>Vegetables are considered a mainstay of the American diet</u>. This is understandable because they contain many <u>nutrients and vitamins</u>. And though Americans consume vegetables grown all over the world, there are some that are generally thought of as just American. <u>American vegetables</u> are of two main varieties: <u>(1) leafy and (2) plant</u>. Two common <u>examples</u> of plant vegetables are <u>tomatoes and corn</u>. Corn is usually either <u>white or yellow</u>. The latter is quite tasty when <u>boiled or roasted</u>.

### 1b.2  Outlining and Mapping

Outlining or mapping can help you organize, reduce, and present information in a visual format. Two critical questions will assist you in preparing information to present in this format: (1) What are the important parts? (2) How do the parts fit together?

**Outlining** is a frequently used process of organizing information. It involves (1) grouping details into categories and (2) arranging those categories in a logical order with letters and numbers. Outlining helps you see relationships and determine what is and what is not important. You may use either a topical ideas outline or an outline of complete sentences. Never use both formats in the same outline. Follow these steps to outline information:

**Step 1:** Read the section (or paragraph or page) to be outlined.

**Step 2:** Write the title or topic at the top of the page.

**Step 3:** Identify relationships in the writing, with at least two parts in each grouping. Determine which parts go together and how each part is related to the other. Then, pair items of equal importance: main ideas with main ideas, major details with major details, minor details with minor details, and examples with examples.

**Step 4:** Order information from most to least important, and use Roman numerals, letters of the alphabet, and Arabic numerals to show levels of importance. List main topics, then subtopics, then supporting details (major then minor), then examples. As you move farther to the right in your outline, the information becomes less and less important.

**Step 5:** Check your outline. *Ask: Have I identified main categories and assigned Roman numerals? Have I grouped and arranged items within each category and assigned letters of the alphabet and Arabic numerals?*

Here is a sample outline:

American Vegetables

I. Two major varieties
   A. Leafy
   B. Plant
      1. Tomatoes
      2. Corn
         a. White
         b. Yellow
            (1) Roasted
            (2) Boiled

**Mapping** is another way of visually organizing information. It helps you see how the author organizes ideas and how these ideas are related to each other. The contents of a map are similar to what you would place in a topical outline. Follow these steps to construct a concept map:

**Step 1:** Read the passage to be mapped.

**Step 2:** Circle the key words and ideas in the passage. Limit ideas to one or two words or brief phrases.

**Step 3:** Place the topic at the top or center of the map.

**Step 4:** Determine the relationships between ideas. Place main ideas, supporting details, and examples so that they appear in a most to least important order.

**Step 5:** Use circles and boxes to enclose key ideas, and use lines and arrows to connect the circles and boxes. These figures should show levels of ideas and relationships between ideas. *Ask: Do I see which ideas are related, on the same level?*

There is more than one way to map. Thus, your map is personal. It doesn't have to look like anyone else's. Look at these examples:

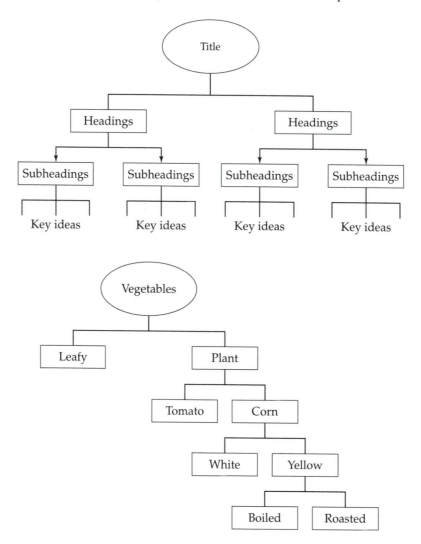

## 1b.3 Charting and Diagramming

Diagramming and charting are two more ways to organize and display information graphically. **Charting** works well when you want to compare and contrast ideas. Once you set up your chart and fill in the information, you can clearly see similarities and differences. Follow these steps to chart information:

**Step 1:** Categorize your subject into its major parts.
**Step 2:** Identify key features. *Ask: How are the features alike? How are they different?*
**Step 3:** Place major categories horizontally (across).
**Step 4:** Place features in left-hand column (up and down).

Here is a sample chart incorporating the elements in the preceding map:

|  | VEGETABLES | |
| --- | --- | --- |
| *Features* | *Leafy* | *Plant* |
| Color<br>Preparation<br>Cooking<br>Examples | green<br>chopping<br>steamed<br>cabbage | yellow, white<br>shucking<br>roasted, boiled<br>corn |

**Diagramming** is yet another way to present information visually. It is useful for showing how something is done. Diagrams make the steps in a process stand out so that you can see the flow of information clearly. Follow these steps to diagram information:

**Step 1:** Read the information carefully.
**Step 2:** Identify the steps, their function, and their place in the process. *Ask: Do steps give directions? Do they require a decision or show a beginning or ending?*
**Step 3:** Place steps in geometric shapes. For example, you might use slanted rectangles for directions, rectangles for calculations, diamonds for decision points, and ovals for starts or stops.
**Step 4:** Verify the accuracy of your flowchart. *Ask: Are all steps included, and are they placed correctly in the process?*

Look at the following diagram, which shows the same steps for mapping information.

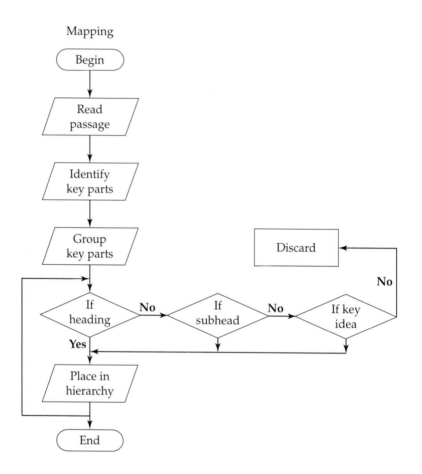

Mapping

## 1b.4 Paraphrasing, Summarizing, and Annotating

In paraphrasing, summarizing, and annotating, you analyze written information and make it your own. This improves your overall understanding. Ask yourself: What are the key points? and What does it all mean?

**Paraphrasing** means putting the author's ideas in your own words. This shows that you understand the author's exact message. Follow these steps to paraphrase information:

**Step 1:** Read the passage two or three times, looking up any unfamiliar words.

**Step 2:** Study the key parts of sentences carefully and make sure that you understand the author's message. Pay close attention to punctuation. This can help you locate the parts. *Ask: Which part is most/least important? What is the author really saying?*

**Step 3:** Close the book; then rewrite the message in your own words. To help with paraphrasing, you might try using synonyms or a different sentence structure.

**Step 4:** Check your response. **Ask:** *Do the author and I say the same thing?*

**Summarizing** allows you to focus on the main points of the original writing. Selectively gather the major ideas from the reading and express these ideas in your own words. A good summary is about one-third the length of the original material and contains the same ideas you would use for an outline or map. Follow these steps to summarize information:

**Step 1:** Read the paragraph.

**Step 2:** Identify the key information. Omit all details except for a few really important ones.

**Step 3:** Group related ideas together with words that tie ideas together. Some examples of these words are *also, however, nevertheless,* and *first.*

**Step 4:** Write your summary. Be sure to include only the important details. Make sure you are properly paraphrasing, and use quotation marks around everything you have copied directly from the text.

**Annotating** forces you to point out important information, such as *definitions, examples,* and *lists.* It helps you identify the gist of what the author is saying or note what the information does (e.g., it defines or presents background information). Annotating requires that you highlight important material; then you summarize or paraphrase key information and write it in the margin of your textbook. When you finish, use this information to help organize notes on what you have read. Follow these steps to annotate a passage:

**Step 1:** Read the whole passage to be annotated.

**Step 2:** Break the passage into sections and work on only one section (usually a paragraph) at a time.

**Step 3:** Determine what you want to highlight and/or write: key ideas, definitions, or what the section does.

**Step 4:** Paraphrase or summarize the information you choose to use; then write it in the margin of your text.

**Step 5:** Review and take notes on what you have annotated. This will help you remember and understand more clearly what you are reading.

Read the passage below, and then study the paraphrase, summary, and annotation that follow.

### Old Folks Are Worth a Fortune

*Old folks are worth a fortune: with silver in their hair, gold in their* 1
*teeth, stones in their kidneys, lead in their feet, and gas in their stomachs. I have become a lot more social with the passing of the years; some might even call me a frivolous old gal. I'm seeing five gentlemen every day.*

2      *As soon as I awake, Will Power helps me get out of bed. Then I go to see John. Then Charley Horse comes along, and, when he is here, he takes a lot of my time and attention. When he leaves, Arthur Ritis shows up and stays the rest of the day. (He doesn't like to stay in one place very long, so he takes me from joint to joint.) After such a busy day, I'm really tired and glad to go to bed with Ben Gay. What a life!*

3      *P.S. The preacher came to call the other day. He said that at my age I should be thinking about the hereafter. I told him I do, all the time. No matter where I am—in the parlor, upstairs in the kitchen, or down in the basement—I ask myself, "Now, what am I here after?"*

### Paraphrase of Paragraph 3

*The minister dropped in the other day. He told me that anyone my age should be concerned with the hereafter. I said to him that I do—constantly. Whether I am in the parlor, kitchen, upstairs, or in the basement, I wonder what am I here after.*

### Summary of the Passage

*"Old folks are worth a fortune" because they have silver hair, gold teeth, kidney stones, leaded feet, and gassy stomachs. Daily, the "frivolous old gal" meets five lively gentlemen: Will Power, John, Charley Horse, Arthur Ritis, and Ben Gay. The visiting preacher said at her age she "should be thinking about the hereafter"; she said wherever she goes she wonders what is she here after.*

### Annotation of Paragraphs 1 and 2

*Paragraph 1 uses examples to show why old folks are worth a fortune (silver, gold, stones, lead, and gas).*

*Paragraph 2 identifies daily routine with five lively gentlemen (Will Power, John, Charley Horse, Arthur Ritis, and Ben Gay).*

### EXERCISE 1.7   READING PROCESSES

*Read the passage below and complete the information-processing activities that follow.*

1      It could take years to pass a new health care plan. Perhaps you would like something to drink while you're waiting.

2      In the future, every American will likely be guaranteed certain health benefits. Until then, everyone can benefit from the vitamins and nutrients in 100 percent Florida Orange Juice. It's loaded with vitamin C, which is vital for healthy skin and gums. It gives you folic acid, a member of the B-vitamin family that is particularly important for women of childbearing age. It's also a good source of potassium, a mineral that is necessary for normal muscle function. On top of that, orange juice is fat-free, cholesterol-free, and sodium-free.

So while the politicians are busy hammering out all the important   3
health care issues, you can be sure that you are doing everything possible
to take care of yourself.

1. Highlight the key ideas in the passage. Look for main ideas, definitions, examples, lists, and repeated words.

2. Complete the outline below.

   The Benefits of Orange Juice

   I. Vitamins and nutrients

      A. _____

      B. _____

      C. _____

   II. Other qualities

      A. _____

      B. _____

      C. _____

3. Complete this concept map below for paragraph 2.

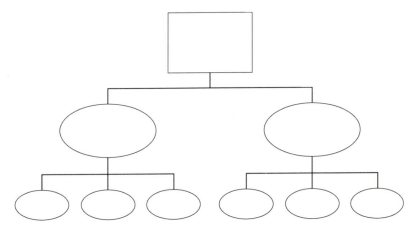

4. Write a paraphrase of paragraph 3.

   _____

   _____

   _____

5. Write a summary of the passage.

   _____

   _____

_____

_____

_____

_____

_____

_____

_____

6. Write an annotation of paragraph 2.

_____

_____

_____

_____

## EXERCISE 1.8   READING PROCESSES

*Read the passage below and complete the information-processing activities that follow.*

# The Conditioning Effect

*Stephen R. Covey*

1     While we have accepted the tremendous power of conditioning in our lives, to say that we have no control over that influence creates quite a different map. There are actually three social maps—theories of determinism—to explain the nature of man. They are genetic determinism, psychic determinism, and environmental determinism.

2     Genetic determinism basically says your grandparents did it to you. That's why you have such a temper. Your grandparents had short tempers and it's in your DNA. It just goes through the generations and you inherited it. In addition, you're Irish, and that's the nature of Irish people.

3     Psychic determinism basically says your parents did it to you. Your upbringing, your childhood experience laid out your personality and shaped your character. That's why you're afraid to be in front of a group. It's the way your parents brought you up. You feel terribly guilty if you make a mistake because you "remember" deep inside the emotional scripting when you were very weak and tender and unprotected. You "remember" the emotional punishment, the disapproval, the comparison with somebody else when you didn't perform as well as expected.

Environmental determinism basically says your boss is doing it to    4
you—or your spouse, or that bratty teenager, or your economic situation,
or national policies. Someone or something in your environment is to
blame for your situation.

Each of these maps is based on the stimulus/response theory we    5
most often think of in connection with Pavlov's experiments with dogs.
The basic idea is that we are conditioned to respond in a particular way to
a particular stimulus.

1. Highlight the key ideas in the passage. Look for main ideas, examples, definitions, lists, and repeated words.

2. Complete this outline of paragraph 1.
   I. Three social maps

   A. _____

   B. _____

   C. _____

3. Complete the concept map below.

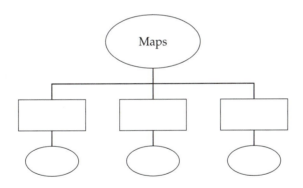

4. Complete the chart below.

| FEATURES | THREE SOCIAL MAPS | | |
|---|---|---|---|
| *Types* | _____ | _____ | _____ |
| *Basis* | Inherited | _____ | _____ |
| *Responsible Party* | _____ | _____ | Boss, spouse . . . |

5. Write a paraphrase of paragraph 5.

_____

_____

_____

6. Write a summary of the passage.

_____

_____

_____

_____

_____

7. Write an annotation of paragraphs 1 and 2.

Paragraph 1: _____

_____

Paragraph 2: _____

_____

# Mastery Test 1

*Read the passage below and answer the questions that follow.*

## Groundwater: Our First Priority

*Dale Hesser*

1

People depend on pure, clean, drinkable water. Without it, we cannot survive. In some parts of Earth, clean water is very scarce. In certain areas of developing countries, people spend much of each day hauling water from wells several kilometers from their homes. In the United States, many people find it hard to tolerate even a temporary water shortage.

2

Prior to the agricultural and industrial revolution in the United States, there was plenty of water for all. Now, however, population and standard of living have threatened to use up drinking water supplies. Agriculture and industry use about 95 percent of that supply. Household uses have risen greatly. Adding to the problem is the fact that many aquifers have become polluted, thus decreasing the usable supply.

3

Water is easily polluted. It is known as "the universal solvent." This does not mean that every substance can be dissolved in it, but a large percentage of substances do dissolve in water. Water is a good solvent of natural materials, especially those containing oxygen, such as alcohols, sugars, and organic acids. Water is also good for dissolving some salts. Among these salts are the positively charged ions of metals, which in certain amounts are poisonous to humans. These ions include copper, cadmium, mercury, and lead. Lead pipes were used at one time to transport water supplies.

4

Water also has the rare property of being able to dissolve, in small amounts, substances not generally considered to be water-soluble. One of these, benzene, is a threat to the water supply in many areas. Some other insoluble products react with water to produce new substances that are soluble. Still other substances, such as petroleum products, simply float on the surface. Some pollutants are not poisonous but create a large biological oxygen demand, which has the effect of removing oxygen from the water and making it more difficult for the water to support life and purify itself naturally.

## COMPREHENSION EXERCISE
*Circle the letter of the best answer.*

1. What can you discover from reading only the title and first paragraph of the passage?
   a. Groundwater is not easy to find.
   b. There are ways to purify water.

    c. Though sometimes scarce, groundwater is a priority because it is needed for survival.

    d. There are some problems with today's water supply.

2. Which of the following is the best checkpoint for monitoring this selection?
    a. each page
    b. each paragraph
    c. each sentence
    d. each line

3. What would be a good reason for reading this article?
    a. to understand problems with the groundwater supply
    b. to find out why groundwater may be scarce
    c. to complete the assignment
    d. to learn about the benefits of water

4. Which of the following is a good question to ask about paragraph 3?
    a. What substances are water-soluble?
    b. What are four types of salts?
    c. What percentage of substances dissolve in water?
    d. Why is water so easily polluted?

5. Fill in the map below with key ideas from paragraph 3.

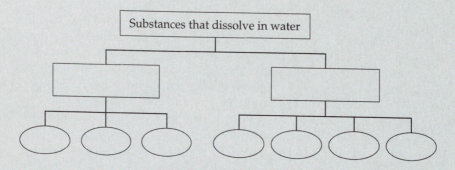

6. Which of these headings would work well for charting threats to the water supply in paragraph 2?
    a. industrial revolution, population, standard of living
    b. groundwater, yesterday, today, tomorrow
    c. groundwater, problems, solutions
    d. agriculture and industry, household, aquifers

7. Which of these is a good paraphrase of paragraph 1?
    a. Needing pure water to live, people think about it all over the world.
    b. Water is needed for life on Earth.

  c. People can't live without water on Earth.
  d. Water, which is necessary for life, requires much manpower in Third World countries, and many Americans are disturbed by brief shortages.

8. Write a summary of paragraph 4.

  _____

  _____

  _____

  _____

  _____

  _____

  _____

9. Which of the following is a good annotation of paragraph 2?
  a. What are problems associated with the water supply?
  b. Why has the water supply decreased?
  c. The problems and solutions of the water source.
  d. The three factors that contribute to the decrease in today's water supply.

10. What are the benefits of processing information?
  a. to understand and to remember what you read
  b. to identify key ideas
  c. to check the contents of the article
  d. to understand the steps to previewing

  Score: Number correct _____ (out of 10) $\times$ 10 = _____

# 2 Processing Words:
## *Understanding the Basics*

The basic requirements for all word-processing activities rest on your knowledge of words. Your ability to recognize and define words is essential to success in reading. For this reason, this section presents vocabulary development and a brief overview of two important word sources: the dictionary and the thesaurus.

## 2A VOCABULARY DEVELOPMENT

There are several ways to develop a strong vocabulary. The three ways covered here are (1) understanding word parts, such as roots and affixes; (2) using context clues; and (3) applying a vocabulary card system.

### 2a.1 Roots, Prefixes, and Suffixes

The **root** is the main part of a word. **Affixes,** called **prefixes** and **suffixes,** are additions to root words. They change the meaning of the root and sometimes the part of speech of the word.

| ROOT | MEANING | EXAMPLE |
|------|---------|---------|
| cred | believe | credible, incredible |
| cycle | circle | cyclic, bicycle |
| derma | skin | dermatologist, pachyderm |
| geo | earth | geology |
| graph | write | telegraph, graphic |
| ped | foot | pedal, centipede |
| script | write | postscript |
| voc | call, voice | vocal |

A **prefix** is a syllable added to the beginning of a root word without a change in spelling.

| PREFIX | MEANING | EXAMPLE |
|---|---|---|
| a-, il-, im-, in- | not | amoral, immature |
| bi- | two | bicycle |
| circum- | around | circumference |
| com-/con- | together, with | commute |
| de- | out, away from | deport |
| ex- | take out | export |
| pre- | before | preview |
| pro- | for | pronoun |
| re- | over, again | repeat |
| un- | not | unhappy |

A **suffix** is a syllable added to the end of a root word. This addition results in a change in meaning and often in the spelling of the root word. (See *sparsity*, from *sparse*, below.) Also, the new word formed from the addition of a suffix may become a different part of speech.

A **noun** names a person, place, or thing.

A **verb** states an action or state of being.

An **adjective** describes a noun or pronoun.

An **adverb** describes a verb, an adjective, or an adverb.

The part of speech is indicated in parentheses following each example below.

| WORD ROOT | SUFFIX | MEANING | NEW WORD |
|---|---|---|---|
| like (verb) | -able, -ible | ability to do | likeable (adjective) |
| pay (verb) | -er, -or, -ee | one who | payee (noun) |
| help (verb) | -ful | full of | helpful (adjective) |
| sparse (adjective) | -ity | state of | sparsity (noun) |
| memory (noun) | -ize | process | memorize (verb) |
| quiet (adjective) | -ly | quality | quietly (adverb) |
| kind (adjective) | -ness | state of | kindness (noun) |

A single word may have both a prefix and a suffix.

| PREFIX | ROOT | SUFFIX |
|---|---|---|
| un- | think | -able |
| in- | cred | -ible |
| il- | legal | -ly |

## EXERCISE 2.1   PREFIXES AND SUFFIXES
*Circle the letter of the best answer.*

1. A **tricycle** has
   a. one wheel.
   b. three wheels.
   c. two wheels.
   d. four wheels.

2. **Geomorphology** is related to
    a. the earth.
    b. the sun.
    c. the moon.
    d. the sky.

3. **Dermasoft** is a lotion for
    a. hair.
    b. skin.
    c. nails.
    d. boots.

4. To **vocalize** means to
    a. run.
    b. use the voice.
    c. remain silent.
    d. stand.

5. A **manuscript** is a
    a. wheel.
    b. person.
    c. scribe.
    d. book.

6. A **telegraph** is used to
    a. receive information.
    b. send information.
    c. package information.
    d. discover information.

7. A **podiatrist** is concerned with
    a. feet.
    b. cars.
    c. eggs.
    d. babies.

8. **Incredible** means
    a. believable.
    b. not believable.
    c. likeable.
    d. miserable.

9. **Circumnavigate** refers to travel
    a. under something.
    b. above something.
    c. around something.
    d. through something.

10. A **pretest** is taken
    a. toward the end.
    b. at the beginning.
    c. at the end.
    d. in the middle.

## EXERCISE 2.2　SUFFIXES
*Circle the letter of the new part of speech that results from the addition of a suffix.*

1. Envy → enviable
    a. noun
    b. verb
    c. adjective
    d. adverb

2. Slow → slowly
    a. noun
    b. verb
    c. adjective
    d. adverb

3. Thank → thankful
    a. noun
    b. verb
    c. adjective
    d. adverb

4. Happy → happiness
   a. noun                    b. verb
   c. adjective               d. adverb

5. Energy → energize
   a. noun                    b. verb
   c. adjective               d. adverb

6. Employ → employee
   a. noun                    b. verb
   c. adjective               d. adverb

7. Hero → heroic
   a. noun                    b. verb
   c. adjective               d. adverb

8. Awkward → awkwardly
   a. noun                    b. verb
   c. adjective               d. adverb

9. Loyal → loyalty
   a. noun                    b. verb
   c. adjective               d. adverb

10. Create → creative
    a. noun                   b. verb
    c. adjective              d. adverb

## 2a.2   Context Clues

Context clues are the author's tips to the meaning of words that are used in text. The **context** includes the sentence, paragraph, and/or passage in which an unfamiliar word is found. It may also include punctuation clues. The word *present*, for example, is meaningless out of context. However, when placed in the context of a sentence, its meaning becomes clear: *I will present the award* shows a **verb** meaning "to give" whereas *I want the present* shows a **noun** meaning "gift." Several of the various types of context clues are presented below.

| CONTEXT CLUE | DEFINITION AND EXAMPLE |
|---|---|
| **Punctuation** | The actual definition is separated from the text by commas, dashes, or parentheses.<br><br>*Thomas is **loquacious** (talkative).* |
| **Contrast words** | This definition is an antonym or word(s) opposite in meaning to the unknown word. Aids to recognition include *not, on the other hand, however, despite,* and *although.*<br><br>*Thomas is **loquacious**; <u>however</u>, his friend has <u>very little to say.</u>* |

| | |
|---|---|
| **Synonyms** | The definition has a meaning similar to the unknown word. |

*Thomas is **loquacious,** or <u>talkative</u>, like Alma.*

**Examples**      Specific examples provide an illustration of the unfamiliar word. Aids to recognition are key words like *after, for example, including, to illustrate, for instance,* and *such as.*

*The meat was cooked with **condiments** <u>such as garlic, thyme, mustard and catsup</u>.*

**Inferences**      Personal background, knowledge, and experience are used to figure out the meaning of the unknown word after clues from the words or phrases surrounding the unknown word are identified.

*Thomas is so **loquacious** that <u>his tongue appears to go limp from so much movement</u>.*

## EXERCISE 2.3   READING CONTEXT CLUES
*Circle the letter before the word that gives the meaning of the italicized word, and write the type of context clue in the space provided.*

1. The **adverse** effects of this weather, including chapped lips, frostbitten hands, and cold feet, have caused many to stay indoors.
   a. mysterious
   b. harmful
   c. pleasant

   Type of context clue: _____

2. When Eddie lived on the streets, he asked friendly women for money and then **implored** their spouses for more.
   a. warned
   b. begged
   c. explored

   Type of context clue: _____

3. Despite her age, Ms. Smith stays active. She is not **stagnant** like so many others who live in the nursing home.
   a. inactive
   b. animalistic
   c. elderly

   Type of context clue: _____

4. Because the mother refused to buy candy, the **irate** child fell to the floor kicking and screaming.
   a. nervous
   b. courageous
   c. angry

   Type of context clue: _____

5. The temperature **fluctuates** with the seasons.
   a. goes up and down
   b. is unclear
   c. remains flat

   Type of context clue: _____

6. Marvin is truly **resilient;** he has bounced back after losing all his money and serving a five-year prison term.
   a. depressed
   b. able to recover
   c. happy

   Type of context clue: _____

7. I believe Sue's mother is a classic **hypochondriac;** she cries often, complains always, sleeps all day, sniffles when you sniffle, and takes many medicines.
   a. one who suffers from imaginary illnesses
   b. one who is allergic to others
   c. one who fears flying

   Type of context clue: _____

8. Because Jack was late every day last week, he told his boss a complete **fabrication** to keep from being fired from his job.
   a. truth
   b. explanation
   c. lie

   Type of context clue: _____

9. The teacher did not give a **succinct** answer to the student's questions; instead she gave a long, meaningless response.
   a. brief
   b. conscious
   c. ordinary

   Type of context clue: _____

10. **Nepotism**—favoritism to relatives and friends—is commonplace among public service workers.
    a. favoritism to relatives and friends

b. unfavorable responses

c. code of honor

Type of context clue: _____

## EXERCISE 2.4  WRITING CONTEXT CLUES

*In each space below, write a sentence using the type of context clue shown.*

1. Punctuation: _____

   _____

2. Contrast word: _____

   _____

3. Synonym: _____

   _____

4. Example: _____

   _____

5. Inference: _____

   _____

## 2a.3  The Vocabulary Card System

In building a strong vocabulary, you will sometimes want to remember new words that you are exposed to in your classes as well as in other situations. One way to add these new words to your active vocabulary is to use the vocabulary card system. Follow the steps below using index cards.

**Step 1.** Write (a) the new word and (b) its pronunciation in parentheses on the front of the card.

**Step 2.** Record the following on the back of the card: (a) a brief definition, (b) a sentence using the word, and (c) a mnemonic or picture image to help you remember the meaning of the word.

**Step 3.** During free moments, practice quizzing yourself as you would with flash cards, reshuffling the cards after each use.

**Step 4.** Once you know certain definitions by heart, band these words in another stack and review them often. Continue studying unknown words, occasionally moving known words into the review stack until you have learned all the words in the set. Use these words often in your everyday conversations.

**Step 5.** Repeat this procedure with another set of words.

Look at these sample vocabulary cards:

---

**crotchety**

(krach'it-e)

---

**Card 1 (front)**

---

picture image

 **full of stubborn notions**

Tom's <u>crotchety</u> grandmother
won't do anything she's told.

---

**Card 1 (back)**

---

**finesse** (fi-nes')

---

**Card 2 (front)**

---

rhyming word
mnemonic

**the ability to handle delicate and
difficult situations skillfully**

Rescuing hostages takes **finesse.** the finest, the best

---

**Card 2 (back)**

## EXERCISE 2.5   MAKING VOCABULARY CARDS

*Practice making vocabulary cards with the words below.*

1. acute          4. mementos

2. decadent       5. perspective

3. mantra

## EXERCISE 2.6   USING THE VOCABULARY CARD SYSTEM

*Use the vocabulary card system to learn twenty words you would like to know.
Good word sources include the Internet, television, and newspaper and magazine articles. Test your success with a partner.*

## 2B WORD SOURCES

You can use a dictionary and a thesaurus to develop a strong vocabulary.

### 2b.1 Using a Dictionary

A dictionary is a book of word definitions. It also gives varied information about words. It can, for example, help you pronounce a word, locate synonyms, spell words, know the parts of speech, determine word origins, and divide words into syllables. However, before you look up an unfamiliar word in a dictionary, ask these questions:

Is the word already defined in context by the surrounding words and phrases?

Can I determine the word's meaning from its context?

Can my knowledge of affixes and roots help me unlock the word's meaning?

If these efforts fail, then use your dictionary.

Knowing the parts of a dictionary, which in some ways is similar to a telephone directory, will help you get the most from your efforts. These are the features of a dictionary:

1. **Guide words** at the top show the first and last words on each page.
2. The **main entry word,** the major word being defined, is boldfaced, hanging over into the left-hand margin, and listed in alphabetical order.
3. The **pronunciation** shows the way the word should sound. The pronunciation is usually given in parentheses following the entry word, with accented syllables and marked vowels to show emphasis and stress.
4. The **etymology** shows the origin of the word (e.g., *L.* for Latin, *OE* for Old English).
5. A word's **part of speech** shows how it can be used in the system of English grammar (*noun, verb, adverb, adjective,* and *pronoun*).
6. The **definition** gives the meaning of the word, with the most common definition listed first.
7. **Special usage labels** that give added information about the word include *slang, colloquial, obsolete, dialect,* and *archaic.*
8. **Synonyms** are words having a similar meaning.
9. The **pronunciation key,** a list of common words representing the varied sounds found in the words being defined, is usually located at the bottom of every other page.

### EXERCISE 2.7   THE DICTIONARY

*Study the dictionary entry below and match each lettered part to its numbered description above. Write the correct number in the space after each letter.*

a. _____                          b. _____

c. _____                          d. _____

e. _____                          f. _____

g. _____

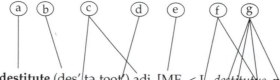

destitute (des'tə toot') adj. [ME. < L. destitutus, pp. of
destituere, to set, place: see STATUTE] 1. not having; being
without; lacking (with of ) [destitute of trees] 2. lacking the
necessities of life; living in complete poverty 3. [Obs.]
abandoned -vt. tut'ed, 'tut'ing [Rare] 1. to deprive 2. to
make destitute -SYN. see POOR

## EXERCISE 2.8   ALPHABETICAL ORDER

*Write the following words in alphabetical order.*

façade          1. _____

anonymity       2. _____

anomalous       3. _____

actuary         4. _____

omnipotent      5. _____

epicure         6. _____

ephemeral       7. _____

juxtapose       8. _____

epilogue        9. _____

epiphyte       10. _____

## EXERCISE 2.9   FINDING PRONUNCIATIONS IN A DICTIONARY

*Using the pronunciation in your dictionary, write the phonetic
pronunciation of each word.*

1. façade        _____

2. anonymity     _____

3. anomalous     _____

4. actuary          _____

5. omnipotent      _____

6. epicure          _____

7. ephemeral       _____

8. juxtapose       _____

9. epilogue         _____

10. epiphyte       _____


## EXERCISE 2.10   USING A DICTIONARY

*Use your dictionary to complete the chart below: First locate the entry word and its usage label definition. Then write a brief definition and the remaining requested information under the appropriate column headings. (The third word is done for you.)*

| ENTRY WORD (1) | GUIDE WORDS (2) | PRONUN- CIATION (3) | ETYMOL- OGY (4) | PART OF SPEECH (5) | DEFINITION (6) | USAGE LABEL (7) |
|---|---|---|---|---|---|---|
| *goof* | ____ | ____ | ____ | ____ | ____ | ____ |
| *hustle* | ____ | ____ | ____ | ____ | ____ | ____ |
| *keel* | kayak keep | kel | M.E. | VI | to turn over | Coll. |
| *measly* | ____ | ____ | ____ | ____ | ____ | ____ |
| *noble* | ____ | ____ | ____ | ____ | ____ | ____ |
| *party* | ____ | ____ | ____ | ____ | ____ | ____ |


## 2b.2   Using a Thesaurus

A **thesaurus** is a book of synonyms. It contains many families of words that are similar in meaning. Using a thesaurus can help you express yourself more precisely, avoid overuse of the same words, find antonyms for a word, and convey more specific shades of meaning. The index in the back section lists words in alphabetical order along with page numbers to help you locate words quickly. These are the parts of a thesaurus entry:

1. The **entry word** is listed with words of similar meaning.
2. The **part of speech** is identified.

3. **Synonyms** (similar words) are separated by semicolons.
4. **Cross-reference word(s)** are different main words that contain synonyms for the entry word. These are shown in small capital letters.
5. **Special usage labels** show how a particular word may be used (e.g., *colloquialism, slang*).
6. **Antonyms** are words with an opposite meaning.

## EXERCISE 2.11   THE THESAURUS

*Study the following thesaurus entries and match each lettered part to its numbered description above. Write the correct number in the space after each letter below.*

a. _____                                    b. _____

c. _____                                    d. _____

e. _____                                    f. _____

### CONTACT

*Nouns*—contact, contiguity, abutment, TOUCH, CONNECTION; osculation; meeting, encounter, border[land], frontier, tangent. See NEARNESS.

*Verbs*—be in contact, be contiguous, join, adjoin, abut; butt; TOUCH, meet, encounter, run *or* bump into, meet up with, come *or* chance upon, happen on, run *or* come across, fall on; osculate, come in contact, march with, rub elbows *or* shoulders, keep in touch, hobnob. See JUNCTION.

*Adjectives*—in contact, contiguous, adjacent, touching; bordering, neighboring; conterminous, end to end, osculatory; tangent, tangential; hand to hand; close to, in touch with, shoulder to shoulder, cheek by jowl.

*Prepositions*—against, upon.

*Antonyms*, see INTERVAL, DISTANCE.

conductor, n. guide, escort, DIRECTOR; manager, operator, supervisor; guard; drum major, leader, maestro, choirmaster; transmitter, conveyor. *Colloq.*, time beater. See MUSIC, TRANSPORTATION.

## EXERCISE 2.12   USING A THESAURUS

*Use your thesaurus to find substitutes for the boldfaced words in these sentences.*

1. Nobody should ever have to experience the pain of **talking** to a **person** who likes **talking** about herself.

   a. talking _____

   b. person _____

   c. talking _____

2. Without moving an inch, I **moved** that we order a moving van to **move** all employees who agreed to **move** to our new location.

   a. moved _____

   b. move _____

   c. move _____

3. The **pretty** girl is **pretty** efficient at finding **pretty** clothes.

   a. pretty _____

   b. pretty _____

   c. pretty _____

4. She accidentally **injured** my foot while we were **walking** down the **street** behind the floats.

   a. injured _____

   b. walking _____

   c. street _____

5. If you **run** and run cold water on your **cold** hands now, they might not **hurt** later.

   a. run _____

   b. cold _____

   c. hurt _____

## EXERCISE 2.13   USING YOUR DICTIONARY AND THESAURUS

*Use your dictionary and thesaurus to correct or to express more precisely the boldfaced words in these sentences.*

1. Anna was **glad** that she **got** a **nice pear** of diamond earrings for her birthday.

   a. glad _____

   b. got _____

c. nice _____

d. pear _____

2. Michael is **moving good,** but Chicago **steal** might **loose.**

   a. moving _____

   b. good _____

   c. steal _____

   d. loose _____

3. Some **old speakers** are **interesting;** others are **poor.**

   a. old _____

   b. speakers _____

   c. interesting _____

   d. poor _____

4. The **wise man left** his **big** throne.

   a. wise _____

   b. man _____

   c. left _____

   d. big _____

5. We **wood** have been **happy** if we had **one** the **lottrey.**

   a. wood _____

   b. happy _____

   c. one _____

   d. lottrey _____

# Mastery Test 2

*Read the passage below and use context clues and your knowledge of roots, prefixes, and suffixes to determine the meaning of each boldfaced word.*

## Home for the Holidays

When Millard Fuller was a six-year-old growing up in Lanette, Alabama, his father taught him the meaning of profit and loss. And the boy 1 learned his lessons well. When he finished law school in 1960, Fuller said that he and a partner were already **grooming** a $50,000 mail-order business they had formed while in school into a **multimillion**-dollar sales empire: "My goal was to make a lot of money—and I succeeded."

But in his efforts to get rich, Fuller neglected something else in his life: his family. His wife, tired of **competing** with and losing to the firm, 2 left him. Fuller knew his **priorities** had to change. He chased down his wife in New York, and together they made a **decision.** Fuller would sell his **interest** in the business. They would give up the big house, the cars, and the boats and focus on the family. So, Fuller and his wife **retreated** to a farm in rural Georgia, where he discovered both an **appalling** lack of decent housing and a new mission in life: to help the poor build **affordable** homes. With that, Habitat for Humanity was established in 1976.

Since then, people of all faiths, races, and beliefs—including former President Jimmy Carter—have helped the **organization** construct some 3 70,000 homes around the world. Says Fuller, "To get the most out of life, **entrepreneurs** must **enrich** others just as they enrich themselves."

## VOCABULARY REVIEW
*Circle the letter for the best definition of each boldfaced word as it is used in the passage.*

1. **Grooming** means
   a. tending a horse.
   c. putting everything in place.
   b. preparing to get married.
   d. organizing and caring for.

2. **Retreated** means
   a. visited a quiet place.
   c. returned.
   b. withdrew to a safe place.
   d. received treats.

3. **Enrich** means
   a. to make rich.
   c. to give value to.
   b. to fertilize.
   d. to sweeten.

4. **Interest** means
   a. business license.
   b. a right or claim to something.
   c. a feeling of concern.
   d. money paid for the use of money.

5. **Priorities** means
   a. prior plans.
   b. acts of minor importance.
   c. prior abilities.
   d. matters of importance.

6. **Appalling** means
   a. feeling blue.
   b. losing time.
   c. causing shock.
   d. turning modern.

7. **Decision** means
   a. a clearing of one's thoughts.
   b. a feeling of satisfaction.
   c. a conclusion reached.
   d. a choice of going home.

8. **Entrepreneur** means
   a. a French businessman.
   b. a superfast reader.
   c. a person who starts a business.
   d. a family manager.

9. **Affordable** means
   a. able to form.
   b. able to sell.
   c. able to purchase.
   d. able to carry.

10. **Competing** means
    a. trying to take over.
    b. trying to train.
    c. trying to honor.
    d. trying to win.

11. **Organization** means
    a. the condition of being organized.
    b. the act of grouping.
    c. the condition of working together.
    d. the act of sharing.

12. **Multimillion** means
    a. one million.
    b. many millions.
    c. more than a million.
    d. less than a million.

Circle the words that have a prefix attached.

13. grooming            14. retreated

15. enrich              16. interest

17. priorities          18. affordable

19. organization        20. multimillion

Score: Number correct _____ (out of 20) × 5 = _____

Name _____, Course & Section _____, Date _____

# 3

# Text Processing I:
## *Relating the Facts*

*Relating the facts* in reading refers to looking at the way the author organizes and connects ideas in writing. Seeing these relationships helps you get a better understanding of what you read. The information below will acquaint you with the parts that make up the whole—the paragraph, essay, or longer written work. The parts include the topic, central idea, main idea, supporting details, signal words, and paragraph patterns. Together, these items work to form the author's message. Your understanding of them will help you fit the pieces of the writing and reading puzzle together.

## 3A MAIN IDEAS

One of the most important aspects of reading is finding the main idea. This is the point that the author makes in the writing. The main idea is a sentence—not a word or phrase—that tells what a paragraph or group of paragraphs is about. It is always a general idea that focuses on a particular subject. The first steps, then, in finding the main idea require you to know how to do three things: (1) separate general from specific ideas, (2) identify the topic, and (3) locate key ideas in sentences.

### 3a.1 General and Specific Ideas

To separate general from specific ideas, you must know the difference between the two. **General ideas** are broad ideas that include group words such as *people*, *animals*, and *sports*. In contrast, a **specific idea** is narrow and particular. It refers to the individual items that may be included in a general idea. Examples of specific ideas for the general idea *people* include *men*, *women*, *boys*, *girls*, *children*, *students*, and so on. Follow these steps to identify general and specific ideas:

**Step 1.** Look for words, ideas, concepts that make up a broad category.
   *Ask: Does the idea include many individual items?*

**Step 2.** Determine what the specific ideas are. ***Ask:*** *What are the specific ideas, examples, or parts that make up the general idea?*

**Step 3.** Check your response. ***Ask:*** *Can I clearly see a difference between the general and specific ideas?*

Figures 3.1 and 3.2 show the relationship between general and specific ideas.

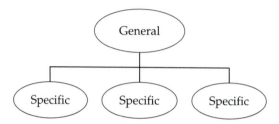

**Figure 3.1** Relationship Between General and Specific Ideas

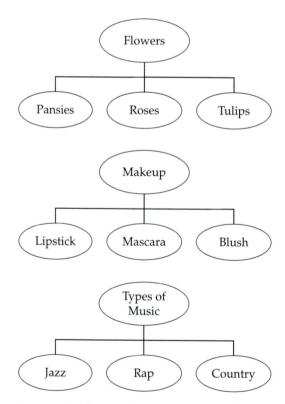

**Figure 3.2** Maps of General and Specific Ideas

## EXERCISE 3.1  GENERAL IDEAS

*Circle the general idea in each word grouping.*

1. Easter   Christmas   holidays   Halloween
2. algebra   mathematics   trigonometry   calculus
3. puppy   kitten   animal babies   calf

Did you choose *holidays, mathematics,* and *animal babies* as the most general items in this sample? These terms represent the correct response for items 1, 2, and 3 because each of these can be broken down further into specific ideas or examples.

## EXERCISE 3.2  SEQUENCING SENTENCES

*Sequence these sentences from general to specific.*

_____  A. There are several methods of cooking vegetables for maximum nutrition.

_____  B. One method is to cook vegetables only until tender in a minimum amount of water.

_____  C. You may cook squash, for example, in just enough water to prevent scorching, using a pan with a tight-fitting lid.

In this second sample, the sequence should be A, B, C. The first sentence is general. It includes terms that could be narrowed down, such as *several methods* and *vegetables.* The second sentence gives a specific example of one of the several methods (*until tender in a minimum amount of water*). But the third sentence is even more specific because it provides detailed information about cooking a particular vegetable, namely, *squash. Enough water to prevent scorching* and *pan with tight-fitting lid* provide more specific information.

## EXERCISE 3.3  RECOGNIZING GENERAL IDEAS

*Circle the letter of the general idea in each word grouping.*

1. a. grapes            b. apples
   c. fruit             d. plums

2. a. vegetables        b. corn
   c. squash            d. beets

3. a. juice             b. beverages
   c. coffee            d. tea

4. a. clothes           b. shirt
   c. shorts            d. jacket

5. a. joy               b. love
   c. hate              d. emotion

6. a. presidents        b. Lincoln
   c. Clinton           d. Washington

7. a. iris                        b. pupil
   c. eye parts                   d. lens

8. a. sofa                        b. furniture
   c. dresser                     d. table

9. a. vehicles                    b. car
   c. van                         d. truck

10. a. kidney                     b. heart
    c. organs                     d. liver

## EXERCISE 3.4    WRITING GENERAL IDEAS

*Write a general term for each of the following word groupings.*

1. _____ nurse   firefighter   judge   police officer

2. _____ leopard   tiger   lion   cougar

3. _____ football   soccer   baseball   basketball

4. _____ ant   wasp   beetle   locust

5. _____ opium   cocaine   nicotine   marijuana

6. _____ cobra   python   adder   rattler

7. _____ Nancy   Hillary   Barbara   Jacqueline

8. _____ mustard   catsup   relish   mayonnaise

9. _____ nutmeg   oregano   paprika   basil

10. _____ macaroni   spaghetti   linguini   ravioli

## EXERCISE 3.5    GENERAL AND SPECIFIC IDEAS WITH SENTENCES

*Sequence these sentences from general (1) to most specific (3).*

1. _____ a. In the spring, basketball playoffs are covered on the major networks as well as on the sports channel.

   _____ b. Most professional sports delight their fans by showing seasonal competitions on television.

   _____ c. In January, football's Super Bowl game is watched by millions on NBC.

2. _____ a. Phone service can be slow, and you should not be surprised if you constantly get a busy signal; just keep redialing.

   _____ b. It's not easy to reach people; there are still problems with communications.

   _____ c. Meeting with potential clients in a Third World country can be challenging.

3. \_\_\_\_ a. For instance, Tate went with his group on a catamaran
   journey to a private snorkeling spot and then on to
   St. Kitts for some shopping.

   \_\_\_\_ b. To be truly successful, an employee incentive experience
   must include multiple activities.

   \_\_\_\_ c. It's about creating one-of-a-kind activities, such as scav-
   enger hunts, parties in special places, and private yacht
   charters.

4. \_\_\_\_ a. More sophisticated travelers are discovering that for the
   price of a hotel room they can rent an apartment.

   \_\_\_\_ b. Families and older couples feel that the biggest
   advantage to renting an apartment is being able to
   prepare meals.

   \_\_\_\_ c. An apartment has all the comforts of home—full
   kitchen, living room, patio, and maybe even laundry
   facilities.

## 3a.2 The Topic

The next step in identifying the main idea is to find the **topic** of the paragraph. The topic is the broad or general subject about which the writer
has chosen to write. It may appear as a word or phrase found in a title, in
a paragraph, or throughout the reading. Identification of the topic in a
paragraph can lead you to the **topic sentence.** Follow these steps to identify the topic:

**Step 1.** Read the paragraph.
**Step 2.** Determine the subject of the paragraph. *Ask: Who or what is the
author writing about? Is any word or its substitute (a synonym or pronoun) frequently repeated?*
**Step 3.** State the topic in a word or a phrase.
**Step 4.** Check your response. *Ask: Is this really the author's subject? Is the
subject too broad or too narrow?*

## EXERCISE 3.6   SEQUENCING TOPICS

*Sequence these topics from broad (1) to narrow (3).*

1. \_\_\_\_ a. shoes        \_\_\_\_ b. sneakers        \_\_\_\_ c. Nikes

2. \_\_\_\_ a. dessert       \_\_\_\_ b. pie             \_\_\_\_ c. apple pie

3. \_\_\_\_ a. exercise      \_\_\_\_ b. aerobics        \_\_\_\_ c. jogging

4. \_\_\_\_ a. animal        \_\_\_\_ b. mammal          \_\_\_\_ c. whale

Did you number each of the four items above 1, 2, and 3?

## EXERCISE 3.7    PARAGRAPH TOPIC

*Circle the topic of the following paragraph.*

> Acute pain serves a useful purpose and should be taken seriously. It can be a warning sign of a dangerous illness, such as a heart attack or a blood clot. Dr. Dan Jones, a local emergency physician, says that some of the more common problems are seen in hospital emergency departments.

Did you circle *acute pain* in the paragraph? The word *pain* alone would have been too general. The word *it* in the second sentence is a substitute for *acute pain* in the first sentence.

## EXERCISE 3.8    IDENTIFYING GENERAL AND SPECIFIC IDEAS

*Each set of words below contains a general idea and a specific idea. Sequence the items in each set from general (1) to most specific (3).*

1. _____ a.  the Beatles

   _____ b.  musical groups

   _____ c.  musical groups from England

2. _____ a.  the solar system

   _____ b.  the planets

   _____ c.  Mars

3. _____ a.  western states

   _____ b.  states

   _____ c.  California

4. _____ a.  flowers

   _____ b.  tulips

   _____ c.  exports from Holland

5. _____ a.  disease

   _____ b.  tuberculosis

   _____ c.  airborne disease

6. _____ a.  electronics

   _____ b.  electronic equipment

   _____ c.  videocassette recorder

7. _____ a.  *Dead Presidents*

   _____ b.  movies about presidents

   _____ c.  movies

8. _____ a. illness

   _____ b. psychosis

   _____ c. mental illness

9. _____ a. colleges

   _____ b. schools

   _____ c. community colleges

10. _____ a. father

    _____ b. male family members

    _____ c. family

## EXERCISE 3.9   RECOGNIZING PARAGRAPH TOPICS

*Label the three subjects following each paragraph from "Homebrew Erykah Badu" as follows: T for topic, S for too specific, and G for too general.*

1. Take a splash of Sarah, a bit of Billie, and a shot of Chaka and add echoes of Ella. Mix liberally with some down-home blues, and you're close to the Badu brew. It is a potent musical gumbo best served hot.

   _____ a. the Badu brew

   _____ b. a potent musical gumbo

   _____ c. talented female singers

2. A live Erykah Badu performance is an experience. With her trade-mark candle and lighted incense, her foot-high headdress and her Afrocentric clothes, she creates her own space and invites the audience into her reality.

   _____ a. Erykah Badu

   _____ b. a live Erykah Badu performance.

   _____ c. Erykah Badu's trademark

3. Badu was born Erica Wright, but she decided to change her name as a teenager. Her mother objected to her changing her first name, so Erykah changed the spelling. The "Badu" part came from her favorite jazz sound. And she discovered later, from her father, that in Islam the word means "to manifest truth."

   _____ a. Badu's name change

   _____ b. Badu's name

   _____ c. the Badu part

4. Badu, the Dallas native, studied theater at Grambling State University in Louisiana, and she is a trained dancer. Only a few years ago, she was working three jobs in Dallas. She was teaching during the day, performing at nightclubs in the evening, and waitressing on the third shift to make sure she could pay her bills.

_____ b. the Dallas native

_____ a. Erykah's background

_____ c. Erykah's three jobs

5. Erykah's willful determination may be in direct contrast to the laid-back song stylings on her CD, but don't believe the hype. Badu isn't simply some whacked-out cosmic butterfly. There's a shrewd businesswoman hiding under that headdress, the kind of determined artist who took a nineteen-song demo to the record company, wrote all of the songs but one on her CD, wrote and directed the video for *On & On*, and co-directed the video for her single, "Next Lifetime."

_____ a. a shrewd businesswoman

_____ b. Erykah's willful determination

_____ c. determination

## EXERCISE 3.10   RECOGNIZING PARAGRAPH TOPICS

*Identify the topic of each of the following paragraphs.*

1. A credit profile contains varied types of information that you may consider personal or even private. The first item in a credit profile is your name and any variations of your name under which you may have been known. Examples of other information in a credit profile are social security number, address, place of employment, and date of birth. Also included in a credit profile are charge accounts, credit accounts, a detailed list of your open and closed loans, and public-record items—bankruptcies, tax liens, and court judgments.
   Margie Jasper, "Your Credit Profile Rights"

   Topic: _____

2. As simple as it sounds, exercise is the best natural anti-anxiety agent we have. Exercise reduces tension, drains off excess aggression and frustration, enhances well-being, improves sleep, lessens the tendency to overeat, aids in concentration, and reduces distractions. It is healing to the body, and therefore to the mind. Getting exercise at least every other day should be part of your plan to reduce anxiety and control worry. But you can also exercise on the spot to reduce some worry. If you are having a bad day at the office, try walking up and down a flight of stairs five times. Your mind will be less troubled

when you come back to your desk. The change in body chemistry resulting from exercise calms the mind.

—Edward M. Hallowell, "Worry"

Topic: _____

3. Prayer or meditation can change the state of your brain as well. Talk to God when you feel worried. If you are not religious, learn how to meditate. Brain scans show beneficial changes in the brain during meditation and prayer. These changes are similar to most of our measures of improved health, including long life and reduced incidence of illness. And extended worry decreases with regular prayer or meditation.

Edward M. Hallowell, "Worry"

Topic: _____

4. From Lake Louise, travel time to Jasper is about three hours, or as long as you desire. Icefields Parkway, connecting Alberta's Banff and Jasper National Parks, is a 142-mile stretch that parallels the Rockies' most jagged and awesome peaks. Decades ago, only pack trains traveled the route, and a fast trip from Jasper to Lake Louise took almost three weeks. Today, 50 years after it opened, Icefields Parkway has allowed some 50 million tourists to visit areas once seen only by the hardiest of travelers.

Topic: _____

5. Hopson says a definite turnoff for a man is a woman who constantly compares him to an ex-boyfriend, an ex-husband, her girlfriend's man, or anybody else. Comparing how a man measures up (and doesn't) is a sure way to make him spit fire. "Women have to be careful not to stereotype or generalize," Hopson says. "A woman can't assume a man is going to be a certain way because other men have been that way. Men are complex creatures and have to be treated as such."

Topic: _____

## 3a.3 The Key Idea in a Sentence

To understand how a topic sentence functions in a paragraph, become familiar with the key idea in a sentence. The key idea is the major point the author makes. It contains the essential parts of the sentence stripped of modifiers or other descriptive terms and phrases. This leaves only the subject and the author's focus or controlling idea. To find the key idea of a sentence, follow these steps:

**Step 1.** Read the sentence carefully. *Ask: Do I understand the contents of this sentence?*

**Step 2.** Identify the subject. *Ask: Who or what is the sentence all about?*

**Step 3.** Determine the author's focus or controlling idea. *Ask: How does the author feel about the subject? What is the attitude or opinion expressed? What is the verb in the sentence?*

**Step 4.** Eliminate the modifiers and descriptive words and phrases. *Ask: Have I included only the essential parts of the sentence: the subject and the focus?*

**Step 5.** Check your response. *Ask: Did I locate the bare essence of the sentence? Do I need to reword this sentence to express the author's main point?*

### EXERCISE 3.11    FINDING KEY IDEAS

*Read each sentence below and locate the key idea. Underline the subject and the point the author makes about it.*

1. The lady who wore the yellow pinstriped suit to church last Sunday is unhappy because her pet rabbit was bitten by a poisonous snake.

2. Despite the fact that my house was blown away during the horrible storm last night, I am still alive; nothing else really matters.

If you chose "The lady" and "is unhappy" in sentence 1 and "I" and "am still alive" in sentence 2, you chose the correct key ideas. You eliminated the extra information (modifiers—words, phrases, clauses) and keyed in on those ideas the author considered important.

### EXERCISE 3.12    IDENTIFYING KEY IDEAS IN SENTENCES

*Underline the key ideas in the following sentences.*

1. Just as the quarterback had gotten away from two others the following day, he was able to escape two tacklers in last Friday's game against the opposing team.

2. Spending countless hours in the learning lab, Janice now understands mathematics, which is a requirement for college students in schools around the country.

3. It is no surprise that Ernest Hemingway, who wrote *The Old Man and the Sea*, won the Pulitzer Prize for literature in 1953.

4. Although I have tried repeatedly to locate another word like *Mississippi*, I cannot find one; perhaps the four *i*'s and the four *s*'s give it an unusual quality.

5. Becoming famous for writing the ragtime song *Maple Leaf Rag*, Scott Joplin, who is known by music lovers around the world, will surely be noted in history as one of the great composers of the twentieth century.

## 3a.4 The Stated Main Idea

The main idea may be stated in a **topic sentence** in the paragraph. This sentence is usually found at the beginning of a paragraph. However, it could very well be located in the middle or at the end. This important statement is not only general, but it also sums up most of the specific details in a paragraph. Its contents include the topic and the author's thoughts about the topic. Follow these steps to identify the topic sentence:

**Step 1.** Read the paragraph.

**Step 2.** Identify the topic of the paragraph. *Ask: Who or what is the author writing about?*

**Step 3.** Determine the point the author attempts to make about the topic. *Ask: What does the author want me to understand about the topic? Does the author achieve his or her purpose? What is the author's message to me? What is the key idea that is repeated or explained in depth?*

**Step 4.** Locate the general statement that sums up all the details and key ideas in the paragraph. *Ask: Which sentence is most general and best sums up all details and key ideas in the paragraph?*

**Step 5.** Check your response. *Ask: Do the details and key ideas in the paragraph support this point? When I read the sentence by itself, does it appear to explain the paragraph well?*

## EXERCISE 3.13   FINDING TOPIC SENTENCES

*Read each group of sentences below. Look for and underline the topic sentence, which should be neither too narrow nor too broad, yet general enough to cover all of the details.*

1. In the winter people of all ages walk at the mall.
   The beach is a popular place to walk in the summer.
   In the spring, all kinds of people walk in parks.
   Children can walk in the park with their dog or a friend.
   Along the streets is where many people walk in the fall.
   People walk many places all year.

2. Behavior, after all, is a primary form of communication for school-age children.
   Here are a few of the more common classroom styles.
   The class clown tends to be an outgoing child in need of attention.
   The quiet one is shy, introverted, and insecure about speaking up in school.
   The daydreamer who tunes out or doodles in class may have a concentration problem.
   The eager beaver tends to be a high achiever who is naturally motivated.

In the first group, the last sentence is the most general because it includes all places where people walk during the year: winter, malls; summer, beach; spring, park; and fall, streets. The other sentences are too narrow because they give only one place and season to support the topic sentence.

In the second group, the second sentence is the main idea because it is the most general. It includes children grouped into the four categories depending on their classroom behaviors: the class clown, the quiet one, the daydreamer, and the eager beaver. The first sentence introduces the paragraph and states the topic. The other sentences are too narrow. They highlight only one type of behavior to support the topic sentence.

### EXERCISE 3.14   STATED MAIN IDEAS

*For each paragraph below, underline the topic sentence and then write the topic in the space provided.*

1. Drugs are destroying our young college athletes. One example is Jack Jones, a great football player for Jackson State. At twenty, he helped his team win an NCAA championship while high on cocaine. Becoming addicted in high school, Jones later left college for the streets of San Francisco. Another example is Barry Ellison, a celebrated tennis star at a renowned Eastern university. After injuring his left arm at age 20, Barry was treated with prescription drugs by the team's physician. Barry, too, became addicted and dropped out of college the next year.

   Topic: _____

2. Hatha yoga, one of the best overall body toners, helps to move energy through your body. If your joints feel hot and stiff, try this simple Hatha yoga technique: Close your eyes, and visualize cool streams of water running through your entire body. Combine this with a gradual opening and closing of the hands, and say, "I release the past, I release the stiffness, and I allow streams of cool, nourishing energy to flow through my body." When visualization and energy are continually used, they are far more helpful than a medicinal drug—and a lot less toxic!
   Natural Medicine Chest, "Start Moving to Stop Pain"

   Topic: _____

3. Though acceptance therapy is not yet widely practiced, it shows promise of reaching many couples not helped by behavioral modification or other traditional methods. A pilot study of twenty couples considering divorce found that after six months of acceptance therapy, ninety percent reported dramatic increases in satisfaction, and, a year later, none had split up. The National Institute of Mental Health is now funding clinical trials for acceptance therapy involving 180 couples. Results of that study are five years away, but therapists are already bringing some of the ideas into their practices. "What we're

most excited about," says Jacobson, "is that this method is successful with many of the couples least helped by behavioral therapy, like older people in more traditional marriages."

Joanne M. Schrof, "Married with Problems"

Topic: _____

4. Spousal abuse can take many different forms. One of the most frequent signs of spousal abuse is physical injury. The abused spouse suffers from unusual broken bones, bruises, burns, and cuts. Usually the person responsible for the abuse claims that the victim had an accident even though no ordinary accident could cause such injuries. Emotional neglect is a second type of spousal abuse. The abuser simply ignores the spouse and refuses to respond to bids for attention. Emotional abuse is another common form of mistreatment. In this case, the abuser does serious damage to the spouse's self-esteem.

Topic: _____

5. Far too many people in this country are killing themselves by smoking. For this reason, several products are now available to help people stop smoking. Nicoderm, for example, is the name of a patch that distributes mini-doses of nicotine to help smokers quit. There is also a chewing gum containing nicotine. This product allows quitters to gradually cut down the amount of nicotine they get from cigarettes. Then there are audio and videotapes that use suggestion to encourage people to quit. There are also special cigarette filters that reduce the amount of smoke and nicotine that gets to the smoker's mouth.

Topic: _____

6. One study in Washington State found that patients were more satisfied with their chiropractor's manner than with their medical doctor's. Patients may even be too satisfied. One frequent complaint about chiropractors is that treatment goes on for too long. Patients become dependent on regular manipulation, and their therapists are all too happy to please them. Alan Adams of the Los Angeles College of Chiropractors estimates that perhaps 10 to 15 percent of his colleagues are guilty of this.

Topic: _____

## 3a.5 Implied Main Idea

Sometimes the main idea of a paragraph is implied, and there is no topic sentence. In this case, you must consider all of the supporting details when you write a sentence describing the topic. Follow these steps to write an implied main idea:

**Step 1.** Read the paragraph.
**Step 2.** Identify the topic of the paragraph.

**Step 3.** Determine the point the author attempts to make about the topic. **Ask:** *What does the author want me to understand about the topic? What is the author's message to me? What key ideas are repeated or explained in depth?*

**Step 4.** Use the major supporting details and key ideas to create a general statement that represents the point the author makes about the topic. **Ask:** *Does this sentence sum up the details and key ideas? Does a general term replace a list? Does the sentence express the author's point?*

**Step 5.** Check your response. **Ask:** *Does my sentence capture the main points stated in the paragraph? When I read the sentence to myself, does it appear to explain the paragraph well?*

## EXERCISE 3.15   IDENTIFYING AN IMPLIED MAIN IDEA

*Read the groups of sentences below. Think about the meaning of the paragraph. Then read the lettered options and explanations for choosing the correct implied main idea.*

1. Supervisors complain that workers are late for work.
   Supervisors say that workers on early morning shifts are often too sleepy or too sluggish to be productive.
   Supervisors say that workers turn in incomplete time sheets.
   Supervisors complain that workers abuse time-off privileges during breaks and lunch.
   According to supervisors, workers turn in poor-quality work.
   a. Supervisors are opinionated.
      *(Too broad—no mention of complaints or workers; the topic could be anything.)*
   b. Supervisors have strong feelings about workers.
      *(Too broad—"feelings" could be negative or positive.)*
   c. Supervisors accuse workers of sleeping on the job.
      *(Too narrow—this is only one of the many complaints.)*
   d. Supervisors have many complaints about workers.

2. Go to the library to read, study, or do homework.
   Instead of socializing, use your free time to study with your classmates.
   Discuss your reading and quiz each other before tests.
   If you have questions, use your free time to see your instructor.
   Go to the learning lab for tutoring if you need extra help.
   a. Students can do a number of things while in college.
      *(Too broad—mention of success or use of free time on campus is missing.)*
   b. Discussions and quizzes will help students pass tests.
      *(Too narrow—the sentence presents only one part of the list.)*
   c. Students should find the library and the instructor's office.
      *(Too narrow—the sentence presents only one part of the list.)*

  d. To be successful, students must make good use of their free time
      on campus.

## EXERCISE 3.16   IMPLIED MAIN IDEAS

*Circle the letter of the implied main idea for the sentences in the paragraphs
below. Then write TB (too broad) or TN (too narrow) in the blank before each of
the remaining options.*

1. Women accuse men of not talking enough.
   Women say that men do not share their feelings.
   Women complain that men work too hard.
   Women say that men choose work over family.
   According to women, men cannot be trusted.

   _____ a. Women are opinionated.

   _____ b. Women have strong feelings about men.

   _____ c. Women accuse men of working too much.

   _____ d. Women have many complaints about men.

2. The play area will include swings, a slide, and monkey bars.
   An open area will be staged for playing baseball and soccer.
   The picnic area will be furnished with ten picnic tables.
   A locked building will store equipment and supplies.
   The entire playground will cover half a block.

   _____ a. The layout of the playground means paying attention to
                detail.

   _____ b. The layout of this playground is designed for playing,
                eating, and storing supplies.

   _____ c. The playground will include swings, sliding boards, and
                monkey bars.

   _____ d. The layout of playgrounds requires much prior planning.

3. During the first stage of liver disease, the liver becomes fatty, but no
   symptoms appear.
   Abstinence can reverse this damage.
   The second stage is hepatitis, or inflammation.
   If drinking continues, the liver enlarges, causing pain.
   Cirrhosis is the third and most advanced stage of liver disease.
   Scar tissue replaces working liver cells.
   If untreated, cirrhosis is fatal.

   _____ a. Cirrhosis is fatal.

   _____ b. Before the hepatitis stage, the liver becomes fatty, and later,
                cirrhosis sets in.

_____ c. Alcohol damages the liver in three stages.

_____ d. Alcohol damages select organs of the body.

4. Physical abuse involves severe physical punishment for a child's actions.
   The parent, for example, may lose control and hit the child.
   The second type of abuse is emotional: the parent says cruel things to the child.
   Specifically, the parent may tell the child she's ugly.
   Emotional abuse harms as much as physical abuse does.
   Sexual abuse is the third type.
   In this case, a relative or family acquaintance forces the child to have sexual relations.

   _____ a. A child can be abused in several ways.

   _____ b. Emotional and sexual abuse are detrimental to a child.

   _____ c. Child abuse can be characterized as physical, emotional, or sexual.

   _____ d. Physical abuse involves the parent's losing control and hitting the child.

5. Pet foods can be stored in lidded storage tubs, lidded trash cans, or other similar large-capacity containers.
   Keeping dry foods, such as kibble, moisture-free will maintain its texture and taste.
   Mice or other sneak thieves won't be encouraged to chew into paper bags or to climb into uncovered containers.
   There is less likelihood of your pet sneaking food during non-mealtimes.
   —Ann Marie Radaskiewicz

   _____ a. Keeping pet food in a closed container makes sense for a number of reasons.

   _____ b. Keep your pet from sneaking food during non-mealtimes.

   _____ c. Pet foods should be stored.

   _____ d. Mice like pet food, too.

## EXERCISE 3.17   WRITING AN IMPLIED MAIN IDEA

*Read each of the following paragraphs and determine the topic and implied main idea.*

1. Regardless of weather conditions, many dogs sleep outdoors year round. And even when circumstances allow them to have dog houses, some are still unprotected because they have no door to close

to ward off the elements. Secondly, for some, table scraps are the order of the day while others consume their share of the dreaded dry kibble, purchased in giant bags to last the entire month. Variety is unheard of. And for those who are favored with the canned or packaged meat varieties, they are (regardless of size) given only one serving, one can or one patty. Last, and even more degrading, some dogs stay home tied up all day, maybe longer, to be released at their owner's whim. My, what a life!

Topic: _____

Implied topic sentence: _____

2. Students who return to school after age 25 often take a reading course to brush up on their skills. These older students have had much experience in the world of work and family and, therefore, bring this knowledge to their classes. They know exactly what they want from college. They use their time wisely because their busy lives force them to do so. Family, exercise, study, and jobs must be carefully balanced if these students are to succeed. Students who are middle-aged and older often study harder and get better grades, not only for personal satisfaction, but also from a sense of competition with their younger classmates.

Topic: _____

Implied main idea: _____

3. Some individuals become homeless because they have no network of friends and relatives. If they also have no financial cushion, they drop through the cracks and end up on the streets. Some have mental illnesses serious enough to prevent them from keeping a job. In the past, they might well have been institutionalized. Others are mentally capable but have physical conditions that prevent them from working. Without medical coverage, their health continues to worsen. Some homeless individuals abuse alcohol or drugs and may require long-term treatment to overcome their addictions.

Topic: _____

Implied main idea: _____

4. Each year thousands of people seriously consider furthering their education by attending college. However, the Department of Labor estimated that 80 percent of the new jobs require vocational or technical training, but not a college degree. Second, even in some jobs that usually require a college degree, people with drive and determination can often succeed without a college degree. President Harry Truman, for example, never attended college. Most important,

many recent college graduates who hoped to find work related to their field of study have been unable to do so.

Topic: _____

Implied main idea: _____

5. If you have a sour outlook on life, very little will ever seem funny. You have to shake yourself up a bit and say, "Look, let's take off these dark glasses and see what there is around here that is funny." Only then can you see or hear something that will give you a great big laugh. Perhaps the first thing you need to do is to look for things that are funny in yourself. Next, you may look for things that are funny in the people and things around you.

Topic: _____

Implied main idea: _____

6. Baby-training tapes are the creation of Seattle developmental psychologist Brent Logan, founder of Prelearning, Inc., a prenatal-education research institute. "This is not a yuppie toy," says its inventor. "We have barely literate families who are using the tapes." To date, 1,200 children—the oldest of whom is now 4—have "listened" to the recordings. Last year 50 of the youngsters, ranging in age from 6 months to 34 months, were given standardized language, social, and motor-skills tests. Their overall score was 25 percent above the national norm.

Topic: _____

Implied main idea: _____

### 3a.6  The Central Idea

Longer readings, such as articles or essays, contain what is called a **central idea** or **thesis**. It tells what the entire reading is about. Like the main idea of a paragraph, the central idea gives more information about the topic. For instance, it provides the author's viewpoint or expresses how the author feels about the topic. The central idea is often referred to as the central point, central theme, or thesis. It resembles a description of a movie in *TV Guide* and may be stated in one of the sentences in a paragraph or implied. In some instances, clues to the central idea may come from titles. Follow these steps to determine the central idea:

**Step 1.**  Read the title and first paragraph. *Ask: What does this title mean? What does it tell me about the selection? Are there clues that express the author's feelings about the topic in this paragraph?*

**Step 2.** Try to predict what the whole selection is about. *Ask: What is the entire reading about? Is there a relationship between the title and the first paragraph?*

**Step 3.** Read the entire selection. For each paragraph, try to determine what the author is really saying. *Ask: What's the author's point? What's the message?*

**Step 4.** Write a sentence to express the central idea. Look away from the reading and pretend that you are telling someone what you have just read. *Ask: What was this all about?*

**Step 5.** Check your response. *Ask: Is this what the whole selection is all about? Do the main ideas provide additional detailed information about this statement?*

### EXERCISE 3.18   FINDING THE CENTRAL IDEA

*Practice applying the steps above to determine the central idea in Constance F. Geiger's article "The Payoff."*

# The Payoff

*Constance F. Geiger*

Improving your diet today could help prevent heart disease, stroke, and a number of different cancers. It doesn't take a drastic change in lifestyle to help ward off disease; make small changes you can live with. Eating more of protective foods, such as fruits, vegetables, and grains, is easy when you expand your selection beyond apples and oranges to include fun, unfamiliar produce.  1

"Five a day" is just a start. Studies of disease incidence by population suggest that the more fruits and vegetables we eat per day, the better our chances for staving off cancer. According to Ritva Butrum, Ph.D., head of research at the American Institute for Cancer Research, "Scientists are seeing even greater promise for stopping cancer before it starts." How? By taking advantage of the wide variety of protective substances found only in vegetables, fruits, and grains.  2

For every decade after age 30, your calorie needs decrease by 2 percent. This means that if you eat the same amount at age 50 as you did at age 30, you'll gain a pound every two months—6 pounds per year. Starving yourself or trying fad diets aren't solutions. Include more activity in your life instead. Use the stairs, walk more, drive less, and do your own yard work. You'll feel better, think better, and look better. Schedule time for exercise—remember, you only need about 30 minutes a day, three times a week.  3

The central idea is this: All it takes for you to prevent disease and to improve your health and the quality of your life is a good diet and moderate exercise.

## EXERCISE 3.19    FINDING THE CENTRAL IDEA

*Read the following article and apply the steps above to determine the central idea.*

# Blues Roots

*Bob Millard*

1      Exactly who first sang and played the blues, exactly where, and exactly when will probably always be a musical mystery. The first written references to the blues appeared in the 1890s, and the publication of W. C. Handy's "Memphis Blues" introduced the music to a commercial audience in 1912.

2      Oral history and the music itself, however, suggest an earlier origin in the African American field hollers, church singing, and popular music of the mid-nineteenth-century South. Musicologists point out that several important features of the blues, including its characteristic tonal shadings, call-and-response structure, repeated refrains, and use of the falsetto voice, derive from African musical tradition.

3      Social, economic, and cultural factors fostered the development of three regional styles of early blues. Mississippi Delta musicians Robert Johnson, Johnny Shines, and others used percussion-like strumming and bottleneck guitar chords with a vocal style that combined singing and speech. In Georgia and the Carolinas, blues artists such as Blind Boy Fuller and Blind Willie McTell drew upon ragtime and popular music to shape a crisp melodic and rhythmic style. The guitar picking and high vocals of Blind Lemon Jefferson are probably the most celebrated example of Texas blues.

4      From the 1920s, blues recordings brought black female artists Ma Rainey, Bessie Smith, and others to national attention. Around the same time, the migration of African Americans from the rural South to northern cities during the Great Depression gave rise to distinctive urban styles in Memphis, Atlanta, Kansas City, St. Louis, and, particularly, Chicago. The best known Chicago blues artists from this period include Tampa Red, Memphis Minnie, and "Sonny Boy" Williamson.

5      Beginning in the late 1940s, Muddy Waters, Howling Wolf, and others took traditional blues to an even wider audience. The jazz, soul, rhythm and blues, and rock music of later eras continue to show the powerful influence of the blues.

Topic: _____

Central idea: _____

_____

Details are cornerstones, the crucial bits of information that make up a paragraph. Examples of details are definitions, facts, opinions, examples, or other clarifying explanations. For this reason, they can be seen, circled, or highlighted. It's important to know how to separate the major details from the minor ones. Here's where **signal words** come in. These special words, in many instances, can lead you to the major details.

## 3b.1 Signal Words

Signal words are clues that the author uses to help you to understand sentences and paragraphs better. They are sometimes referred to as **transitions** or **connectives.** Common examples are *and, since,* and *such as.* Of equal importance, a major function of signal words is to alert you to certain relationships within and between sentences. As a result, these signals lead you to main ideas and supporting details. Like traffic signals, these special words tell you when to stop (*finally*), when to move ahead (*also*), when to turn around (*however*), and more.

Several types of signal words and specific examples of each type are shown in the chart below.

| TYPES | EXAMPLES |
|---|---|
| Cause-effect | accordingly, as a result, because, cause, consequently, effect, in conclusion, leads to so, thus, therefore |
| Chronology/process | after, as, before, currently, during, finally, first, last, next, now, recently, today, then, until, when, while, twenty years ago |
| Classification | categories, divisions, groups, kinds, types, parts |
| Comparison | alike, also, as well as, comparable, equally, in the same way, like, similarly |
| Contrast | although, but, conversely, different, even though, however, in contrast, instead, nevertheless, on the contrary, on the other hand, unlike, while, yet |
| Example | for example, for instance, including, such as, to illustrate, to show |
| Listing | also, another, to begin with, first, second, third, finally, last, furthermore, moreover, next, then |

Note that some signal words can serve more than one function. For example, *first, second, third, next, then,* and *finally* can signal a process or a listing pattern.

## EXERCISE 3.20   FINDING SIGNAL WORDS IN SENTENCES

*The following sentence pairs show the function of signal words in sentences. Read each sentence pair with and without the signal words, and circle the letter of the one which best expresses the relationship between the ideas. The signal words are printed in boldface type.*

1. a. The car is out of gas; it will not run.
   b. The car is out of gas; **therefore,** it will not run.

2. a. Denotation refers to the most basic definition of a word; connotation refers to the feelings that a word arouses.
   b. Denotation refers to the most basic definition of a word, **but** connotation refers to the feelings that a word arouses.

By referring to the chart of signal words above, you can see that *therefore* in sentence 1 signals a cause-effect relationship, showing the effect of the car's being out of gas. You see also that *but* in sentence 2 signals a contrast, or opposite, relationship that points out the differences between denotation and connotation.

## EXERCISE 3.21   FINDING SIGNAL WORDS IN PARAGRAPHS

*The following paragraphs show how signal words function in a paragraph. The topic sentence is underlined. Think about which paragraph is more effective.*

WITHOUT SIGNAL WORDS

<u>Four major factors contribute to the difficulty of reading material</u>. The factor is the difficulty and familiarity of the concepts presented. If the concepts are unfamiliar or difficult, you will have to read at a slower pace in order to comprehend. The factor is the level of the vocabulary. If the vocabulary used is unfamiliar to you, the material will be harder to understand and comprehension will drop. The complexity of the style will affect the difficulty of the material. The factor is the reader's ability to use key techniques necessary to reading efficiency.

WITH SIGNAL WORDS

<u>Four major factors contribute to the difficulty of reading material</u>. The **first** factor is the difficulty and familiarity of the concepts presented. If the concepts are unfamiliar or difficult, you will have to read at a slower pace in order to comprehend. The **second** factor is the level of the vocabulary. If the vocabulary used is unfamiliar to you, the material will be harder to understand and comprehension will drop. **Third,** the complexity of the style will affect the difficulty of the material. The **final** factor is the reader's ability to use key techniques necessary to reading efficiency.

Did you notice how the signal words guided you in seeing the relationship between the topic sentence and the other parts of the paragraph? Did you also notice how the signal words clearly introduced the details that backed up the claim stated in the topic sentence (the four major factors contribute to the difficulty of the reading material)? The supporting details are the following: first, the difficulty and familiarity of concepts; second, level of vocabulary; third, complexity of style; and final, the use of key techniques).

## EXERCISE 3.22   WRITING SIGNAL WORDS

*Write an appropriate signal word from the chart in each blank.*

1. To keep his voice in good condition, Ken sings a song every day; yesterday, _____, he sang "Misty."

2. Ellen's weight-loss program is ineffective. She lost six pounds last week _____ regained it this week.

3. _____ mixing the ingredients and pouring the casserole in the pan, we put it in the oven and baked it for fifty minutes.

4. Anna lost her driving privileges _____ she was involved in too many accidents.

5. Somebody burned popcorn in the microwave; _____, the security guard had the appliance removed from the building.

6. _____ I fell asleep last night, I set my alarm for 5:00 A.M.

7. Both twins had phobias. One twin was afraid of closed-in places and, _____, the other was afraid of the dark.

8. Some students always participate in class; _____, instructors are not satisfied unless the whole class is participating.

9. The word *broker* was first used to mean a vendor of wine; over the years the term has come to mean any small retailer, _____, a pawnbroker.

10. Three types of vocabulary are evident in content area texts. The _____ type, general vocabulary, consists of everyday words.

## EXERCISE 3.23   SELECTING SIGNAL WORDS

*Write an appropriate signal word from the chart in each blank.*

1. There are several precautionary measures you can take to protect your car from the heat. _____, keep windows slightly cracked when parked in the hot sun. This allows the hottest air to escape and fresh air to circulate. _____, try shading the interior with a windshield shade for the front and newspaper or cloth for other large glass areas. _____, occasionally apply a protective coating to vinyl and leather interiors to replace plastics or oils that dry out with heat.

2. Lawyers for the banks often have trouble building a defense _____ juries tend to sympathize with the borrowers. The courts are

increasingly holding bankers not just to the details of their written contracts _____ to their verbal promises as well. _____, banks have grown more and more cautious about lending money to start businesses and gentler in their handling of delinquent borrowers. Any such rise in pleasantness is good for lenders and borrowers alike _____ the costs of jumbo lawsuits are simply passed along to the average banking customer.

Margie Jasper, "Your Credit Profile Reports"

3. There are several steps to follow in making coconut ice cream balls. _____, place coconut in a shallow dish. _____, use an ice cream scoop and a large melon baller to create ice cream balls. _____, roll ice cream balls in coconut, pressing firmly, until coated. _____, place coated ice cream balls on cookie sheet and return to freezer for 1 to 2 hours or until firm. To serve, make a mountain of ice cream balls in a serving dish. _____, add coconut curls, if desired. (To make coconut curls, use a vegetable peeler to cut thin strips from the long edge of a shelled coconut that has been broken into large pieces.) Makes 25 2-inch balls.

Jeanne Ambrose, "Holiday Magic"

## 3b.2  Major Details

A major detail is just what its name implies: important. It is a supporting detail that helps develop and explain the main idea. It answers *who, what, when, where, why, how* about the central idea (essay) and the main idea (paragraph). Follow these steps to identify major details:

**Step 1.**  Read the paragraph carefully.

**Step 2.**  Determine the main idea.

**Step 3.**  Ask the following questions about the main idea and look for the idea/thing that follows in parentheses:

Who/What is involved in the action? (person/thing)

What happened? (event/action)

When did the event/action occur? (time)

Where did the event/action take place? (place)

Why did the event/action occur? (reason)

How did the event/action take place? (procedure)

**Step 4.**  Look for signal words that may alert you to the important key ideas ( *first of all, in addition, second, most important, of equal importance*, etc.).

**Step 5.**  Look for opening phrases that may introduce these details (*several kinds, three factors, many ways*, etc.).

**Step 6.**  Check your response. *Ask: Are these ideas given the most attention? Are these ideas connected to a major point? Are these items in a list? Are punctuation clues present (colon, commas, dashes, etc.)?*

## 3b.3 Minor Details

Minor details are not that important. In fact, you might skip them when you read. Their general function is to provide extra information about a subject and to help round out the paragraph. Follow these steps to identify minor details:

**Step 1.** Read the passage.

**Step 2.** Look for fillers. *Ask: Does this idea round out the paragraph? Does it provide an interesting tidbit of information?*

**Step 3.** Look for more information about a major detail. *Ask: Does this explain or clarify a major detail? Does this repeat or reexplain an example that has already been given?*

**Step 4.** Check your response. *Ask: Does this information help me understand the main idea, or is it something extra?*

### EXERCISE 3.24  FINDING DETAILS

*Read the sentences in the following paragraph and place a check mark beside all the details that directly support the underlined topic sentence.*

_____ a. Behavior, after all, is a primary form of communication for school-age children.

_____ b. Make clear its meaning and you'll be better equipped to help your child succeed academically.

Here are a few of the more common classroom styles.

_____ c. The class clown tends to be an outgoing child in need of attention.

_____ d. The shrinking violet is shy, introverted, and insecure about speaking up in school.

_____ e. In a comfortable setting at home or with close friends, however, she may be full of talk.

_____ f. The daydreamer who tunes out or doodles in class may have a concentration problem.

_____ g. For this type, the work may be too easy or too advanced.

_____ h. The eager beaver tends to be a high achiever who's naturally motivated.

_____ i. But he can be hard on himself if he doesn't meet his own standards.

The major details are sentences a, c, d, f, and h because they support, help to prove, or clarify the topic sentence. Sentence a, for example, links behavior with "classroom styles" in the topic sentence. Without sentence a, the topic sentence would be unclear. The other major details show the specific styles of classroom behavior—the class clown, the shrinking violet, the daydreamer, and the eager beaver. All other details (b, e, g, and i) are minor because they give additional information about the major details and help to round out the paragraph.

## EXERCISE 3.25    FINDING DETAILS

*In the blanks that follow each paragraph, write the letters of the details that directly support the underlined topic sentence.*

1.  <u>The Capital One Internet provider has several outstanding features</u>. (a) Its cost is reasonable. (b) The monthly service fee is $10. (c) It provides unlimited usage. (d) Whether you log on for hours or minutes at a time, you are assessed no additional charge. (e) It is user-friendly. (f) Directions are provided on each page to guide you to the many sites on the Internet. (g) It can be accessed easily. (h) A two-step diagram leads you effortlessly into virtual reality.

    1. _____                    2. _____

    3. _____                    4. _____

2.  <u>The punter on a football team kicks the ball at five important intervals during a game</u>. (a) First, he kicks the ball to start the game. (b) This is called the kickoff. (c) After the loss of three downs, he kicks the ball on the fourth down. (d) Since the team has only four chances, or downs, to gain ten yards to keep possession of the ball, this kick occurs more frequently than any other during the course of the game. (e) He also kicks the ball to score a three-point field goal. (f) This occurs when the team cannot get close enough to the end zone to score a touchdown. (g) However, once the team scores a touchdown, he kicks the ball for the extra point. (h) This one-point kick can mean the difference between winning and losing the game. (i) Last, after the touchdown and extra point try, he kicks the ball to the opposing team. (j) This requires unusual skill, for the kicker has to aim the ball away from a dangerous kick-off return man, like Deion Sanders, who is potentially capable of running the ball the full length of the field for a touchdown. (k) Except for a blocked kick, this is the kicker's greatest fear.

    1. _____                    2. _____

    3. _____                    4. _____

    5. _____

## EXERCISE 3.26    FINDING DETAILS

*Place a check mark in front of the details that directly support the underlined topic sentence in each paragraph.*

1.  <u>Not surprisingly, North Carolina has suffered devastating animal-waste-related environmental disasters</u>. _____ (a) More than a hundred hog operations have been caught illegally dumping manure

into waterways during the past few years. _____ (b) Moreover, about half of the lagoons in the state are leaking. _____ (c) In 1999 alone, 35 million gallons of animal waste poured into state waterways, killing 10 million fish. _____ (d) This is three times more than the oil spilled by the *Exxon Valdez.* _____ (e) The single biggest spill came on June 21, when 25 million gallons of raw sewage flowed into the New River after a manure pit ruptured at a plant run by Oceanview Farms.

Ken Silverstein, "Meat Factories"

2. _____ a. Golf was the fastest-growing sport of the past decade, but these days the hot contender for the 2000s is croquet. Croquet's attractions are many. _____ (b) For one, game times are shorter than in golf. _____ (c) The greens fees are cheaper. _____ (d) Men and women can compete on an equal footing. _____ (e) The cutthroat competition for the wicket satisfies the blood lust of most corporate sharks, and players wear tailored clothes of white linen. _____ (f) Small wonder that since 1977 the number of croquet clubs in the United States has increased from 5 to 300—many of them crowded with former golfers.

Susan B. LaPorte, "Those Wicket, Wicket Ways"

3. There are several steps a consumer can take to decrease the environmental cost of the T-shirt. _____ (a) First, choose T-shirts made of 100 percent natural cotton, which is grown without poisons or fertilizers. _____ (b) The rates of water use and soil erosion for natural cotton are less than half those for regular cotton. _____ (c) Second, look for cotton labeled "transitional." _____ (d) This means it's currently being grown without poison while awaiting natural approval. _____ (e) Or try unbleached, undyed, untreated cotton, or cotton that's been bred to grow in rare earth colors. _____ (f) Better yet, have your logo silk-screened with water-based inks.

Mindy Pennybacker, "The Hidden Life of T-shirts"

4. What is it about lighting a candle that strikes a thoughtful mood in just about everyone. _____ (a) Maybe it's that the act can't be hurried, making it unusual in our push-button culture. _____ (b) Because it takes time and studied intent to strike a flame, hold that flame to a candlewick, and wait for light, the act feels purposeful. _____ (c) And that makes it a natural host for symbolic meaning. _____ (d) Even newer seasonal holidays, such as the Afro-American holiday Kwanzaa, rely on the ritual of candlelighting to convey their message. _____ (e) Each of the seven candles in a Kwanzaa kinara represents a different ethic or principle. _____ (f) Each day's lighting is lit up with seriousness and meaning.

**EXERCISE 3.27    FINDING MAJOR DETAILS**

*For each paragraph below, underline the topic sentence and enclose major details in brackets [ ].*

1. Pet-food products are the single largest category of supermarket items. Pet food takes up an average of 240 linear feet of supermarket shelf space. This is more space than is taken up by baby food or by any other category.

2. Ending verbal abuse means being in control of what we say. To avoid hurtful remarks sparked by job fatigue, try making a transition from the workplace to the home. Initiate a quiet-time routine with your children when you get home. Have them read to you, watch television with you, or join you on a walk. Create peaceful time for all of you. To avoid lashing out at a child in anger when you feel your temper rising, speak with the misbehaving child at a later time. Avoid any contact until then. "Sometimes when I get angry, I'll count to ten and send my son to his room. If I do slip, I apologize," says Judith. "I keep trying to work on me because I want him to be the best he can be."

   Bebe Moore Campbell, "When Words Hurt"

3. If you are planning to have a child, get a head start on those excessive child-rearing costs. An infant's first year can cost nearly $5,000. From birth until voting age, expect child-rearing expenses to top the $100,000 mark. Begin by preparing five years in advance of a planned birth. A $10,000 initial investment with small, yet consistent, follow-up deposits can nearly triple by the time you take your baby home from the hospital. Next, consider using an existing investment account renamed "baby money." Invest wisely to cover baby costs until the child is five years old. Better yet, dip into the savings annually for a helping hand each year until your child is a teenager.

4. Dr. Rosalind Cartwright is a dream researcher. She has developed a dream therapy for changing dreams. According to Dr. Cartwright, dream therapy involves four simple steps you can learn on your own. The first step is to recognize when you are having a bad dream. This type of dream is defined as one that will make you feel helpless or upset the next morning. The second step is to identify what it is about the dream that makes you feel bad. For example, look for reasons for feeling weak instead of strong or out of control instead of in control. Next, stop any bad dream. You do not have to continue your bad dream, for you are in charge. The last step is to change the negative part of the dream. Sometimes you may have to wake yourself up and change the dream before you return to sleep. Other times it is possible to change the dream while you are still asleep.

## 3b.4 Paragraph Patterns

Paragraph patterns show the different ways authors organize information in paragraphs. These patterns help you see the author's plan of action and relationships among ideas. The author often gives clues, or signals, to help you to discover the pattern used. Some of these clues include **signal words** (*also, because, however, therefore*), **descriptive terms** (*likes, differences, causes, effects*), and **introductory words and phrases** (*several factors, some reasons, types, kinds, categories*). Six basic paragraph patterns correspond to those in the signal-word chart on page 75.

| PATTERN | EXPLANATION |
|---|---|
| Cause and effect | Shows actions and their consequences—why actions or events occur (cause) and what happens as a result (effect). |
| Chronology/process | Shows a series of steps or stages or events in a directional (how to do something) or operational (facts arranged with reference to time, dates, or numbers) function. |
| Classification | Shows things being categorized or divided into parts, types, or kinds. |
| Comparison-contrast | Shows how things are alike (comparison) or different (contrast). |
| Example/illustration | Shows specific events, objects, people, topics, instances—often arranged in order of importance. |
| Listing | Shows a series of details, beliefs, conditions, and actions that support a main idea. |

Follow these steps to identify paragraph patterns:

**Step 1.** Read the paragraph carefully.
**Step 2.** Identify the main idea.
**Step 3.** Locate and circle signal words, if any. When no signal words are given, look for other word and direction clues from paragraph meaning.
**Step 4.** Check to see if the signal words introduce major supporting details (*first, second, moreover.*)
**Step 5.** Match the signal word(s) to the paragraph pattern.

The following paragraphs illustrate various patterns. As you read each paragraph, observe the effect of the boldfaced signal words and challenge yourself to identify the key ideas that support the underlined topic sentence.

## Cause and Effect

*People who are overweight simply eat too much, right? Wrong. <u>There are</u>* <u>*other **causes** for gaining weight besides eating more.*</u> ***One*** *is eating the wrong kinds of food, such as fatty and sugary foods.* ***Another*** *may be eating at the wrong times, like just before going to bed. And **a third cause** of gaining weight is not getting enough exercise.*

This paragraph uses a simple cause-effect pattern that shows only one effect but multiple causes. The author identifies three causes for weight gain (the effect). Therefore, gaining weight is the single effect, and the reasons for gaining weight are the causes. The causes, which answer *why*, are preceded by the boldfaced signal words in the paragraph. A map of the paragraph might look like this:

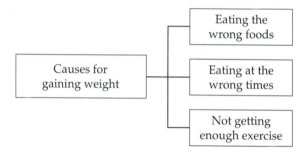

## Cause and Effect

*Not all arthritis sufferers wake up stiff and achy, needing to pop a few aspirin to start the day. <u>Its effects can be worse.</u> The disease can **cause** swelling in and around joints. It can **also** attack bone and internal organs, **causing** them to malfunction. Its **effect** on daily activities, **such as** brushing teeth or putting on shoes, can be more exhausting.*
Kathleen Heins, "Composing a Cure for Arthritis"

This paragraph shows a single cause and multiple effects. Arthritis is the cause, and the effects show what happens as a result of the cause. Signal words include *cause, effect, also,* and *such as.* A map of the paragraph might look like this:

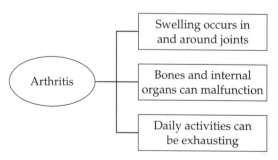

## Cause and Effect

*Child abuse has many tragic **results**. Children who are abused often believe they are unworthy. This **causes** low self-esteem that can **lead to** alcoholism, drug addiction, or even suicide. **In many cases,** the abuse is physically harmful and can even be fatal. **In addition,** many abused children grow up to become abusers of their own children.*

In this paragraph, the author generally describes the results, or effects, of child abuse. However, there are cycles of causes and effects here because one effect becomes the cause of another effect. In this multiple cause-effect relationship, for example, the effect "unworthy feelings" leads to low self-esteem that, in turn, becomes the effect that leads to alcoholism, drug addiction, and suicide. Again, the boldfaced signal words show the various cause-effect relationships in the paragraph. A map of the paragraph might look like this:

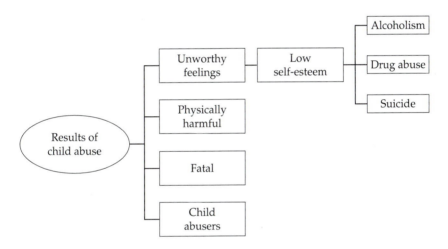

## Chronology / Process

*In Latin America, the holiday season is steeped in tradition. It **begins** on December 16 with* <u>Las Posadas (The Inns),</u> *a reenactment of the Christmas story that often **lasts nine days. Each night,** children and adults dressed in costumes and carrying candles go from door to door, looking for lodging. **At the last house,** they are invited in for music, food, and games. Las Posadas **ends at midnight** on Christmas Eve with the Misa de Gallo, or rooster mass. **Afterward,** church bells ring and fireworks explode as people return home for a festive meal.*
Sharon Overton, "The Festival of Las Posadas"

This paragraph presents a time-order sequence that tells what happens during the holiday season in Latin America. Notice that the events occur in sequential order. The boldfaced signal words help point out this series of activities from the beginning to the end. A map of the paragraph might look like this:

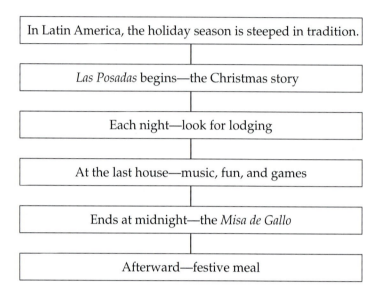

| In Latin America, the holiday season is steeped in tradition. |

| *Las Posadas* begins—the Christmas story |

| Each night—look for lodging |

| At the last house—music, fun, and games |

| Ends at midnight—the *Misa de Gallo* |

| Afterward—festive meal |

### Chronology/Process

*In the fifteenth century, the Ottoman (Turkish) Empire was planning to take over Constantinople. The Turkish troops attacked Constantinople in 1402 and again in 1422, but they did not succeed. Then in 1451, Sultan Mohammed II attacked the city again. In April 1453, the Turkish army attacked the city's thick walls with its new cannon. The defenders, however, repaired the walls every night. Furthermore, they attacked back several times. Still, after some time, the 7,000 defenders became exhausted. They never thought of giving up, however, because they had faith in an old prophecy. The prediction stated that Constantinople could never fall while the moon was becoming full. Unfortunately, on May 22, 1453, the full moon went into an eclipse. The defenders felt frightened and helpless. Three days later, Mohammed II attacked the city again. In a very short time, the Turkish army overpowered Constantinople's troops.*

This paragraph presents a time-order sequence describing the Ottoman Empire's battle with Constantinople. The events occur in a particular time order that begins in 1402 and ends in 1453 during the fifteenth century. The boldfaced dates and signal words help to point out this time-order sequence. A map of the paragraph might look like this:

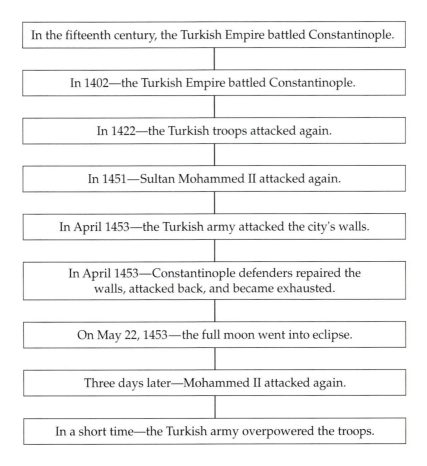

In the fifteenth century, the Turkish Empire battled Constantinople.

In 1402—the Turkish Empire battled Constantinople.

In 1422—the Turkish troops attacked again.

In 1451—Sultan Mohammed II attacked again.

In April 1453—the Turkish army attacked the city's walls.

In April 1453—Constantinople defenders repaired the walls, attacked back, and became exhausted.

On May 22, 1453—the full moon went into eclipse.

Three days later—Mohammed II attacked again.

In a short time—the Turkish army overpowered the troops.

## Classification

*Familiarize yourself with the **four different types** of interviews: unstructured, structured, group, and behavioral. In the unstructured interview, the interviewer might say to you, "Tell me something about yourself." In the structured interview, the interviewer will simply ask direct questions. The group interview can be most intimidating because you are being judged by three or more people. The trick is to relax and answer questions as if talking to one person. In the behavioral interview, you are given a situation and asked how you would handle it.*
Beatryce Nivens, "Six Steps to a Winning Job Interview"

In this paragraph, the interview is classified, or categorized, into four different types: unstructured, structured, group, and behavioral. A brief explanation, or description, helps define each type and distinguish each type from the other. The only signal is that given in the topic sentence— *four different types*. A map of the paragraph might look like this:

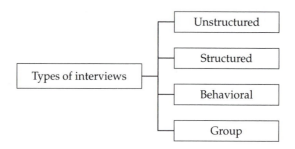

### Example / Illustration

*There are questions you may be asked during an interview that, by law, you need not answer.* **Some examples** *may refer to your children, if you are a parent. "How many children do you have now?" "What type of day care do you have for your children?" If you are not a parent, you may be asked questions* **such as** *these: "Do you plan to have children in the near future?" "Do you use contraceptives?" Other questions may seek information about your marriage or marital status. You may be asked,* **for instance,** *"Why are you divorced (or single)?" "Any marriage plans in the future?" "If your husband moved to another city because of a career relocation, would you join him?"*

This paragraph is developed by use of examples that help prove the topic sentence. The author identifies specific questions that, by law, you do not have to answer during an interview. *Some examples, such as,* and *for instance* are signal words that alert you to the use of the specific examples in the paragraph. A map of the paragraph might look like this:

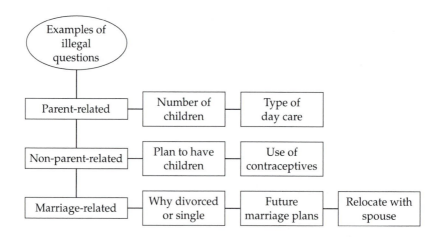

## Comparison-Contrast

*Though different in many ways, the two brothers, Robert and Peter, took over the winemaking business from their Italian-immigrant father, Cesare. Talkative and energetic, Robert oversaw sales and marketing.* **On the other hand,** *Peter, who was quiet and reserved, supervised the wine-making part of the operation. Convinced that California wines could some-day be equal to the finest wines of France and Italy, Robert was itching to change to a European production method and spend more money on mar-keting and sales. A year younger, Peter,* **however,** *was cautious of taking what he felt were unnecessary risks.* **And,** *as is the case in many family businesses when the children butt heads, their father, Cesare, acted as referee as well as final judge of the firm's direction.* **But** *Cesare's death in 1959 left a power vacuum.*

Ellen Hawkes, "Mondavi Family Values"

In this paragraph, the author shows how Robert and Peter are differ-ent. The topic sentence points out that differences will be the focus of this paragraph. Presented point by point for both brothers at the same time, the differences relate to age, job function, attitude, conduct, and lifestyle. Boldfaced contrast signals are used to point out these differences in the paragraph. A map of the paragraph might look like this:

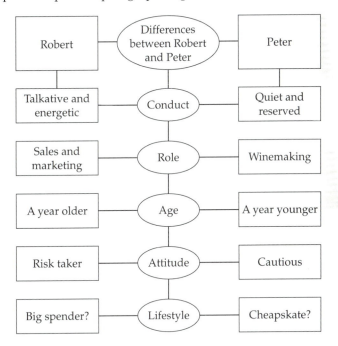

## Comparison-Contrast

*Chapter 11 stores* **differ** *from big chains like Barnes & Noble and Borders Books & Music in size and atmosphere.* **Whereas** *the typical Barnes &*

*Noble store is between 20,000 and 30,000 square feet, Chapter 11 stores are small. "Chapter 11 stores are about 5,000 square feet, with great graphics that quickly let you see where each section is," says Kaufman, the store's owner. "Granted, that doesn't leave much room for in-store coffeehouses, cafes, and performance spaces, **but** nobody seems to miss them." **In comparison,** overhead costs stay low, and so do the prices. To save space, Chapter 11 stores stock only one or two copies of most books, **but** any book can be special-ordered and is usually received within two days.*

Eilene Zimmerman, "Shelving Prejudice"

In this paragraph, Chapter 11 bookstores are compared to other bookstores. Though some points of the comparison are only suggested, the author draws attention to differences in atmosphere, size, overhead, prices, stock size, and method of purchase. The boldfaced signal words highlight these differences throughout the paragraph. A map of the paragraph might look like this:

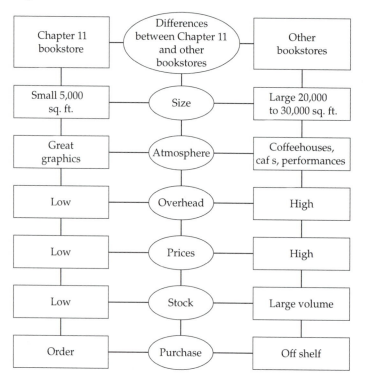

## Comparison-Contrast

*San Francisco, California, Tokyo, Japan, Managua, Nicaragua, and Mexico City, Mexico **all** have something **in common**. They are **all** urban areas that have been hit by major earthquakes. **These cities** are located on or near the edges of active plate margins. A plate is a piece of Earth's crust and upper mantle. Earth can be broken into nine large plates and several smaller plates.*

The paragraph pattern here uses comparison, for the author points out the similarities among the cities. The major similarities include city type, what happened, and why. The boldfaced key words signal the comparison throughout the paragraph. A map of the paragraph might look like this:

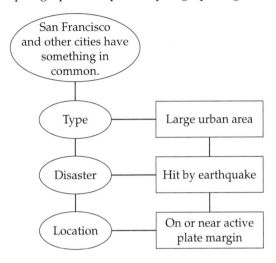

### Listing

*In the course of an evening, watch the different ways car manufacturers position the same automobile.* **One commercial** *will show the car as the at-home Mom's best friend.* **Another** *will picture the car as a classy drive to work for the new executive.* **A third commercial** *can interest younger buyers in how much fun it is to drive the car.* **Still another** *can show the style-conscious model how this same car can be pitted against the more expensive brands.*

In this paragraph, a listing of details is presented to support the topic sentence. In other words, the author lists four ways in which manufacturers position the same automobile. The boldfaced signal words clearly point out the listed items in the paragraph. A map of the paragraph might look like this:

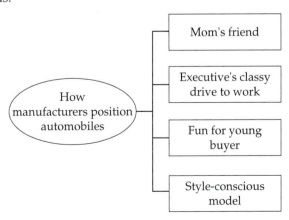

### Listing

*A biologist at NASA (the National Aeronautics and Space Administra-*
*tion), Chris McKay, has suggested* **three theories** *about life on Mars.* **One**
*possibility is that life never developed. A* **second** *possibility is that life*
*arose on Mars just as it did on Earth and survived for at least a billion*
*years. The* **third** *is that life arose and simple organisms developed. When*
*environmental conditions on Mars changed, life ended.*

The three theories mentioned in the topic sentence are listed in the
paragraph. Each theory is introduced with a boldfaced signal word. A
map of the paragraph might look like this:

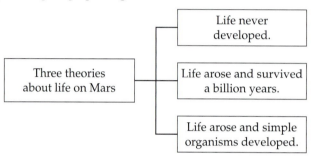

## EXERCISE 3.28   PARAGRAPH PATTERNS AND SIGNAL WORDS

*Read each paragraph below. Then circle the signal word(s) and identify the pat-*
*tern type of each paragraph. A signal-word clue box precedes each paragraph to*
*aid your search.*

1. | five |

Andrew Sorkin of Scarsdale, New York, started a business by combining his personal interests (sports and writing) with management
lessons learned through his Junior Achievement experience. Last year he
organized Pages Publishing Corporation to produce a sports magazine
for the high school market—*The Sports Page*. Andrew's business is unusual for several reasons. First, Pages Publishing is a not-for-profit ven-
ture. Andrew is interested in providing journalism students, rather than
professional writers, with an opportunity to contribute articles to a national magazine. Second, Andrew organized a board of directors consist-
ing of two high school students and six adults from the community to
help him make wise policy decisions. Finally, all students in participating
schools receive the magazine at no charge. The costs of production are
covered through advertising dollars.

Paragraph pattern: _____

2. | five |

Four types of bird wings are easily recognizable because they vary in
size and form. The first type is the elliptical wing. This wing type is like
that of the tiny chickadee. If frightened, this bird can change course
within 0.03 second. Second, there are the high-speed wings that belong to

the fastest birds alive, such as sandpipers. A third type of wing belongs to the soaring birds. Albatrosses, frigate birds, and gannets belong to this group. These birds have the highest aerodynamic efficiency of all but are less skilled than the land soarers. The last type is the high-lift wings, belonging to the vultures, hawks, eagles, owls, and ospreys, predators that carry heavy loads.

Cleveland P. Hickman Jr., et al., "Flight"

Paragraph pattern: _____

3. six

There are roughly twice as many people seeking couples therapy today as there were twenty years ago, and couples now make up the fastest-growing segment of those who come knocking on therapists' doors. Although exact statistics are hard to come by, the number of professionals licensed to practice marital therapy gives some indication of the trend. In 1972, 1,000 counselors were licensed marital therapists. A decade later, there were 9,000. Currently, the number of marital therapists is fast approaching 500,000, and psychology journals regularly remark upon the difficulty of keeping up with demand.

Joannie M. Schrof, "Married with Problems"

Paragraph pattern: _____

4. six

Before he retired in 1995, Jin Matsushita made a good living selling stocks for Yamaichi Securities. He owned 50,000 shares of his employer's stock, worth about $1 million at their peak. Even the stock-market drop in 1989 didn't hurt him badly. He was able to make a $98,000 down payment on a $545,000 condominium on the shore of Tokyo Bay. But last November, Yamaichi went bust, the biggest corporate failure in Japan's history, and now Matsushita says his shares are "just pieces of paper." His condo is worth about 80 percent less than what he paid for it. At 62, Jin Matsushita has gone back to work, mopping floors in a housing complex near his apartment. He has become an example of an idea that was almost unknown in postwar Japan until recently: downward mobility.

Paragraph pattern: _____

5. three

Intense agape (divine love) can border on masochism (self-inflicted pain). For example, an agapic person might wait forever for a lover to be released from prison or from a mental hospital. Another might tolerate an alcoholic or drug-addicted spouse. Still others might be willing to live with a partner who engages in illegal or immoral activities.

Nijole Benokraitis, "Lee's Styles of Loving"

Paragraph pattern: _____

6. four

Osteoarthritis affects about 16 million people, mostly women over age 45. Nicknamed "old age-arthritis," osteoarthritis usually develops with age. It's caused by the breakdown of cartilage, the rubbery material that cushions the ends of bones. It can also be caused by a joint injury, typically through sports. Osteoarthritis is most common in the fingers, hips, knees, and spine. Sufferers feel best when they first get up in the morning and worse as the day goes on and they use their joints.

Kathleen Keins, "Composing a Cure for Arthritis"

Paragraph pattern: _____

7.  two

Ralph Tupaz and Irene Gonzalez, the union man and the environmentalist, seem worlds apart. Tupaz is a middle-aged family man who has worked for fifteen years at the giant Chevron oil refinery in El Segundo, California. Gonzalez, however, a 21-year-old student at the University of California at Irvine, comes from a family that blames nearby refineries for constant respiratory problems and headaches. The two were asked to name the biggest problem facing the country. "Job security," Tupaz said confidently. "Pollution," Gonzalez replied. Has the environment gotten better or worse? "Better," he said, "especially here." "Worse," she declared.

David Moberg, "Brothers and Sisters"

Paragraph pattern: _____

## EXERCISE 3.29   PARAGRAPH PATTERNS AND SIGNAL WORDS

*Map each paragraph from Exercise 3.28 by filling in the key ideas below.*

1.

2.

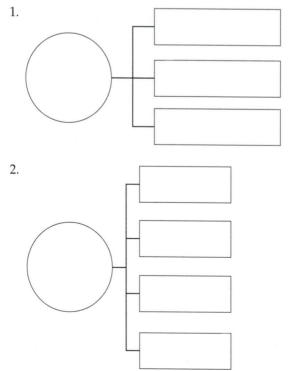

3.

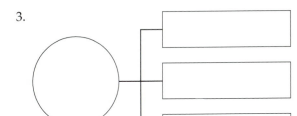

4.

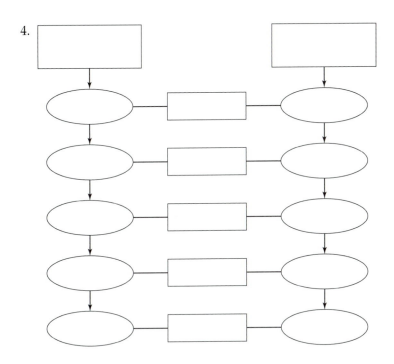

5.

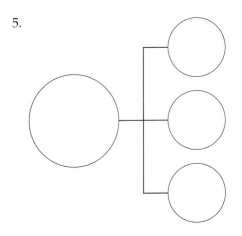

6.

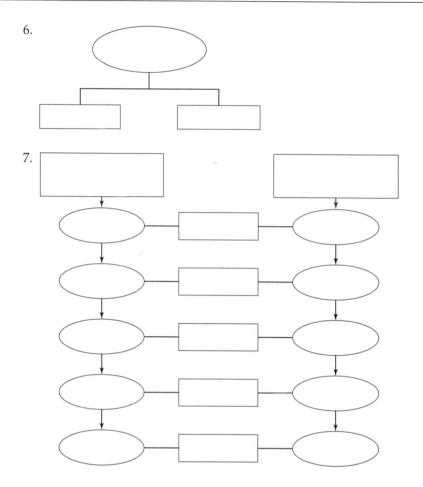

7.

## EXERCISE 3.30  PARAGRAPH PATTERNS AND SIGNAL WORDS

*Read each paragraph below. Then circle the signal word(s) and identify the pattern type. A signal-word clue box precedes each paragraph to aid your search.*

1. four

Many of Earth's natural resources cannot be replaced in the foreseeable future. Some of these resources include fossil fuels such as oil, coal, and natural gas. Also included are minerals such as salt, gold, silver, and copper. Clay, sand, and gravel are still other resources that are not renewable. Most of these resources are found underground. Before they can be used, they must be found, mined, and processed.

Dale Hesser, "Minerals"

Paragraph pattern: _____

2. six

A substance is not mineral unless it meets five requirements. (1) Minerals are nonliving. (2) They are formed in nature. (3) They are solids. (4) Atoms of a mineral have the same crystalline pattern. (5) The chemical

composition of a mineral is the same with only minor variations. Applying these requirements to Earth materials, we can now define a mineral.
Dale Hesser, "Minerals"

Paragraph pattern: _____

3. four
Sedimentary rocks are classified as clastics and nonclastics. Clastics are rocks made of fragments of rocks and minerals and broken shells. These fragments are carried by water, wind, or glaciers and are deposited as the speed of the transporting agent decreases. They include sandstone, siltstone, and shale. Nonclastics are sedimentary rocks that are deposited from solution or by lifelike processes. They are either chemically or organically formed. They include limestone, flint, rock salt, and alabaster.
Dale Hesser, "Sedimentary Rock"

Paragraph pattern: _____

4. two
A name is sometimes a ridiculous fate. For example, a man afflicted with the name of Kill Sin Pimple lived in Sussex, England, in 1609. In the spring of that year, the record shows, Kill Sin served on a jury with his Puritan neighbors, including Fly Debate Roberts, More Fruit Fowler, God Reward Smart, Be Faithful Joiner, and Fight the Good Fight of Faith White. Poor men. At birth, their parents had turned them into religious bumper stickers.
Lance Morrow, "The Strange Burden of a Name"

Paragraph pattern: _____

5. six
There are two ways to get knocked out: to the body and to the head. Getting knocked out to the body paralyzes you for ten or twenty seconds. It's extremely painful when you're down, but after you get up it's as if nothing happened. Getting knocked out to the head is the opposite. It doesn't hurt. You're just put to sleep. One time I got hit with a bomb and went down unconscious. The first thing I remember was the referee counting 4. So I got to one knee and waited for the count to reach 8. But the next thing I knew, the referee counted 10 and waved the fight over. I said, "What happened to 6, 7, 8, and 9?" So, you see, you can go in and out of consciousness for a while even though you don't know it. It's probably going to give you a headache when you wake up the next morning.
Cal Fussman, "What It Feels Like"

Paragraph pattern: _____

6. two
People diagnosed with antisocial personality disorder have several very specific characteristics that separate them from people with other personality disorders. For example, they are often punished and rejected by their families and friends. They often violate the rights of others and

break the law without feeling guilty. They are often superficially charming, have at least average intelligence, are often alcoholics, and do not form meaningful bonds with others. Both men and women suffer from antisocial personality disorder; however, it is more common in men.

Paragraph pattern: _____

7.  three

At the trial, a jury of twelve people listens to the arguments of both attorneys and hears the testimony of the witnesses. Then the jury goes into a private room to consider the evidence and decide whether the accused is guilty of the crime. If the jury decides that the accused is innocent, he or she goes free. However, if the person is convicted, the judge sets a date for the accused to appear in court again for sentencing. At this time, the judge tells the convicted person what the punishment will be. The judge may sentence the guilty person to prison, impose a fine, or place him or her on probation. Thus, a trial by jury relies on both the jury and the judge to see that justice is served.

Paragraph pattern: _____

## EXERCISE 3.31   PARAGRAPH PATTERNS AND SIGNAL WORDS

*Map each paragraph from Exercise 3.30 by filling in the key ideas below.*

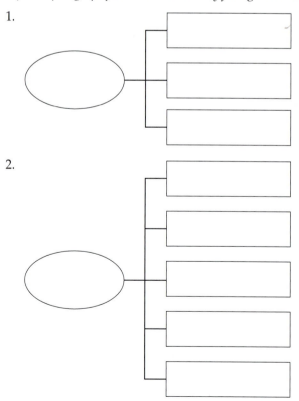

1.

2.

3.

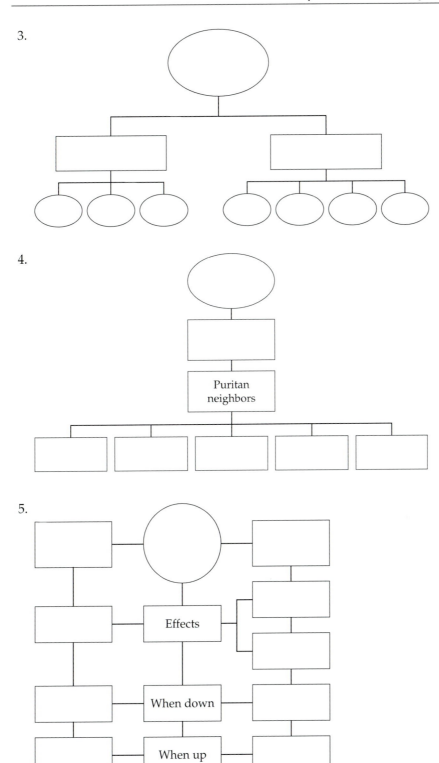

4.

5.

6.

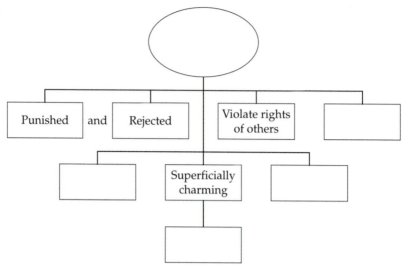

Punished    and    Rejected    Violate rights of others

Superficially charming

7.

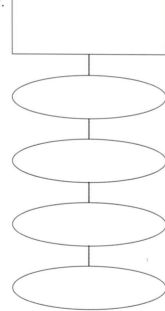

# Mastery Test 3

*Read the passage below and answer the questions that follow.*

## Being on Time: A Cultural Difference

In the United States, it is important to be on time, or punctual, for an appointment, a class, or a meeting. However, this may not be true in all countries. An American professor discovered this difference while teaching a class in a Brazilian university. The two-hour class was scheduled to begin at 10 A.M. and end at 12 P.M. On the first day, when the professor arrived on time, no one was in the classroom. Many students came after 10 A.M. Several arrived after 10:30 A.M. Two students came after 11 A.M. Although all the students greeted the professor as they arrived, few apologized for their lateness. Were these students being rude? He decided to study the students' behavior.     1

The professor talked to American and Brazilian students about lateness in both an informal and a formal situation: at lunch with a friend and in a university class, respectively. He gave them an example and asked them how they would react. If they had a lunch appointment with a friend, the average American student defined lateness as 19 minutes after the agreed time. On the other hand, the average Brazilian student felt the friend was late after 33 minutes.     2

In a U.S. university, students are expected to arrive at the appointed hour. In contrast, in Brazil, neither the teacher nor the students always arrive at the appointed hour. Classes not only begin at the scheduled time in the United States, but they also end at the scheduled time. In the Brazilian class, only a few students left the class at noon; many remained past 12:30 to discuss the class and ask more questions. While arriving late may not be very important in Brazil, neither is staying late.     3

The explanation for these differences is complicated. People from Brazilian and North American cultures have different feelings about lateness. In Brazil, the students believe that a person who usually arrives late is probably more successful than a person who is always on time. In fact, Brazilians expect a person with status or prestige to arrive late. In the United States, however, lateness is usually considered to be disrespectful and unacceptable. Consequently, if a Brazilian is late for an appointment with a North American, the American may misinterpret the reason for the lateness and become angry.     4

As a result of his study, the professor learned that the Brazilian students were not being disrespectful to him. Instead, they were simply behaving in the appropriate way for Brazilian students in Brazil. Eventually, the professor was able to adapt his own behavior so that he could feel comfortable in the new culture.     5     *(430 words)*

## COMPREHENSION EXERCISE
*Circle the letter of the best answer.*

1. What is the central idea of the passage?
   a. Brazilian students are late, but American students arrive in class on time.
   b. The importance of being on time differs among cultures.
   c. An American professor studied the habits of students from another culture.
   d. The professor was able to adapt his own behavior to the Brazilian culture.

2. What is the key idea of the following sentence from paragraph 1? "On the first day, when the professor arrived on time, no one was in the classroom."
   a. The professor arrived on time.
   b. When the professor arrived, no one was in the classroom.
   c. No one was there.
   d. On the first day, no one was in the classroom.

3. Which of the following relationships is signaled in the first paragraph?
   a. classification
   b. comparison
   c. contrast
   d. cause-effect

4. In paragraph 2, the author asks the students how they would react in a given situation. What is the relationship between the author's question and the student's answer?
   a. classification
   b. comparison
   c. contrast
   d. cause-effect

5. Which of the following best describes the organization pattern of paragraph 3?
   a. classification
   b. comparison
   c. contrast
   d. cause-effect

6. Draw a map of the contents of paragraph 3.

7. What is the implied main idea of paragraph 3?
   a. Arrival and departure times of American and Brazilian schools are the exact opposite.
   b. In the United States, classes begin at the scheduled time.

   c. In Brazil, neither the teacher nor the students arrive on time.

   d. While arriving late may not be very important in Brazil, neither is staying late.

8. The last sentence in paragraph 3 is a
   a. major detail.
   b. minor detail.
   c. topic sentence.
   d. key idea.

9. What is the organization pattern of paragraph 4?
   a. classification
   b. comparison
   c. contrast
   d. example

10. Which of the following sentences contains the main idea of paragraph 4?
    a. sentence 1
    b. sentence 2
    c. sentence 3
    d. sentence 4

Score: Number Correct _____ (out of 10) × 10 = _____

# 4

# Text Processing II:
## *Connecting with the Author*

In this chapter, you will become better acquainted with the author and the art of writing. Both critical reading and critical writing will help you get more from the reading than what the author states directly. With critical reading, you will learn to use what the author states directly in order to shape your own ideas. You will go beyond the page to make inferences, draw conclusions, predict outcomes, and form generalizations. With critical writing, you will analyze the author's writing techniques and determine the value of the information to you. Here you will focus on the author's purpose, audience, style, tone, mood, and varied types of language usage. You will learn to recognize fact and opinion, figurative expressions, and propaganda.

## 4A CRITICAL READING

In reading critically, you create a meaningful link with the author by discovering unstated ideas that the author expects you to know and understand. By making predictions, drawing inferences and conclusions, and generalizing, you become skillful at investigating—interpreting and evaluating—what you read. This, then, adds another important dimension to your reading.

### 4a.1 Inferences

**Drawing inferences** is reading between the lines to make a reasonable guess about the author's meaning. In making inferences, you use the author's words to arrive at a point that is strongly suggested but never directly stated and not necessarily true. For this reason, you can get more from the author's stated message than what is actually there. Because inferences are implied, you cannot underline or highlight them. However, you can underline or highlight definite evidence to support your inferences. To make inferences, follow these steps:

**Step 1.** Read the information. Make sure you understand the directly stated information, even if it means rereading.

**Step 2.** Combine the following to draw your inference: (a) the directly stated information, (b) your background knowledge and experience, and (c) your reasoning.

**Step 3.** Add up all the facts and state your inference. *Ask: Is this what the author means?*

**Step 4.** Test your inference. Double-check the evidence from the material you read. *Ask: Is this a valid assumption from the reading?*

**Note:** Your background knowledge alone is not enough. You must have evidence from the reading to support your inference.

### EXERCISE 4.1   MAKING INFERENCES
*Circle the letter before each inference you can draw from the following sentences.*

1. Poultry is on sale today for 29 cents a pound at Food Mart.
   a. Chicken usually costs more than 29 cents a pound.
   b. Now is a good time to stock up on turkey legs.
   c. Beefsteak costs more than 29 cents a pound.
   d. Food Mart has good buys on all meat products.
   e. Milk can be purchased at bargain prices at Food Mart.
   f. Food Mart carries a large supply of meat products.
   g. The popularity of poultry has grown worldwide.
   h. Food Mart expects to sell many chickens today.
   i. Managers at Food Mart have ordered a larger than usual supply of poultry products.
   j. The lines at Food Mart checkout counters are expected to be about the same as usual today.

You should have circled only letters *a, b, c, h,* and *i.* These are the only inferences you can draw from the information given. The key words are *sale* and *poultry.*

2. Mark's sweaty palms were itching in class yesterday.
   a. Mark is going to have good luck.
   b. Mark has a nervous condition that causes his hands to sweat.
   c. Mark needs a manicure.
   d. Mark overslept and had no time to lotion his hands.
   e. Mark found it difficult to concentrate on classwork.
   f. Mark went straight to the doctor's office after class.
   g. Mark probably wore his tight leather gloves again.
   h. Mark's hands were hot.
   i. Mark was uncomfortable.
   j. Mark is allergic to hot classrooms.

You should have circled letters *e* and *i* only. The evidence is too weak to support the other statements. However, unless Mark is not human, itching hands will affect his ability to concentrate and his level of comfort. We cannot assume that because Mark's palms were sweaty, they were hot. They may just as well have been cold and produced a "cold" sweat.

3. Mom is angry because Dad forgot to pay the car insurance again this month.
   a. Dad is working overtime too often.
   b. We will probably have a car accident.
   c. Car insurance is not a priority for Dad.
   d. Mom was upset because the bill wasn't paid.
   e. Mom is a poor driver.
   f. My parents are negligent.
   g. Dad always makes mistakes.
   h. The car will stay parked in the garage this month.
   i. Dad has Alzheimers.
   j. Mom considers car insurance important.

You should have circled only letters *c, d,* and *j.* These are the only inferences that can be drawn from the evidence given. Undoubtedly car insurance is not a priority for Dad since he didn't pay the bill. Mom's anger supports *d* and *j.*

## EXERCISE 4.2   MAKING INFERENCES
*Draw a likely inference from the situation presented in each sentence below.*

1. When Ida opened the door to her apartment, her friends were there; gifts and a cake with glowing candles sat on the table.

   Inference: _____

2. Arguing loudly and eyeing the skid marks on the road, the drivers waited for the police to arrive.

   Inference: _____

3. Dressed in black, the teary-eyed woman with a veil over her face received words of comfort from relatives and friends.

   Inference: _____

4. Just before class, Sam came down with a headache, upset stomach, dizziness, and fatigue, and his classmate had "butterflies" in the stomach, jitters, and sweaty palms.

   Inference: _____

5. To feel grown up, to be a part of the in crowd, and to relax and forget about troubles—these are my reasons for excess.

   Inference: _____

## EXERCISE 4.3   EVALUATING INFERENCES
*Place a check mark in the blank beside each inference you can draw from the contents of the following paragraph.*

When Sue asked to work a part-time job ironing clothes for the neighbors, Mom ordered her to wash and iron the clothes at home.

"I want to see if you are ready to iron clothes for a living," her mother quipped. Sue was angry about this. She wanted wages for her work. No one was paying for ironing at home. As Sue ironed, Mom stood nearby, criticizing her every move for several hours. "Sue, hold the iron like this, not like that. Sprinkle the clothes first; then spray the starch." Mom insisted that Sue iron each garment twice. Still ironing—half asleep—at 2:00 A.M., Sue cried out to her mother: "I have changed my mind; I hate ironing!"

_____ 1. Sue's mother does not want Sue to iron for the neighbors.

_____ 2. Ironing is not one of Sue's regular chores.

_____ 3. Sue wants to iron clothes for a living.

_____ 4. Sue does not realize how difficult ironing can be.

_____ 5. Sue's mother is a divorced parent.

_____ 6. Sue wants to purchase school clothes and a car.

_____ 7. Sue is probably a teenager.

_____ 8. Mother has her own way of doing things.

_____ 9. Sue is an only child who does not receive an allowance.

_____ 10. Sue's mother is a critical, demanding person.

## EXERCISE 4.4   MAKING INFERENCES

*The poem "Sure You can Ask Me a Personal Question" by Diane Burns is a Native American's response to a person's stereotypical comments made during a conversation. As you read the poem, use your inference skills to determine what the other person is saying to the Native American speaker. Write your inference on the line before each response.*

1. _____ How do you do?

2. _____ No, I am not Chinese.

3. _____ No, not Spanish.

4. _____ No, I am American Indi—uh, Native American.

5. _____ No, not from India.

6. _____ No, not Apache.

7. _____ No, not Navajo.

8. _____ No, not Sioux.

9. _____ No, we are not extinct.

10. _____ Yes, Indian.

11. _____ Oh?

12. _____ So that's where you got those high cheekbones.

13. _____ Your great grandmother, huh?

14. _____ An Indian Princess, huh?

15. _____ Hair down to there?

16. _____ Let me guess. Cherokee?

17. _____ Oh, so you've had an Indian friend?

18. _____ That close?

19. _____ Oh, so you've had an Indian lover?

20. _____ That tight?

21. _____ Oh, so you've had an Indian servant?

22. _____ That much?

23. _____ Yeah, it was awful what you guys did to us.

24. _____ It's real decent of you to apologize.

25. _____ No, I don't know where you can get peyote.

26. _____ No, I don't know where you can get Navajo rugs real cheap.

27. _____ No, I didn't make this. I bought it at Bloomingdale's.

28. _____ Thank you. I like your hair too.

29. _____ I don't know if anyone knows whether or not Cher is really Indian

30. _____ No, I didn't make it rain tonight.

31. _____ Yeah. Uh-huh. Spirituality.

32. _____ Uh-huh. Yeah. Spirituality. Uh-huh. Mother Earth.

33. _____ Yeah. Uh-huh. Uh-huh. Spirituality.

34. _____ No, I didn't major in archery.

35. _____ Yeah, a lot of us drink too much.

36. _____ Some of us can't drink enough.

37. _____ This ain't no stoic look.

38. _____ This is my face.

## 4a.2 Conclusions

**Drawing a conclusion** means to follow the logic in the reading to arrive at an unstated end result. Conclusions describe the outcome you can predict on the basis of the facts. By using information and reasoning together, you follow a sequence of actions and decide what finally happens. To draw valid conclusions, follow these steps:

**Step 1.** Read the stated information. Make sure you understand the stated information even if it means rereading. *Ask: What does this information mean?*

**Step 2.** Gather the evidence from the reading. *Ask: What evidence can I use to draw a conclusion?*

**Step 3.** Use your background knowledge and reasoning skills to sequence the supporting ideas. *Ask: Are these events placed in the right order?*

**Step 4.** Draw conclusion(s) based on the evidence. *Ask: Is this a valid conclusion? Does this information support my conclusion?*

**Step 5.** Verify your conclusion. *Ask: Is this the author's final point? Did I base this decision on the evidence?*

### EXERCISE 4.5    IDENTIFYING CONCLUSIONS
*Circle the likely conclusion you can draw from each statement below.*

1. I am so depressed; my grades came today.
   a. The speaker is a student.
   b. The person did not perform as well as expected.
   c. The instructors did not like this student at all.
   d. The speaker missed the final examination.
   e. The grades were delivered by mail.

You might have circled *a, b,* and *e.* The other conclusions cannot be drawn based on the evidence.

2. I had a sleepless night last night because of parents calling to complain about their children's grades.
   a. Parents were upset because their children received low grades.
   b. Parents wanted the instructor to change the grades.
   c. The speaker is an instructor.
   d. The children lied about the final examination.
   e. The parents disrespected the person's right to a good night's sleep.

You should have circled *a, b, c,* and *e.* All are valid conclusions that may be drawn from the stated evidence. On the surface, *d* appears to be valid, but there is not enough evidence to support this conclusion.

## EXERCISE 4.6   DRAWING CONCLUSIONS

*Write a likely conclusion for each word grouping below.*

1. Jack is speeding again; if he isn't careful, he _____

   _____.

2. If Mr. Brown continues to smoke three packs of cigarettes a day, he

   _____.

3. If Jan continues to eat whole pizzas every night, she _____

   _____.

4. When it is raining or snowing, Bill _____

   _____.

5. Most infants can stand alone before their twelfth month, and

   between their twelfth and thirteenth month, many infants _____

   _____.


## EXERCISE 4.7   EVALUATING CONCLUSIONS

*Place a check mark beside each sentence that states a valid conclusion that may be drawn from the following passage.*

Trudie Ross could see that one of her customers was grating on her other patrons and employees. "This man came in the café every day just to read the newspapers," says Ross, who owns the Newsstand Café in Denver. Other customers quietly nibbled on sandwiches and sipped coffee drinks while browsing the thousands of magazines she stocks. But not the toxic customer. "He always complained that others had torn out his favorite sections. He was generally unpleasant to be around."

After putting up with his negative comments and disruptive behavior for months, Ross had a brainstorm for how to take action without causing a scene or embarrassing him in public. She just politely asked him to stop coming into her café. "I approached him and said that we needed a 'time-out' from each other," said Ross, who asked him to stay out of her café for a few months.

To her surprise, it worked. "We haven't seen him in weeks," said Ross. "It's wonderful." Her regular customers and employees have praised her for taking action. If you have a toxic customer, don't throw him out, but clearly and politely ask him to go away—just for a while.

Jane Applegate, "The Toxic Customer"

_____ 1. Business owners must consider the feelings of others.

_____ 2. The toxic customer is angering patrons at a café nearby.

_____ 3. Irritable people are aware of the negative effect they have on others and are not surprised when they are asked to leave.

_____ 4. Many paying customers would have eventually stopped going to Ross's café.

_____ 5. The café atmosphere has changed greatly since the toxic customer stopped coming in.

_____ 6. Ross had never experienced anything like this before.

_____ 7. A retired professor, the toxic customer appeared to have had a personal problem.

_____ 8. One of Ross's mottoes is "Think before you act."

_____ 9. The toxic customer made few, if any, friends at the café.

_____ 10. The author liked the way Ross handled the situation.

## 4a.3 Predictions

**Making predictions** means taking the author's message to another level. You are using information in the present to foretell the future. Predictions are based on factual information that may change over the course of time. To make predictions, follow these steps:

**Step 1.** Read the stated information. Make sure you understand, even if it means rereading.

**Step 2.** Analyze the stated information carefully. Use your reasoning skill to complete an "if-then" statement ("If I fall asleep, then I will snore"). *Ask: Does this information lead me to conclude similarly that if it's cloudy, then it will probably rain?*

**Step 3.** State your prediction. *Ask: Can this result follow from the information given?*

**Step 4.** Test your prediction. *Ask: Based on the present, is this likely to happen in the future?*

### EXERCISE 4.8   MAKING PREDICTIONS
*Circle the most likely prediction for each of the numbered sentences.*

1. The couple fought all night long.
   a. The couple will eventually divorce.
   b. The couple will make up and start over again.
   c. The couple will move into another apartment.
   d. The couple will begin to make plans for parenthood.

The most likely prediction is *a*. But, who knows?

2. The pouring rain affected the driver's vision considerably.
   a. The driver pulled over to the side of the road.
   b. The driver continued to drive at full speed.

c. The driver turned off the windshield wipers.

d. The driver put on the brakes quickly.

The most likely outcome is *a*.

## EXERCISE 4.9   MAKING PREDICTIONS

*In the spaces provided, write your prediction for the two actions that will occur next.*

1. Once inside the supermarket, Ted _____

   and _____ .

2. Diane filled out an application for her apartment,

   _____ , and _____ .

3. People turned out in large numbers to meet the famous author;

   they _____ and _____ .

4. When the airplane landed, the passengers _____

   and _____ .

5. At Bee's drive-in restaurant, the menu for today is chicken necks

   and gizzards; customers _____ and

   _____ .

## EXERCISE 4.10   MAKING PREDICTIONS

*Read the paragraph below; then place a check mark beside the valid predictions you can make.*

One of the top stories of the year was that of a baby boy born to a mother alone in the woods. Not thinking the birth was so near, the mother had left the city on a two-day camping trip to the Ozarks. There she would meditate and commune with nature. This ritual was to prepare her for the upcoming event—the birth of her newborn. After two days in the wooded mountains, the mother, quite relaxed, would leave for home that next morning. She packed her bags before retiring for the evening and fell fast asleep. Around midnight, however, a pull in her tummy awakened her. She excused this as the green apple she had eaten earlier and dozed off again. About two hours later, she was awakened again, only this time to excruciating pain. Too weakened to call for help, she lay there suffering. What seemed like hours later, she managed to reach the phone on the wall beside the bed and dial 911.

_____ 1. The baby will experience psychological trauma later.

_____ 2. The doctor was sued for miscalculating the baby's time of arrival.

_____ 3. The mother and baby were rushed to the hospital.

_____ 4. The angry father divorced the mother a few months later.

_____ 5. News reporters consider this a great human interest story.

_____ 6. After hearing this story, stalkers will be more and more on the lookout for pregnant women in distress.

_____ 7. The son will be told the story of his birth many times by different people.

_____ 8. An event such as this will probably not happen again anytime soon.

_____ 9. Whenever the mother eats a green apple (if she eats one), she will think about her ordeal.

_____ 10. The mother will have much calling and talking to do when she gets home from the hospital.

## 4a.4 Generalizations

Identifying generalizations is another way to analyze the author's writing. Generalizations are statements about a group based on the actions of one or more persons who belong to that particular group (for example, "All children like to play"). Pay particular attention to any writing that relies on generalizations to support a point. To identify valid generalizations, follow these steps:

**Step 1.** Look for a stated/implied group in the statement. *Ask: Does this statement mention a number of individuals or things placed together in one category* (parents, nurses, students, etc.)?

**Step 2.** Determine whether the statement describes an action of all members of the group. *Ask: Are all members said to do the same thing?*

**Step 3.** Determine whether the statement is valid. *Ask: Does the author use words that allow no room for exceptions* (all, always, never, none, totally, should)?

**Step 4.** Verify the generalization. *Ask: Is this true of all members of the group?*

### EXERCISE 4.11   EVALUATING GENERALIZATIONS
*Place a check mark before the valid generalizations below.*

_____ 1. All parents should spank their children for rude behavior.

_____ 2. When drowning, a swimmer should call out to the lifeguard.

_____ 3. Most doctors who overcharge their patients do not stay in business for very long.

Did you choose 1 and 3 as generalizations? The third example is the only valid generalization.

## EXERCISE 4.12 RECOGNIZING GENERALIZATIONS

*Place a check mark beside generalizations and a second check mark beside those that are valid. Circle any key words that are clues to the correct response.*

_____ 1. Families should eat at least one meal together every day.

_____ 2. Doctors have proved over time that they just cannot write.

_____ 3. It seems that illegible penmanship is a requirement for entering the medical profession.

_____ 4. Most high school students dread the thought of spending four more years in school.

_____ 5. Abusive pet owners should be sentenced to life in prison.

_____ 6. All owners of automobiles must wear a seat belt.

_____ 7. A computer fanatic will surf the net all night long.

_____ 8. Genetic counselors predict which couples will have a healthy baby.

_____ 9. Procrastinators will never complete a worthwhile task.

_____ 10. Television news commentators have changed over the years.

## 4B CRITICAL WRITING

Critical writing is another way to connect with the author. It involves looking critically at what the author has to say by questioning, comparing, and evaluating the message to determine its value to you. This is done by paying special attention to the author's writing techniques and choice of language.

### 4b.1 Fact and Opinion

Being able to distinguish between fact and opinion makes you an informed reader. You know if the writing represents the author's bias and whether or not you want to accept it. Most textbook writers use facts, but many other types of writing may be loaded with opinions. In case of the latter, writers sometimes use direct quotations from informed sources to lend credibility to their work, helping their writing to become more factual, more believable.

**Facts** are statements that can be verified or checked for accuracy. Thus, a common characteristic of facts is concreteness. As a result, facts are observable through the senses, measurable through experiment, and obtainable through research. Facts must be proved and, therefore, may be labeled either true or false. Words that represent facts have a **denotative,** or literal, meaning as found in a dictionary definition.

**Opinions** are statements that reveal a personal preference and which thus cannot be proved. Unlike facts, opinions often have a **connotative,** or implied, meaning and may include the following:

- Statements about others (*you, everybody, people*)
- Comparisons (*better, best; worse, worst; least, more, most*)
- Abstract or descriptive terms (*eager, pretty, love, something*)
- Future reference (*tomorrow, in the future*)
- Verbs and adverbs that suggest doubt or possibility (*appears, believes, feels, apparently, possibility, probably*)
- Conditional terms (*could, if, might, suppose*)

To distinguish between fact and opinion, follow these steps:

**Step 1.** Read the statement carefully.

**Step 2.** Circle key words and phrases. *Ask: Where are the key words and phrases?*

**Step 3.** Determine the type of information. *Ask: Is this information verifiable? Is the information a personal preference?*

**Step 4.** Identify facts. *Ask: How can this information be verified—by experiment? by observation? or by research?*

**Step 5.** Identify opinions. *Ask: Are differing opinions likely?*

**Step 6.** Verify your findings. *Ask: Is this verifiable information? = a fact. Is this personal preference? = an opinion.*

### EXERCISE 4.13   FACT AND OPINION
*Place a check mark beside the sentence that states a fact.*

_____ 1. Seven bird nests are in the elm tree in my backyard.

_____ 2. Everybody owes somebody something.

Did you check sentence 1? This statement is a fact because everything is observable and measurable. You can see and count the seven bird nests in the tree. The second sentence, however, states an opinion. You cannot verify such abstract terms as *everybody, somebody,* or *something*. And, surely, the sentence is a statement of personal preference. Some people, even you, may agree with this statement, but many others are likely to disagree.

### EXERCISE 4.14   IDENTIFYING FACT AND OPINION
*Place a check mark beside each sentence that states a fact.*

_____ 1. Every child likes candy.

_____ 2. Eyeglasses cost too much in today's economy.

_____ 3. An Associate of Arts degree can be earned in two years.

_____ 4. I love peanut butter and jelly sandwiches.

_____ 5. Bob Ofit has tracked down films all over the world.

_____ 6. Tomorrow we are going to the zoo.

_____ 7. More people live in California than in Idaho.

_____ 8. I believe I can fly.

_____ 9. You really don't need to become a pharmacist.

_____ 10. Wealthy people are happier than poor people.

_____ 11. A pound of salt weighs the same as a pound of nails.

_____ 12. It takes less than a week for a tomato to spoil.

_____ 13. If I cry today, it will probably rain tomorrow.

_____ 14. What the world needs now is love.

_____ 15. The players are enthusiastic about the game.

## 4b.2 Analyzing the Author's Purpose

Audience, style, mood, and tone all work together to support the author's purpose. In fact, this is another way the author is able to influence you, the reader. The alert reader is aware of the author's influence in promoting the message. Study the following definitions to become more aware of ways an author can attempt to influence your thoughts and actions.

- **Purpose** is the author's reason(s) for writing: to inform, to teach, to sell, to entertain, to persuade, to inspire, and so on. *Ask: What is the writer's reason for writing this?*
- **Mood** is the way the author hopes to make you feel: happy, sad, joyful, enthusiastic, depressed, frightened, and so on. *Ask: How does the writer want me to feel?*
- **Audience** is the person or people the author targets in the writing: general interest (anybody) or a particular group, such as students, mothers, nurses, teachers, motorcyclists, or pilots. *Ask: For whom is this written?*
- **Style** consists of the characteristics peculiar to a particular writer, including the length and difficulty of paragraphs, sentences, and words. *Ask: What makes this writer different from other writers? What "personality" does the writer have?*
- **Tone** is the author's attitude or feeling about the subject: it may be admiring, amused, angry, excited, humorous, informative, insensitive, instructive, neutral, objective, persuasive, serious, sympathetic, and so on. Note: A writer who expresses no feelings about the subject is using an objective or neutral tone. *Ask: How does the writer want me to feel about the subject?*

## EXERCISE 4.15   IDENTIFYING THE AUTHOR'S PURPOSE

*Read the following excerpt about garlic and circle the best answer to each question.*

# All About Garlic

*Carol Edgar*

1        As ancient as civilization itself, that oh-so odorous herb called garlic has returned to American kitchens with new potency. It's conveniently coincidental that garlic satisfies not just our quest for taste, but our quest for health as well. Long used to ward off vampires, illness and other evils, it's easy to smell why garlic is now genuinely valued for its antibiotic and bacterial effects on diseases ranging from arthritis to arteriosclerosis. (You can even buy garlic capsules at your local health-food store.)

2        At only a calorie or two per clove and pennies a head, garlic ranks as one of the most efficient ways of adding taste to food. Be sure to use it fresh; good cooks dislike the prepared forms. When buying garlic, look for firm, plump bulbs with skins that are clean, dry, and unbroken. The white varieties are generally milder than the rose-color garlics, and giant elephant garlic is one of the mildest of all. Store garlic not in the refrigerator (where it will mildew) but in a dry place with lots of circulating air. Fresh garlic will keep for six to eight weeks, so buy only as much as you can use fairly quickly.

1. Mood: How does the author want to make you feel?
   a. happy                          b. enlightened
   c. depressed                      d. irritable

2. Audience: To whom is the author writing?
   a. a general audience             b. a student
   c. a homemaker                    d. one who likes garlic

3. Style: What makes the author's writing different from that of other writers?
   a. many descriptive words         b. difficult vocabulary
   c. short, choppy sentences        d. long, complicated paragraphs

4. Tone: How does the writer want you to feel about garlic?
   a. interested                     b. nervous
   c. angry                          d. amused

5. Purpose: Why did the author write this article about garlic?
   a. to humor the reader
   b. to entertain the reader
   c. to persuade the reader to use garlic
   d. to inform the reader about the benefits of garlic

## 4b.3 Figurative Language

**Figurative language** is used by writers to paint a picture with words for the reader. This type of vivid language creates images in the mind of the reader and helps bring clarity and understanding to ideas. Four types of figurative expressions are commonly used:

- A **simile** is an indirect comparison using the word *like* or *as:* "She smells like a rose." "He's as thin as a broom."
- A **metaphor** is a direct comparison: "The teacher is a ruler." "He is a brick house."
- **Personification** means giving human qualities to nonhuman objects: "The leaves dance in the wind." "The sun sleeps at night."
- **Hyperbole** means exaggerated expression: "I cried a thousand tears." "He weighs a ton."

### EXERCISE 4.16   FIGURATIVE LANGUAGE

*For each sentence, choose a word from the list below that describes the type of figurative language used, and write the correct letter in each blank. Then write what each statement means.*

| a. simile | b. hyperbole | c. metaphor | d. personification |
| --- | --- | --- | --- |

_____ 1. I paid a fortune for this ring.

Meaning: _____

_____ 2. Her razor-sharp tongue cut my feelings to pieces.

Meaning: _____

_____ 3. The raindrops whisper softly in my ear.

Meaning: _____

_____ 4. The business was the glue that held the family together.

Meaning: _____

_____ 5. A good friend is like a gift-wrapped box.

Meaning: _____

_____ 6. Jack was as cool as a cucumber when he drove up.

Meaning: _____

_____ 7. I have never seen clouds weep the way they did today.

Meaning: _____

_____ 8. Marrying to find happiness is like gambling to become rich.

   Meaning: _____

_____ 9. Sam is a pistol when he gets angry.

   Meaning: _____

_____ 10. She graded a mountain of papers before falling asleep.

   Meaning: _____

## EXERCISE 4.17   WRITING FIGURATIVE LANGUAGE

*Write figurative expressions; either compose them yourself or find examples in the lyrics of your favorite songs.*

1. **hyperbole**

   a. _____

   b. _____

2. **metaphor**

   a. _____

   b. _____

3. **personification**

   a. _____

   b. _____

4. **simile**

   a. _____

   b. _____

## 4b.4  Propaganda

**Propaganda** is a form of writing used often in editorials, commercials, and political campaigns to influence your actions or opinions. This appeal to your emotions is a deliberate attempt to control your thoughts. Whether harmful or not, propaganda must be recognized by the careful reader, so you will remain in control of your actions. Here are several common propaganda techniques:

• **Bandwagon** means following the crowd—everyone is doing it, so you should do it too: "Join the Pepsi generation."
• **Name calling** is the use of words that have a negative connotation: "The aliens are coming!"

- The **plain folks** strategy is used by advertisers to show regular people just like you and me using their products: *Vacationing wife*: "Don't you know nothing—Pepto Bismol is the best laxative. It says so here on the label." *Vacationing husband*: "She never goes on vacation."
- **Stacking the cards** means giving only the best (or worst) point of view: "MCI charges only 5 cents per minute for Sunday long-distance calls." "ATT charges 17 cents per minute for weekday long-distance calls."
- In **testimonials,** authorities or famous people testify to the value of a product: Michael Jordan says, "You had better eat your Wheaties."
- **Transfer** means linking something that is liked or respected with something or someone else: "Mountain Springs water is as American as apple pie."

## EXERCISE 4.18   IDENTIFYING PROPAGANDA

*Identify the type of propaganda used in each statement. Write the correct letter from the box in the space provided.*

| | | |
|---|---|---|
| a. bandwagon | b. name-calling | c. plain folks |
| d. testimonial | e. transfer | f. stacking the cards |

_____   1. We treat all dirt like scum.

_____   2. How do you create a room that says "Wow"? With Benjamin Moore, that's how.

_____   3. Deep-cleaning carpets is almost as easy as child's play.

_____   4. Veterinarians, like Dr. Gretchen Becker, know one thing is almost certain with any cat, besides a unique personality, and that's hairballs. . . . Learn what vets feed their pets.

_____   5. Dermatologists know: Your dry, sensitive skin needs an effective cleanser that's mild. And they recommend . . .

_____   6. It's the kind of cereal you'd invent with your kid. I know—because I did.

_____   7. When you're here, you're family.

_____   8. Millions of people turn to Metabolife to lose weight.

_____   9. Cozy Sunday mornings were made for Mohawk carpet.

_____ 10. Rich, buttery shortbread Sandies from Keebler. Something simple you can do for you. Every day.

_____ 11. The devil is in the details. (It hurts to have a demon doing the work.)

_____ 12. Every minute of every day, someone buys a Clopay garage door. So beautiful, durable, and reliable, you'll want one for your home, too.

_____ 13. Our compact stereo not only produces great sound, it inspires it. *Customer comments:* "I wanted the best for my husband. . . . He loves it! It's the best gift he's ever received."

_____ 14. Presenting SnackWell's Mint Crème: Luscious chocolate cookies, covered with mint crème and smothered in rich, velvety icing. Yet amazingly, reduced in fat. So they're simply better for you. Live WELL. Snack WELL.

_____ 15. The favorite vacuum of thousands of hotels and more than a million professionals and private users. You can use this powerful vacuum to clean your home better than ever.

# Mastery Test 4

*Read the passage below and answer the questions that follow.*

## The Strange Burden of a Name

*Lance Morrow*

A name is sometimes a ridiculous fate. For example, a man afflicted with the name of Kill Sin Pimple lived in Sussex [England], in 1609. In the spring of that year, the record shows, Kill Sin served on a jury with his Puritan neighbors, including Fly Debate Roberts, More Fruit Fowler, God Reward Smart, Be Faithful Joiner, and Fight the Good Fight of Faith White. Poor men. At birth, their parents had turned them into religious bumper stickers.

A name may announce something—or hide something. In the Arab or Chinese societies, for example, a beautiful child may be called by a disgusting name—"Dog," "Stupid," "Ugly," say—in order to ward off the evil eye. Hillary Rodham knew that in some parts of the savage political world, she attracted the evil eye to the 1992 Democratic ticket. So during her overnice, cookie-baker phase, she was purposely "Hillary Clinton," silent, nodding adorer and helpmate of Bill. She half-hid herself in "Hillary Clinton" until the coast was clear. With the Inauguration, the formal, impressive triple name has lumbered into place like a convoy of armored cars: Hillary Rodham Clinton.

The name problem for married women is a clumsy mess. Married women have four or more choices. (1) Keep the last name they were given at birth. (2) Take the husband's last name. (3) Use three names, as in Hillary Rodham Clinton; or, as women did in the '70s, join the wife's birth name and the husband's birth name with a hyphen—a practice that in the third generation down the road would produce multiple-hyphenated nightmares. (4) Use the unmarried name in most matters professional, and use the husband's name in at least some matters personal and domestic. Most men, if they were to wake up one morning and find themselves changed into married women, would (rather huffily) choose Option No. 1.

The words with which people and things are named have a changeful magic. Some cultures invent different names for people in different stages of life. In Chinese tradition a boy of school age would be given a "book name," to be used in arranging marriages and other official matters. A boy's book name might be "Worthy Prince" or "Spring Dragon" or "Celestial Emolument." (Does a father say, "Hello, have you met my boy,

Celestial Emolument?") Hillary Rodham Clinton may find her name changing still further as her political power progresses. Perhaps by next year, she will be known as "H. R. Clinton." Maybe the year after that, she will be "H. R. (Bob) Clinton."

## COMPREHENSION EXERCISE

1. What can you infer in regard to the author's opinion about Hillary Clinton?
   a. She is an honest person.
   b. She is a confused wife.
   c. She will do whatever it takes to get what she wants.
   d. She has high moral standards.

2. Which of the following inferences can you make about names?
   a. Chinese names tell very little about a person.
   b. Names are more important to men than to women.
   c. Parents are overly concerned with the effect that a name will have on a child.
   d. Hyphenated names have a proven history of problems.

3. What do you suppose the expression *like a convoy of armored cars* means?
   a. paraded cars on the assembly line
   b. loaded with explosives
   c. prepared to defend a position
   d. organized to battle for cars

4. What type of language is used in the expression *like a convoy of armored cars?*
   a. personification
   b. propaganda
   c. figurative
   d. objective

5. A Chinese boy's *book name* (such as "Worthy Prince," "Spring Dragon," or "Celestial Emolument") is an example of
   a. personification
   b. propaganda
   c. simile
   d. metaphor

6. What is the author's tone in the last paragraph?
   a. humorous
   b. depressing
   c. angry
   d. persuasive

7. How would you classify the last two sentences in paragraph 4?
   a. suggestions
   b. violations
   c. predictions
   d. generalizations

8. Which of the following is a fact from the selection?
   a. "The words with which people and things are named have a changeful magic."
   b. "The name problem for married women is a clumsy mess."
   c. "Married women have four or more choices."
   d. "Most men, if they were to wake up one morning and find themselves changed into married women, would (rather huffily) choose Option No. 1."

9. What does the author use to show that he has extra information to present?
   a. capital letters
   b. parentheses
   c. quotation marks
   d. fragments

10. What is the author's purpose?
    a. to challenge people to spell names correctly
    b. to inform people about issues concerning names
    c. to persuade people to choose better names
    d. to embarrass people who have unusual names

**Score**: Number Correct _____ (out of 10) × 10 = _____

# PART II

# Applied Reading

This part of the text consists of fifteen reading selections: ten general-interest articles, four textbook excerpts, and one excerpt from a novel. Following each selection are exercises to develop your reading skills. Most of the skills reinforced through these activities were introduced in Part I. However, many of the activities also provide avenues for improving listening habits and reading speed discussed briefly below.

## LISTENING STRATEGIES

There is a big difference between hearing and listening. For the most part, hearing is mechanical. It requires little or no effort, whereas listening requires concentration and great effort. One major difficulty associated with listening is taking side trips, allowing your mind to wander elsewhere instead of concentrating on the speaker and the message. To listen more intensely and decrease the number of side trips, practice the following listening strategies:

- Summarize the speaker's message.
- Predict where the speaker is headed.
- Question the validity of the speaker's words.
- Make a conscious effort to listen more closely.

Two activities following the selections include an effective listening component: postreading and collaborating. In the postreading exercises that require you to work with a partner, you will act as both a listener and a speaker. As a listener, your goal is to make sure that your partner is communicating effectively. You can do this only by practicing good listening skills. Be sure not to interrupt the speaker; just listen carefully and take brief notes. After the speaker finishes, you may ask follow-up questions, repeat key ideas, and provide feedback as needed.

During the collaborating activities, you are again called on to use your listening skills, this time working with a group. To ensure that listening occurs, stay focused on the conversation. Establish eye contact with the speaker, take brief notes, and be a sympathetic listener. Through facial expressions and head nods, you alert the speaker to your understanding or lack thereof.

## MEASURING YOUR READING RATE

You may find it helpful to keep a record of the time it takes for you to read the general-interest selections. A good rate to strive for in this type of reading is between 200 and 300 words per minute. Of course, with the demands of reading on your schedule, a higher rate would be even better.

The major purpose of most of the textbook selections is to give you practice in study-type reading. For this reason, you are not asked to time yourself on these.

An important point to remember about your reading rate is that you should not expect to read every selection at the same rate. In any case, you want your overall rate to improve with practice. Also, you want your reading comprehension score to remain steady or, preferably, to increase. Thus, you should constantly monitor your reading activity by making frequent comparisons between your comprehension score and your reading rate. If your comprehension score decreases, you may need to adjust your reading rate—you could be reading too fast.

The word count is printed in parentheses at the end of each of the following selections. Use a stopwatch or a clock with a second hand to time your reading of the general-interest selections. Then refer to the reading rate chart at the back of the book to get your reading rate, and record it in the Reading Rate Progress Chart.

# READING SELECTIONS

*A = argument, E = exposition, N = narration, P = process, T = textbook

Selection 1

# Eight Terrific Tips
# for Managing Time

*D. M. B. Harrison-Lee and Matt Larson*

## PREREADING EXERCISE

Study the title, the Vocabulary Review, and the first paragraph of the selection. Then write a sentence expressing what you believe this selection is about.

_____

_____

_____

_____

If job, family, and civic and social commitments are running you  1
ragged, take a break and **meditate** on the following ideas for better managing your time—and your life:

   **1. You can't do it all, so get some help.** Ask for and accept help to  2
get things done. Remember, housework is a family responsibility. Consider having your groceries delivered, shopping by catalog, or hiring a student to clean your home.

   **2. Learn to say no.** It's nice to be needed, but no one is **indispen-**  3
**sable.** Defend your calendar, and don't allow others to **impose** on it unnecessarily.

   **3. Get organized.** The time wasted sifting through loose papers and  4
cluttered drawers can be better spent organizing them.

   **4. Acquire tools that increase your effectiveness.** A fax and an-  5
swering machine, cellular phone, pocket organizer, and daily planner can free up time and give you more control.

   **5. Don't put off until tomorrow . . . Procrastination** doesn't buy you  6
time. In fact, it usually costs you more. Pick a time to focus on the task you're tempted to put off, and complete it.

7        **6. Prepare.** Select tomorrow's outfit the night before. Plan a week's dinner menus and slice, dice, and season beforehand. Make a daily "to do" list. Keep a grooming bag packed for trips.

8        **7. Curb on-the-job socializing.** Cut that long conversation short if it's going to keep you from getting your job done.

9        **8. Set priorities.** Being busy shouldn't mean that you ignore or give less to the people or activities that are important to you. Always set aside time for them.

*(260 words)*

## POSTREADING EXERCISE

Now that you have read the selection, revise the sentence you wrote in the prereading exercise.

_____

_____

_____

1. Discuss the revised sentence with a study partner, giving support for your ideas. Your partner will listen, take notes, and use the notes to repeat your key ideas.

2. Now trade places with your partner.

## COMPREHENSION EXERCISE
*Circle the letter of the best answer.*

### SKIMMING FOR FACTS

1. The author recommends that you consider
   a. shopping at midnight.
   b. having your groceries delivered.
   c. hiring a live-in housekeeper.
   d. taking a vacation to meditate.

2. The time you spend sifting through cluttered drawers could be better spent
   a. cleaning them.
   b. organizing them.
   c. spending quality time with the kids.
   d. completing an unfinished task.

3. To the author, "prepared" means
   a. completing all items on your "to do" list.
   b. planning a month's dinner menus.

    c. keeping a snack pack bag ready for trips.
    d. selecting tomorrow's outfit the day before.

4. If you're already busy, you should _____ when asked to do more.
    a. just say no
    b. kindly accept the job
    c. decide if the price is right before accepting
    d. say maybe and forget it

5. You should always save time for _____ that are important to you.
    a. wishes
    b. people
    c. activities
    d. both b and c

**RELATING THE FACTS**

6. What type of tip is given in paragraph 2?
    a. example
    b. addition
    c. comparison
    d. cause-effect

7. According to the author, which of these is a tool to increase effectiveness?
    a. microwave oven
    b. pencil sharpener
    c. measuring cup
    d. cellular phone

8. Which pattern of organization does this selection follow?
    a. listing
    b. comparison-contrast
    c. classification
    d. cause-effect

9. Which relationship is shown in this sentence: "It's nice to be needed, but no one is indispensable"?
    a. cause-effect
    b. addition
    c. contrast
    d. both a and c

10. Map the ideas presented in paragraph 7.

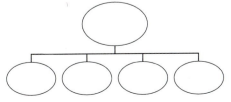

CONNECTING WITH THE AUTHOR

11. The author suggests that major necessities
    a. do not have to prove stressful.
    b. are not really important.
    c. require financial backing.
    d. are costly to the young homeowner.

12. You can infer from paragraph 2 that the author believes that housework is
    a. a major responsibility.
    b. more demanding than employment outside of the home.
    c. better left undone.
    d. a thing of the past.

13. In paragraph 4, the author appears to favor purchasing a
    a. folding table.
    b. file cabinet.
    c. red notebook.
    d. box of paper.

14. In paragraph 7, it appears that the author thinks cooking, dressing, and travel
    a. require less time than everything else.
    b. come first on everyone's list of dreaded activities.
    c. top the list of time-consuming activities.
    d. require no planning.

15. A likely conclusion drawn from paragraph 9 is that
    a. one should take care of oneself first.
    b. people are more important than anything else.
    c. children should be trained.
    d. everybody is a star.

16. The author's writing style is
    a. direct.
    b. unclear.
    c. difficult.
    d. boring.

17. The headings of each section represent
    a. key ideas.
    b. wordy summaries.
    c. paraphrased sentences.
    d. sentence fragments.

18. Which sentence from the selection states a fact?
    a. "Remember, housework is a family responsibility."
    b. "It's nice to be needed, but no one is indispensable."
    c. "Procrastination doesn't buy you time."
    d. None of the above.

19. Who is the author's audience?
    a. busy executives
    b. students
    c. busy people
    d. none of the above

20. The author's purpose in writing this article is to
    a. inform.
    b. demonstrate.
    c. humor.
    d. humiliate.

---

### PROGRESS CHART

*Circle the correct responses for each section below. Add the circles and multiply by 5. Record the total below and in the score chart in the Appendix.*

| Skimming for Facts | Relating the Facts | Connecting with the Author | Total |
|---|---|---|---|
| 1  2  3  4  5 | 6  7  8  9  10 | 11  12  13  14  15  16  17  18  19  20 | |

## REFLECTING

**Mnemonic devices** are words, sentences, rhymes, and jingles to help you to remember. Here are two ways to make mnemonics that help you remember the eight tips for managing time.

1. Write the key word from each numbered tip in the selection.

    a. _____

    b. _____

    c. _____

    d. _____

    e. _____

    f. _____

    g. _____

    h. _____

2. Arrange the key words to form a sentence. (Your sentence does not have to make sense.)

    _____

3. Write the first letter of each key word.

    a. _____

    b. _____

    c. _____

d. _____

e. _____

f. _____

g. _____

h. _____

4. Create a new sentence using words that begin with these letters.

_____

## COLLABORATING

With a group, make a list of problems that students, workers, and parents face in managing time. Include at least five items in each category. For each list, identify tips from the selection that might help eliminate the problems. Write the number of the tip in parentheses beside each problem.

| STUDENTS | TIP | WORKERS | TIP | PARENTS | TIP |
|---|---|---|---|---|---|
| _____ | ( ) | _____ | ( ) | _____ | ( ) |
| _____ | ( ) | _____ | ( ) | _____ | ( ) |
| _____ | ( ) | _____ | ( ) | _____ | ( ) |
| _____ | ( ) | _____ | ( ) | _____ | ( ) |
| _____ | ( ) | _____ | ( ) | _____ | ( ) |

Which tip seems to be most practical? Explain. _____

_____

_____

_____

## WEB WATCH

Go to the Web site at www.QueenDom.com and take a scientific standardized test on procrastination to discover something about yourself and to learn how you can improve. Sites often change, so if this site is no longer available, explore the Internet to find another site related to procrastination or time management.

## VOCABULARY EXERCISE

Complete the puzzle with words from the box.

| | | | |
|---|---|---|---|
| impose | indispensable | meditate | procrastination |

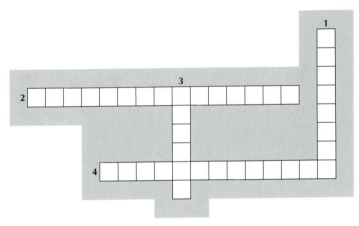

**ACROSS**
2. postponement
4. required

**DOWN**
1. to think deeply
3. to force on another

# Ten Ways to Beat Stress

*Jennie C. Trotter*

**VOCABULARY REVIEW**
**affirmation (af-fir-ma-tion):** positive statement
**brainstorm (brain-storm):** to call up a free flow of ideas
**chanting (chant-ing):** songlike speaking
**evaluate (e-val-u-ate):** to determine the value of
**ironic (i-ron-ic):** contrary to what's expected
**meditation (med-i-ta-tion):** deep, continued thought
**obstacles (ob-sta-cles):** anything that stands in the way of progress

## PREREADING EXERCISE

Study the title of the selection and the Vocabulary Review. Then survey the selection and fill in the map below with key words from the title and major headings.

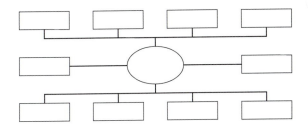

Each of us experiences some kind of stress every day. Try practicing these ten positive ways to cope when you're under pressure.  1

**1. Think positive.** Since most stress starts in the mind, control it by keeping positive thoughts in mind or by viewing the problem from a humorous or **ironic** angle.  2

**2. Visualize.** When you're under pressure, visualize the positive outcome you desire and focus on it often.  3

**3. Let it out.** When anger reaches the boiling point, cool down by punching a pillow, tearing paper, talking to an empty chair, or writing your feelings down.  4

**4. Praise yourself.** Reflect on the rough times you've made it through, and praise yourself for overcoming those **obstacles.** This approach will help you find the positive lesson in the situation.  5

**5. Tune in.** Get in touch with your spiritual self through prayer, **affirmation, chanting,** or **meditation.** If you can't solve the problem or change it or make it better, let it go!  6

7     **6. Seek support.** Talk over your problem with someone. Don't look for instant answers, but enjoy unloading and sharing.

8     **7. Cool out.** Give your mind and body a break by doing something you really enjoy.

9     **8. Take care of yourself.** Get enough rest, eat nutritious meals, and exercise daily to keep your body prepared to deal with stress.

10     **9. Break it down.** Use these four steps to figure out problems: write down the problem, **brainstorm** for solutions, list the consequences, then select and **evaluate** the best solution for you.

11     **10. Help someone else.** Take your mind off your own problems by doing something for someone else.

*(260 words)*

## POSTREADING EXERCISE

Now that you have read the selection, add specific details to the map you produced in the prereading exercise.

## COMPREHENSION EXERCISE
*Circle the letter of the best answer.*

### SKIMMING FOR FACTS

1. According to the selection, where does most stress start?
   a. in the mind
   b. in the workplace
   c. in the body
   d. in the home

2. When should you write your feelings down?
   a. when thoughts flow freely
   b. when dreams become reality
   c. when anger reaches the boiling point
   d. when tears stop falling

3. How can you give your mind a break?
   a. Watch a boring movie.
   b. Do something you enjoy.
   c. Blow your nose—really hard.
   d. Close your eyes.

4. If you can't solve the problem, you should
   a. seek professional help.
   b. study it for a longer period of time.
   c. let it go.
   d. eat a snack.

5. Which of the following is *not* a suggested way to beat stress?
   a. Punch a pillow.
   b. Look for instant answers.
   c. Eat nutritious meals.
   d. Exercise daily.

### RELATING THE FACTS

6. Which pattern of organization does the selection follow?
   a. comparison
   b. contrast
   c. listing
   d. cause-effect

7. Which of the following relationships do the two sentences in paragraph 5 express?
   a. comparison
   b. contrast
   c. cause-effect
   d. process

8. Which of the following relationships is expressed in paragraph 6?
   a. comparison
   b. contrast
   c. process
   d. cause-effect

9. Which of the following types of signals is used in paragraph 7?
   a. comparison
   b. contrast
   c. process
   d. cause-effect

10. Which pattern of development is used in paragraph 10?
    a. chronology
    b. contrast
    c. listing
    d. cause-effect

### CONNECTING WITH THE AUTHOR

11. From the first sentence of the selection, you can infer that
    a. stress is a common occurrence.
    b. stress occurs mostly on holidays.
    c. stress is a good feeling.
    d. stress occurs mostly when you are asleep.

12. In paragraph 2, the author implies that it is important to
    a. review your list of failures constantly.
    b. try to predict accidents before they happen.
    c. laugh at your own careless mistakes.
    d. hold a grudge for a long time.

13. From paragraph 4, you can infer that
    a. bottled-up anger can destroy your health and well-being.
    b. people who endure high levels of stress are angry.
    c. stress produces a long and happy life.
    d. too much worry is a major cause of hair growth.

14. From paragraph 6, you can infer that
    a. it is difficult, if not impossible, to work miracles.
    b. joining a church will end your problems.
    c. you must achieve your goals.
    d. it is easy to solve problems.

15. From paragraph 11, you can conclude that
    a. kindness has many rewards.
    b. selfishness never hurt anybody.
    c. trading problems with someone else is good business sense.
    d. when you help someone, that person is indebted to you for life.

16. From paragraph 7, you might generalize that
    a. everybody meets someone special somewhere.
    b. students should avoid school counselors.
    c. friends are good to have in time of trouble.
    d. people with nagging financial problems should get a quick title loan.

17. How would you describe the author's style?
    a. precise and objective
    b. humorous and subjective
    c. sympathetic and persuasive
    d. instructive and complicated

18. If you were to follow the author's advice in paragraph 4, the actions could be verified through
    a. observation.
    b. testing.
    c. research.
    d. trial and error.

19. Which of the following points does the author make throughout the selection?
    a. There is nothing you can do about stress.
    b. Stress can be controlled.
    c. Getting information about stress is time-consuming.
    d. Most people do not realize the effects of stress.

20. The author's purpose is to
    a. persuade.
    b. inform.
    c. humor.
    d. tell a story.

_____ **PROGRESS CHART** _____

*Circle the correct responses for each section below. Add the circles and multiply by 5. Record the total below and in the score chart in the Appendix.*

| Skimming for Facts | Relating the Facts | Connecting with the Author | Total |
|---|---|---|---|
| 1  2  3  4  5 | 6  7  8  9  10 | 11  12  13  14  15  16  17  18  19  20 | |

## REFLECTING

If Jennie Trotter's view is correct, you too experience stress daily. In fact, William Zinsser, author of *College Pressures*, supports the author's view by identifying four kinds of pressures working on college students today: economic pressure, parental pressure, peer pressure, and self-induced pressure. Think about specific examples of these pressures, and select three stress-related problems you would like to resolve. Use the steps listed below from paragraph 10 of the selection to solve these problems.

1. Write down the problem.

2. Brainstorm for solutions.

3. List the consequences.

4. Select and evaluate the best solution for you.

**Problem 1:** _____

**Consequences:** _____

**Solution:** _____


**Problem 2:** _____

**Consequences:** _____

**Solution:** _____


**Problem 3:** _____

**Consequences:** _____

**Solution:** _____


## COLLABORATING

With a group, discuss individual responses from the Reflecting activity above. Combine the ideas and present them in a chart that uses these headings: Problem, Consequence, and Solution.

## WEB WATCH

On the Internet, explore topics related to stress. Locate two articles on stress and show how the authors' writing styles differ. Pay close attention to the authors' choice of words, the length and difficulty of sentences and paragraphs, punctuation, development of ideas (from general to specific or vice versa), and overall layout. Use these elements of style to identify each author's audience. How certain are you in drawing this conclusion? Explain.

## VOCABULARY EXERCISE

Complete the puzzle with words from the box.

| affirmation | brainstorm | chanting | evaluate | ironic |
|---|---|---|---|---|
| meditation | obstacles | | | |

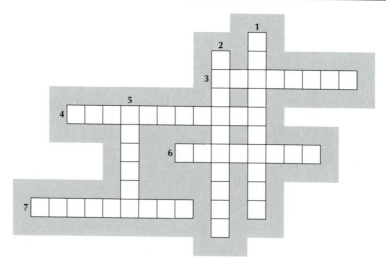

**ACROSS**
3. to determine value
4. a positive statement
6. speaking in song
7. stumbling blocks

**DOWN**
1. to offer multiple ideas
2. deep continued thought
5. contrary to what is expected

# Tips on Reading

## *Biology*

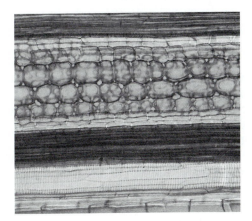

Subjects vary in the natural sciences, as in other fields. The excerpt that follows comes from biology, the study of plant and animal life. "Flight" follows a classification pattern, describing the different types of flight. To get the most from your reading of scientific material, the number one rule is to *read slowly*. Your purpose is to study and learn the material. Thus, you should adjust your reading rate to the difficulty of the content. Before you read difficult material, such as that found in most science textbooks, there are several steps you should follow:

- **Preview the material.** Follow the steps to previewing in Part I of this book. When you preview, pay special attention to how the author organizes information. Look for headings and various organizational patterns such as cause-effect, classification, comparison-contrast, listing, illustration, and process. Look for signal words and phrases that identify spatial arrangement used in descriptions: *to the left, above, below, beside.*
- **Learn the subject-area vocabulary.** Terms may have a special meaning in regard to the subject under discussion. Use the vocabulary card system to study these words prior to reading.
- **Study visuals carefully.** The author may include diagrams or charts that explain processes and concepts.
- **Create your own visual aids** such as pictures, charts, graphs, and diagrams. This information-processing technique helps you see

relationships in the material and adds to your ability to understand and recall information.

- **Take advantage of special textbook features.** Many biology textbooks include marginal notes and chapter prologues. Marginal notes provide interesting sidelights, key ideas, and summarizing information without interrupting the flow of the narrative. Be sure to read these and include them in your notes. The chapter prologue is an essay that relates to the subject of the chapter, presented in an interesting manner to engage your interest and arouse your curiosity.
- **Use reading-processing techniques:** mapping, outlining, annotating, charting, highlighting, and underlining. Ask and answer questions throughout the reading. Also, monitor your reading. At the end of each page, stop and paraphrase the material or write a one-sentence summary. In this way, you reach the end of the material having learned something—not having wasted your time.
- **Use the chapter review questions.** These questions enable you to test your retention and understanding of important material.

Selection 3

# Biology: Flight

*Cleveland P. Hickman, Jr., Larry Roberts, and Francis Hickman*

**VOCABULARY REVIEW**
**aerodynamic (aer-o-dy-nam-ic):** related to the science of forces exerted
   by air and other bodies in motion
**alulas (al-u-las):** end parts of a bird wing
**camber (cam-ber):** an arching curve
**capricious (ca-pri-cious):** subject to change abruptly, uncertain
**dynamic (dy-nam-ic):** related to energy in motion
**static (stat-ic):** related to bodies, masses, or forces at rest
**terrestrial (ter-res-tri-al):** living on land
**turbulence (tur-bu-lence):** violence or disturbance
**velocities (ve-loc-i-ties):** speeds

## PREREADING EXERCISE

Study the Vocabulary Review and the major headings of the selection.
Then use the headings to complete the concept map below.

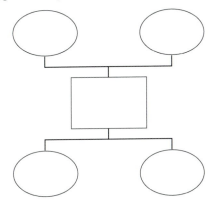

What caused birds to fly and to rise free of the problems on earth, as    1
almost every man has dreamed of doing? The beginning of flight was the
result of complex adaptive pressures. First, the air was an unexplored
space full of flying insect food. Second, it offered escape from **terrestrial**
enemies. Third, it allowed birds to migrate north and south with the seasons. This helped birds to travel rapidly and widely to locate new breed-
ing areas and to profit from a year-round mild climate and food supply.

## BASIC FORMS OF BIRD WINGS

Bird wings vary in size and form. There is a very important reason for this.    2
Special **aerodynamic** requirements are necessary for successful exploration
of different environments. Four types of bird wings are easily recognized.

### Elliptical Wings

3    Birds that must fly in forested areas have elliptical, or oval-shaped, wings. Examples of these birds are sparrows, doves, warblers, woodpeckers, and magpies. This type of wing has a low aspect ratio (ratio of length to width). The wings of the British Spitfire fighter plane of World War II fame closely resembled the outline of the sparrow wing. Elliptical wings are highly slotted between the primary feathers. This helps to stop stalling during sharp turns, low-speed flight, and frequent landing and takeoff. Each separated primary feather acts as a narrow wing with a high angle of attack. This provides high lift at low speed. The high maneuverability of the elliptical wing is modeled by the tiny chickadee. If frightened, this tiny bird can change course within 0.03 second.

### High–Speed Wings

4    There are two types of birds that have high-speed wings. One type is those that feed on the wing. Examples are hummingbirds, swallows, and swifts. A second type is those that make long migrations. Examples of these are plovers, terns, sandpipers, and gulls. Both types have wings that sweep back and thin out to a slender tip. These wings are flat and have a fairly high aspect ratio. However, they lack the wing-tip slotting of the first group. Sweep back and wide separation of the wing tips reduce "tip vortex." This type of **turbulence** tends to develop at wing tips. The fastest birds alive, such as sandpipers (clocked at 175 km per hour/109 miles per hour), belong to this group.

### Soaring Wings

5    The oceanic soaring birds have high-aspect-ratio wings that resemble those of airplanes. This group includes albatrosses, frigate birds, and gannets. Such long, narrow wings lack wing slots. Thus, they are well-suited for high speed, high lift, and **dynamic** soaring. These wings have the highest aerodynamic efficiency of all wings. However, they are less maneuverable than the wide, slotted wings of land soarers. Dynamic soarers take advantage of the highly reliable sea winds. They have learned to use air currents of different **velocities.**

### High–Lift Wings

6    Vultures, hawks, eagles, owls, and ospreys have high-lift wings. These birds are predators. They capture and feed upon other animals and, therefore, carry heavy loads. They have wings with slotting, **alulas,** and distinct **camber.** All of these features promote high lift at low speed. Many of these birds are land soarers. Their broad, slotted wings provide the quick response and maneuverability required for **static** soaring in the **capricious** air currents over land.

*(540 words)*

## POSTREADING EXERCISE

Now that you have read the selection, add specific details to the map you produced in the prereading exercise.

## PROCESSING INFORMATION

1. Read the review questions that follow the Bird Wing Chart below. Use these questions as a guide to highlight the key information in the excerpt.

2. Complete the chart with the highlighted information from the selection.

3. Use the completed chart and the selection to answer the review questions.

| | BIRD WINGS | | | |
|---|---|---|---|---|
| *Features* | *Elliptical* | *High-speed* | *Soaring* | *High-lift* |
| Where birds fly | _____ | _ | ocean | _____ |
| Aspect ratio | low | _____ | _____ | _ |
| Slotting | _____ | none | _____ | _____ |
| Lift | _____ | _ | _____ | high |
| Speed | _____ | _____ | high | _____ |
| Maneuverability | _____ | _ | _____ | _____ |
| Description | _____ | slender | _____ | _____ |
| | _____ | _____ | _____ | alulas |
| | | | _____ | _____ |
| Examples | sparrows | _____ | _____ | _____ |
| | _____ | swallows | _____ | _____ |
| | _____ | _____ | gannets | _____ |
| | _____ | _____ | _____ | _____ |
| | _____ | _____ | _____ | _____ |
| | | _____ | | |

## REVIEW QUESTIONS
*Circle the letter of the best answer.*

1. Birds with high-lift wings fly mostly
   a. over land.     c. over clouds.
   b. over sea.      d. over mountains.

2. Which bird wings do not have slotting?
   a. elliptical and high-speed
   b. high-speed and soaring
   c. elliptical and high-lift
   d. soaring and high-lift

3. The fastest bird alive can fly at speeds of
   a. 50 mph
   b. 85 mph
   c. 109 mph
   d. 150 mph

4. The birds that carry heavy loads are
   a. vultures and gannets.
   b. owls and swifts.
   c. terns and albatrosses.
   d. vultures and hawks.

5. Which wing type is well suited to long migrations?
   a. elliptical
   b. high-speed
   c. soaring
   d. high-lift

6. Which of these factors is responsible for the origin of flight?
   a. technology
   b. disease
   c. training
   d. predators

7. The overall pattern of organization for this selection is
   a. example.
   b. definition.
   c. classification.
   d. comparison and contrast.

8. Soaring-wing birds probably
   a. move fast over sea.
   b. use less energy during flight.
   c. do both a and b.
   d. have long, narrow wings.

9. The wings of the Spitfire fighter plane were designed to resemble
   elliptical wings because the plane had to
   a. move slowly over land.
   b. move rapidly in forest areas.
   c. be able to change course rapidly.
   d. travel long distances.

10. How do the authors begin the selection?
    a. with an introduction
    b. with an assumption
    c. with a cause-effect relationship
    d. with all of the above

---

**Score:** Number correct _____ (out of 10) × 10 = _____

---

## SHORT ANSWER

*Study the information in the Bird Wing Chart again. Then, using your critical thinking and inference skills, fill in the missing information in the sentences below.*

1. Which choice is correct?
    a. The aspect ratio of high-lift wings is probably _____ (high, low).

    b. Birds with high-speed wings probably fly over _____ (land, sea, land and sea).

    c. High-speed wings have _____ (high, low) lift.

    d. High-speed wings have _____ (high, low) maneuverability.

2. Write a brief description of each type of bird wing.

    a. Elliptical: _____

    b. High-speed: _____

    c. Soaring: _____

    d. High-lift: _____

3. Identify birds that have each type of wing listed in question 2.

    a. _____

    b. _____

    c. _____

    d. _____

4. How are elliptical and high-lift bird wings alike?

    _____

    _____

5. How are elliptical and soaring bird wings different?

    _____

    _____

## REFLECTING

List three problems that would exist if our country had no air transportation.

1. _____

2. _____

3. _____


## COLLABORATING

With a group, think of another discovery—like the airplane and the bird wing—that used nature as the basis for its construction. Discuss the discovery, explaining its similarities to the miracle of nature.

**Discovery:** _____

**Model in nature:** _____

**Explanation:** _____

_____

_____

_____


## WEB WATCH

Identify a topic in biology that interests you, such as cloning or DNA. Conduct a search of the topic on the Internet, and read about some recent discoveries in the field.

## VOCABULARY EXERCISE

Complete the puzzle with words from the box.

| | | | | |
|---|---|---|---|---|
| aerodynamic | alulas | camber | capricious | dynamic |
| static | terrestrial | turbulence | velocities | |

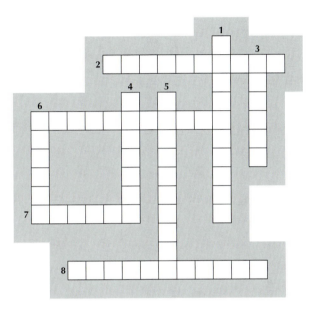

**ACROSS**

2. stormy weather
6. designed to move through air
7. unmoving, still
8. on land

**DOWN**

1. speeds
3. arching curve
4. moving
5. subject to change, uncertain
6. high-lift aid

Selection 4

# The Real Secret to Becoming a Millionaire

*Nancy Nokes*

●●●●●●●●●●●●●●●●●●●●●●●●●●●●●●●●●●●●●●●●●●●●●●●●●●●●●●●●●●●●●●●

**VOCABULARY REVIEW**
**affluence (af-flu-ence):** wealth
**Ferrari (Fer-ra-ri):** sports car
**frugality (fru-gal-i-ty):** careful spending
**impulse (im-pulse):** urge to act without conscious thought
**modest (mod-est):** moderate or reasonable

●●●●●●●●●●●●●●●●●●●●●●●●●●●●●●●●●●●●●●●●●●●●●●●●●●●●●●●●●●●●●●●

**PREREADING EXERCISE**

Study the title, the Vocabulary Review, and the first paragraph of the selection. Then write a sentence expressing what you believe this selection is about.

_____

_____

_____


*Who Wants to Be a Millionaire* may be the hottest show on television these days, but for most people the path to **affluence** doesn't include Regis Philbin and a "lifeline." In his 1996 bestselling book, *The Millionaire Next Door*, Thomas Stanley (with co-author William Danko) explained that most millionaires make their money the old-fashioned way—by earning, saving, and investing.    1

## WHO ARE THE MILLIONAIRES?

The big surprise of Stanley's first book was that the typical millionaire in the United States is not a sports superstar or heir of the family fortune living in a mansion. Rather, the average millionaire has a rather **modest** (by millionaire standards) annual household income of $131,000. He owns a house valued at $320,000. His life is marked by **frugality** and hard work.    2

In his new book, *The Millionaire Mind*, Stanley studies a more select group of millionaires who live in old, well-established neighborhoods. Their homes are more costly. Most are worth over $1 million. And they have higher incomes, averaging $749,000. Yet they also live below their means.    3

4    Why do these people cut out coupons and shop sales? Because they understand the power of money. For example, the typical affluent family in America spends more than $10,000 a year on food and household supplies. Cutting that down by just 10 percent saves $1,000 a year.

## WHAT YOU CAN DO

5    You may never be a multi-millionaire, but you can take positive steps toward a more secure financial future:

Live below your means. These millionaires can afford a new **Ferrari,** but instead buy reliable cars at much lower cost.

Create a savings and spending plan.

Buy carefully and avoid **impulse** purchases.

Learn how to *keep* your money. The millionaires Stanley studies invest carefully and take advantage of tax strategies to help them keep their wealth. In fact, the number one activity they engaged in over a 12-month span was not vacationing or attending charity balls. It was consulting a tax expert.

## DO YOU HAVE A MILLIONAIRE MIND-SET?

6    Stanley's millionaires possess what he calls a *millionaire mind-set*. They are, for the most part, self-made, hardworking, and frugal. See how you would fit in:

1. If you could spend as much as you wanted on a watch, would you buy a:
   a. Rolex ($5,000)
   b. Seiko ($30)

2. If you were about to buy a home, would you:
   a. Build the biggest house you could afford on a lot in a well-to-do suburb.
   b. Buy a comfortable older home in an established neighborhood.

3. Do you typically buy lottery tickets?
   a. No.
   b. Yes.

4. Do you save and invest about 20 percent of your household income annually?
   a. No.
   b. Yes.

5. Have you saved enough money to live without working for ten or more years?
   a. No.
   b. Yes.

6. With the money you invest, are you:
   a. Unwilling to take a chance on losing principal.
   b. Willing to take financial risks.

7. Do you think becoming a millionaire is a matter of:
   a. Luck.
   b. Hard work and planning.

8. If you were trying to impress someone, would you talk about:
   a. How much money your suit cost.
   b. How much your company has accomplished.

   If you answered *b* to most questions, you have a *millionaire mind-set.*   7
If you answered *a* to most, $1 million might not last you very long!

*(530 words)*

## POSTREADING EXERCISE

Now that you have read the selection, revise the sentence you wrote in the prereading exercise.

_____

_____

_____

1. Discuss the revised sentence with a partner, giving support for your ideas. Your partner will listen, take notes, and use the notes to repeat your key ideas.

2. Now trade places with your partner.

## COMPREHENSION EXERCISE
*Circle the letter of the best answer.*

### SKIMMING FOR FACTS

1. How much does the typical affluent family spend each year on food?
   a. $10,000
   b. $3,000
   c. $5,000
   d. $1,000

2. Stanley discovered that the typical millionaire is
   a. a sports superstar.
   b. an heir to a family fortune.
   c. a business owner.
   d. none of the above.

3. The millionaires Stanley studies in his new book have
   a. costly homes.
   b. higher incomes.

c. expensive yachts.
d. both a and b.

4. The most frequent yearly activity of millionaires is
   a. attending charity balls.
   b. traveling over the world.
   c. consulting a tax expert.
   d. studying investment manuals.

5. To achieve a more secure future, you must learn how to
   a. read stock market reports.
   b. make more impulse purchases.
   c. earn more money.
   d. keep your money.

RELATING THE FACTS

6. The main idea of paragraph 2 is
   a. stated in the first sentence.
   b. stated in the second sentence.
   c. stated in the third sentence.
   d. implied.

7. The primary organization pattern in paragraph 2 is
   a. example.
   b. cause-effect.
   c. comparison.
   d. contrast.

8. The primary organization pattern in paragraph 4 is
   a. example.
   b. cause-effect.
   c. comparison.
   d. contrast.

9. Which relationship does the last sentence in paragraph 3 reflect?
   a. cause-effect
   b. contrast
   c. addition
   d. example

10. Map the contents of paragraph 5.

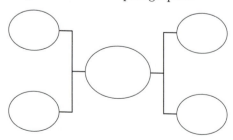

CONNECTING WITH THE AUTHOR

11. The author seems to believe that most millionaires are
    a. well dressed.
    b. extremely lucky.
    c. highly educated.
    d. well disciplined.

12. You can infer from the selection that Thomas Stanley
    a. is a millionaire.
    b. wants to be a millionaire.
    c. doesn't like millionaires.
    d. is interested in millionaires.

13. The author seems to suggest that a Ferrari is a(n)
    a. roomy family car.
    b. expensive car.
    c. stretch limousine.
    d. symbol of power.

14. Stanley implies in paragraph 5 that millionaires
    a. lead a glamorous life.
    b. have no worries.
    c. must work to keep their wealth.
    d. cheat on their taxes.

15. The fact that Thomas Stanley's book is a best-seller suggests that
    a. everybody wants to be a millionaire.
    b. sales will probably increase.
    c. only millionaires are purchasing the book.
    d. there is too much interest in millionaires.

16. A likely generalization from the selection is that
    a. all disciplined people will become millionaires.
    b. poor people ought to become millionaires, too.
    c. good math students should count their own money.
    d. careful spending can bring financial rewards.

17. The author supports her ideas with
    a. research and statistics.
    b. personal experiences.
    c. facts from two books.
    d. all of the above.

18. Which of the following states a fact from the selection?
    a. "You may never be a multi-millionaire, but you can take positive steps toward a more secure financial future."
    b. "*Who Wants to Be a Millionaire* may be the hottest show on television these days, but for most people the path to affluence does not include Regis Philbin and a 'lifeline'".
    c. "Cutting that [cost] down by just 10 percent saves $1,000 a year."

d. "These millionaires can afford a Ferrari, but instead buy reliable cars at much lower cost."

19. The author's tone is
    a. objective.
    b. sad.
    c. angry.
    d. humorous.

20. The author's purpose is to
    a. entertain.
    b. inform.
    c. interpret.
    d. persuade.

## PROGRESS CHART

*Circle the correct responses for each section below. Add the circles and multiply by 5. Record the total here and on the score chart in the Appendix.*

| Skimming for Facts | Relating the Facts | Connecting with the Author | Total |
|---|---|---|---|
| 1  2  3  4  5 | 6  7  8  9  10 | 11  12  13  14  15  16  17  18  19  20 | |

## REFLECTING

Complete the "Do You Have a Millionaire Mind-set" questionnaire. Where do you fit in? Do you desire to change your outlook on financial matters? Explain.

## COLLABORATING

With a small group of four to five members, poll the class on the "Do You Have a Millionaire Mind-set" questionnaire, and then construct a visual (chart or graph) to represent the results of your poll. Write a brief explanation of your graphic.

## WEB WATCH

Locate and compare two reviews of Thomas Stanley's latest book about millionaires. First, name the book; then list at least three points both reviewers make. After reading these reviews, would you purchase the book? Explain.

**Book 1:** _____

   Point 1: _____

Point 2: _____

Point 3: _____

**Book 2:** _____

Point 1: _____

Point 2: _____

Point 3: _____

## VOCABULARY EXERCISE

Complete the puzzle with words from the box.

| affluence | Ferrari | frugality | impulse | modest |
|---|---|---|---|---|

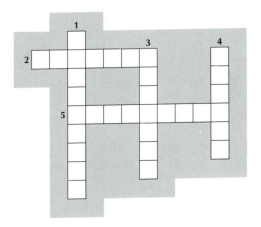

**ACROSS**

2. Bill drives a _____, an expensive vehicle.
5. Her _____ enables her to dine at only the finest of

**DOWN**

1. My landlord is a cheapskate; his _____ has earned him $1 million.
3. With some self-control, you can avoid making most _____ purchases.
4. May's prom dress was _____, not costly like Jackie's.

# What Makes a Good Mother?

*Susan Chira*

- - - - - - - - - - - - - - - - - - - - - - - - - - - - - - - - - - - - - -

**VOCABULARY REVIEW**
**bogeymen (bo-gey-men):** imaginary frightful beings
**comprehensive (com-pre-hen-sive):** wide in scope; inclusive
**condemnation (con-dem-na-tion):** strong disapproval
**confining (con-fin-ing):** limiting
**consistent (con-sis-tent):** fixed, unchanging
**diminish (di-min-ish):** to make or becomer smaller; lessen
**durable (dur-a-ble):** long-lasting, stable
**endure (en-dure):** to last
**forge (forge):** to move forward steadily
**gender (gen-der):** male, female, or neuter classification
**solace (sol-ace):** a comfort or consolation
**trauma (trau-ma):** an emotional shock, distress

- - - - - - - - - - - - - - - - - - - - - - - - - - - - - - - - - - - - - -

## PREREADING EXERCISE

Study the title, the Vocabulary Review, and the first paragraph of the selection. Then write a sentence expressing what you believe this selection is about.

_____

_____

_____

When I was a child, it was clear who the good mother was. She lived 1
in my reader: the homemaker mother of Sally, Dick and Jane. She lived in my television set: Mrs. Cleaver, the ever-aproned, ever-available mother of Wally and the Beav. She even lived in my house.

When I thought about having children, images of my own mother 2
came to mind: the touch of her cool, soft hand on my forehead, our long talks. My memories were of comfort, warmth and safety—the essence of motherhood for me. I worried that my life did not fit that good mother ideal.

I wanted to work, but everything I read kept telling me I should not. 3
Psychologists warned working would destroy children's bonds with their mother, condemning them to a lifetime of emotional **trauma.** Baby-care experts dictated how long mothers should stay home. News reports featured nannies beaming at their charges while the mother was home, then beating them when she left.

4     Yet over time I've found the **bogeymen** created to frighten me back home have disappeared one by one. My husband has brought to fatherhood great zest and a commitment equal to mine. We've slipped nicely into some **gender** roles (he's the tough guy, I the soother); others we've turned inside out (his work hours are shorter than mine). I've learned I don't have to take care of my children and forget everything else to take care of them well. My children know I am their mother. We share a close and **durable** bond. I don't worry that they will be dogged by emotional handicaps because I've worked.

5     My experiences have been matched by what studies have really found about working mothers—as opposed to what we are told they say. In fact, lengthy reviews of the studies have found few **consistent** differences between children of working mothers and mothers who stay at home. They find no convincing links between a mother's work and children's educational achievement, crime rates, drug use, or pregnancy rate.

6     The most **comprehensive** study of child care to date was conducted by the National Institutes of Health. This study has found working doesn't disrupt children's bonds with their parents or **diminish** the influence of parents over children. Other studies suggest the kinds of jobs mothers and fathers have are more important than how many hours they work. What matters is whether work intrudes into home life: Parents whose jobs don't upset their psychological involvement with their children have better behaved kids.

7     Slowly I've come to understand we can invent a new way to be good mothers. We can combine what's best from the old ideal with new possibilities. Most experts agree children need to **forge** a sense of trust and affection with at least one adult. They need a moral compass and limits on their behavior. They must be able to rely on a parent time and again. Psychologists say children sense when their parents are really committed to them. And through the process of "internalization," they form a mental picture and use it as a source of **solace** even when their parents are not there. That's why children's ties with their parents **endure** even when they work.

8     Once parents understand what a child needs, they can determine if someone else can help. A day-care worker can help foster a baby's sense of trust, but only a parent can explain personal moral standards. Only a parent can live that example for her children.

9     It's time to stop the chorus of **condemnation** about working mothers. As a nation we've spent millions of research dollars studying whether day care harms children, instead of finding out how to make sure it doesn't. Ultimately, we must outlaw the belief that good mothers stay at home and bad mothers work; that children of mothers at home thrive and children of mothers who work suffer. Mothers should be free to make choices without being hounded by the **confining** ideal of the good mother. Only then can we become the good mothers we want to be.

*(670 words)*

## POSTREADING EXERCISE

Now that you have read the selection, revise the sentence you wrote in the prereading exercise.

_____

_____

_____

1. Discuss the revised sentence with a partner, giving support for your ideas. Your partner will listen, take notes, and use the notes to repeat your key ideas.

2. Now trade places with your partner.

## COMPREHENSION EXERCISE
*Circle the letter of the best answer.*

### SKIMMING FOR FACTS

1. According to the author, the good mother lived in all of these places *except* in her
   a. house.
   b. television set.
   c. reader.
   d. dreams.

2. Research studies have found no differences between children whose mothers work and those whose mothers stay home in terms of
   a. illegitimacy rates.
   b. crime rates.
   c. career achievement rates.
   d. abortion rates.

3. What fictional character was created to frighten the author back home?
   a. Mr. Research
   b. the bogeyman
   c. the ghost of working mothers
   d. Old Mother Hubbard

4. To the author, the essence of motherhood is
   a. long walks.
   b. a mother's touch.
   c. family dinners.
   d. love and friendship.

5. The most comprehensive study of child care to date was conducted by the
   a. National Institutes of Health.
   b. *Journal of Child Psychology.*
   c. Day-care Centers of America.
   d. Childcare Institute of America.

RELATING THE FACTS

6. Which pattern of development does paragraph 3 follow?
   a. example
   b. comparison
   c. contrast
   d. process

7. Which sentence best represents the main idea of paragraph 3?
   a. the first sentence
   b. the second sentence
   c. the third sentence
   d. the fourth sentence

8. In paragraph 5, which of the following organization patterns does the author use to support her argument?
   a. comparison
   b. contrast
   c. cause and effect
   d. none of the above

9. What is the relationship between the last sentence in paragraph 7 and the sentence before it?
   a. It presents a comparison.
   b. It gives a summary.
   c. It gives an effect.
   d. None of the above.

10. Choose another appropriate title for this selection.
    a. Making a Case for the Working Mother
    b. Working Parents
    c. Research Findings About Mothers
    d. The Expert Opinion of a Working Mother

CONNECTING WITH THE AUTHOR

11. In paragraph 6, the author suggests that when work intrudes into home life, the child
    a. is well disciplined.
    b. becomes first in the parents' life.
    c. spends too little time alone.
    d. sees himself as unimportant and loses self-control.

12. In paragraph 9, the author implies that Americans have
    a. forgotten about mothers.
    b. given working mothers an excellent reputation.
    c. conducted useful research.
    d. made a mistake.

13. In paragraph 7, it appears that the author has
    a. developed a strategy to satisfy grandparents.
    b. devised a plan for nurturing children.
    c. attained satisfaction with being a working mother.
    d. developed a plan for working mothers.

14. From paragraph 7, you can infer that psychologists think that children who sense their parents' commitment to them
    a. quickly forget parental rules.
    b. can always feel the presence of their parents.
    c. can be easily influenced by their peers.
    d. receive quality time from their grandparents.

15. Which of the following can you infer from paragraph 8?
    a. Parents are the primary caretakers of their children.
    b. Parents have the major responsibility for teaching their children right from wrong.
    c. Others must participate in child-rearing practices.
    d. A mother must strengthen the will of her children.

16. What does the author suggest in paragraph 9?
    a. The "good mother" syndrome is a myth.
    b. Mothers are too busy with work to be good parents.
    c. The public should leave parenting to parents.
    d. Day care is a good mother substitute.

17. In which paragraph does the author use parallelism (repetition of key terms) to add drama to her writing?
    a. paragraph 1
    b. paragraph 2
    c. paragraph 3
    d. paragraph 4

18. Which sentence from the selection states a fact?
    a. "It's time to stop the chorus of condemnation about working mothers."
    b. "Only then can we become the good mothers we want to be."
    c. "I worried that my life did not fit that good mother ideal."
    d. "They need a moral compass and limits on their behavior."

19. What does the author mean by "chorus of condemnation"?
    a. choirs singing evil songs about working mothers
    b. people speaking out against the working mother

c. praises surrounding the issue of working mothers

d. songs of praise for mothers who work

20. The purpose of this selection is to
    a. convince the reader that it is all right for mothers to work.
    b. challenge the reader with the author's bias.
    c. inform all mothers of research findings on the issue.
    d. explore the positions for and against working mothers.

## PROGRESS CHART

*Circle the correct responses for each section below. Add the circles and multiply by 5. Record the total here and on the score chart in the Appendix.*

| Skimming for Facts | Relating the Facts | Connecting with the Author | Total |
|---|---|---|---|
| 1  2  3  4  5 | 6  7  8  9  10 | 11  12  13  14  15  16  17  18  19  20 | |

## REFLECTING

Pretend you are the author of the selection, and a mother who is considering going to work has asked for your advice. Write your advice below. Be sure to include ideas from the selection to support your position.

_____

_____

_____

## COLLABORATING

With a group, pretend you are researchers for or against mothers working outside the home. List different positions or viewpoints on the issue, and then present your findings.

1. **For working mothers**

   **Position A:** _____

   **Position B:** _____

   **Position C:** _____

2. **Against working mothers**

   **Position A:** _____

   **Position B:** _____

   **Position C:** _____

## WEB WATCH

On the Internet, locate two articles related to parenting or motherhood. Read both articles and try to determine whether they are objective (factual), subjective (based on feelings and opinions), or biased (one-sided). Give examples from the articles to support your opinion.

## VOCABULARY EXERCISE

Complete the puzzle with words from the box.

| | | | |
|---|---|---|---|
| bogeymen | comprehensive | condemnation | confining |
| consistent | diminish | durable | endure |
| forge | gender | solace | trauma |

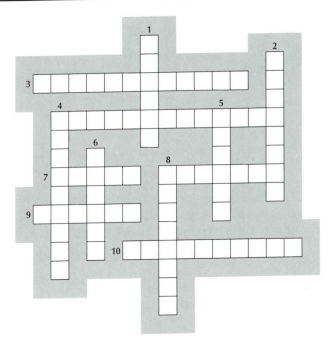

**ACROSS**
3. a putting down
4. all-inclusive
7. to move ahead
8. lasting, sturdy
9. to last
10. regular

**DOWN**
1. classification of male, female, or neuter
2. fictional frightening persons
4. restricted
5. comfort, consolation
6. shock, injury
8. to lessen

# Tips on Reading

## Literature

The literary selection is from *The Bluest Eye* by Toni Morrison. It is an original work of fiction, or imaginative literature, about an African American girl who goes to a psychic hoping to get blue eyes. In general, fiction is based on real-life events, but the author actually creates the story. For greater understanding, look closely at the key features that work together to give you true insight into the story:

- **Characters** are responsible for the action through their words, actions, dress, and thoughts.
- **Plot** features the *climax* or highlight of the story.
- The **theme** is the meaning or a message about life, such as "Good triumphs over evil."
- Style, the author's way of writing, is often influenced by the author's point of view or personal beliefs.
- The **setting** or environment in which the story takes place includes time, place, and mood.

To further your understanding, you might read the story several times, establishing a different purpose for each reading:

- The first reading is strictly for *appreciation and enjoyment*. This is a literal or on-the-surface reading that gives you the freedom to laugh or cry with the excitement, joy, and/or sadness that the story brings.

During this reading, you should experience the story and gain an appreciation for the author's style.

- In the second reading you should *acquire understanding* of what really takes place in the story. Pay close attention to the author's choice of words, looking up any whose meaning is unclear. Put yourself into the world that the author creates. Once you are in this world, picture the sequence of action, the story line, from beginning to end.

- In the third reading you *interpret and evaluate* to understand thoughts and actions that are not readily apparent. At this stage, you make inferences, draw conclusions, predict outcomes, and look critically at the details in the story. Be sure to look for ideas that the author chooses not to state directly, asking yourself questions such as these: *What does the author expect me to know prior to reading? Why does the author use this term? What does this action lead to? Does good triumph over evil? How does the author bring all the parts together?* In answering these questions, put yourself in the place of the author. By combining your senses with your logic, you are processing information to the greatest extent possible, and you are enjoying, appreciating, and understanding literature.

# Literature: The Bluest Eye

*Toni Morrison*

......................................................................................

**VOCABULARY REVIEW**
**ennobled (en-no-bled):** given divine power
**frivolous (friv-o-lous):** foolish
**mortality (mor-tal-i-ty):** the state of being human
**phlegmy (phlegm-y):** containing thick mucous
**poignant (poign-ant):** emotionally touching, moving
**surge (surge):** quick rush

......................................................................................

**PREREADING EXERCISE**

Study the title, the Vocabulary Review, and the first paragraph of the selection. Then write a sentence expressing what you believe this selection is about.

_____

_____

_____

Living there among his worn things, rising early every morning from 1
dreamless sleeps, he counseled those who sought his advice. His business
was dread. People came to him in dread, whispered in dread, wept and
pleaded in dread. And dread was what he counseled.

Singly they found their way to his door, wrapped each in a shroud 2
stitched with anger, yearning, pride, vengeance, loneliness, misery, defeat, and hunger. They asked for the simplest of things: love, health, and
money. Make him love me. Tell me what this dream means. Help me get
rid of this woman. Make my mother give me back my clothes. Stop my
left hand from shaking. Keep my baby's ghost off the stove. Break so-and-
so's fix. To all of these requests he addressed himself. His practice was to
do what he was bid—not to suggest to a party that perhaps the request
was unfair, mean, or hopeless.

The most beautiful-looking ladies sat on toilets, and the most dreadful- 3
looking had pure and holy yearnings. God had done a poor job, and Soaphead suspected that he himself could have done better. It was in fact a pity
that the Maker had not sought his counsel.

Soaphead was reflecting once again on those thoughts one late hot 4
afternoon when he heard a tap on his door. Opening it, he saw a little girl,
quite unknown to him. She was about twelve or so, he thought, and

seemed to him pitifully unattractive. When he asked her what she wanted, she did not answer, but held out to him one of his cards advertising his gifts and services: "If you are overcome with trouble and conditions that are not natural, I can remove them; Overcome Spells, Bad Luck, and Evil Influences. Remember, I am a true Spiritualist and Psychic Reader, born with power, and I will help you. Satisfaction in one visit. During many years of practice I have brought together many in marriage and reunited many who were separated. If you are unhappy, discouraged, or in distress, I can help you. Does bad luck seem to follow you? Has the one you love changed? I can tell you why. I will tell you who your enemies and friends are, and if the one you love is true or false. If you are sick, I can show you the way to health. I locate lost and stolen articles. Satisfaction guaranteed."

5     Soaphead Church told her to come in.

6     "What can I do for you, my child?"

7     She stood there, her hands folded across her stomach, a little stuck out pot of tummy. "Maybe. Maybe you can do it for me."

8     "Do what for you?"

9     "I can't go to school no more. And I thought maybe you could help me."

10     "Help you how? Tell me. Don't be frightened."

11     "My eyes."

12     "What about your eyes?"

13     "I want them blue."

14     Soaphead wet his lips, and let his tongue stroke a gold tooth. He thought it was at once the most fantastic and the most logical request he had ever received. Here was an ugly little girl asking for beauty. A **surge** of love and understanding swept through him, but was quickly replaced by anger. Anger that he was powerless to help her. Of all the wishes people had brought him—money, love, revenge—this seemed to him the most **poignant** and the one most deserving of fulfillment. A little black girl who wanted to rise up out of the pit of her blackness and see the world with blue eyes.

15     His outrage grew and felt like power. For the first time he honestly wished he could work miracles. Never before had he really wanted the true and holy power—only the power to make others believe he had it. It seemed so sad, so **frivolous,** that mere **mortality,** not judgment, kept him from it. Or did it?

16     With a trembling hand he made the sign of the cross over her. His flesh crawled; in that hot, dim little room of worn things, he was chilled.

17     "I can do nothing for you, my child. I am not a magician. I work only through the Lord. He sometimes uses me to help people. All I can do is offer myself to Him as the instrument through which he works. If He wants your wish granted, He will do it."

Soaphead walked to the window, his back to the girl. His mind raced,     18
stumbled, and raced again. How to frame the next sentence? How to hang
on to the feeling of power? His eye fell on old Bob sleeping on the porch.

"We must make, ah, some offering, that is, some contact with nature.     19
Perhaps some simple creature might be the vehicle through which He
will speak. Let us see."

He knelt down at the window, and moved his lips. After what     20
seemed a suitable length of time, he rose and went to the icebox that stood
near the other window. From it he removed a small packet wrapped in
pinkish butcher paper. From a shelf he took a small brown bottle and
sprinkled some of its contents on the substance inside the paper. He put
the packet, partly opened, on the table.

"Take this food and give it to the creature sleeping on the porch.     21
Make sure he eats it. And mark well how he behaves. If nothing happens,
you will know that God has refused you. If the animal behaves strangely,
your wish will be granted on the day following this one."

The girl picked up the packet. The odor of the dark sticky meat made     22
her want to vomit. She put a hand on her stomach.

"Courage. Courage, my child. These things are not granted to faint     23
hearts."

She nodded and swallowed visibly, holding down the vomit.     24

Soaphead opened the door, and she stepped over the threshold.     25

"Good-bye, God bless," he said and quickly shut the door. At the     26
window he stood watching her, his eyebrows pulled together into waves
of compassion, his tongue fondling the worn gold in his upper jaw. He
saw the girl bending down to the sleeping dog, who, at her touch, opened
one liquid eye, matted in the corners with what looked like green glue.
She reached out and touched the dog's head, stroking him gently. She
placed the meat on the floor of the porch, near his nose. The odor roused
him. He lifted his head and got up to smell it better. He ate it in three or
four gulps. The girl stroked his head again, and the dog looked up at her
with soft triangle eyes. Suddenly he coughed, the cough of a **phlegmy** old
man—and got to his feet. The girl jumped. The dog gagged, his mouth
chomping the air, and promptly fell down. He tried to raise himself,
could not, tried again and half-fell down the steps. Choking, stumbling,
he moved like a broken toy around the yard. The girl's mouth was open, a
little petal of tongue showing. She made a wild, pointless gesture with
one hand and then covered her mouth with both hands. She was trying
not to vomit. The dog fell again, a spasm jerking his body. Then he was
quiet. The girl's hands covering her mouth, she backed away a few feet,
then turned, ran out of the yard and down the walk.

Soaphead Church went to the table. He sat down, with folded hands     27
balancing his forehead on the balls of his thumbs. Then he rose and went
to a tiny night table with a drawer, from which he took paper and a
fountain pen. A bottle of ink was on the same shelf that held the poison.

With these things he sat again at the table. Slowly, carefully, admiring his penmanship, he wrote the following letter:

28    Att: TO HE WHO GREATLY **ENNOBLED** HUMAN NATURE BY CREATING IT

29    Dear God:

The purpose of this letter is to familiarize you with facts which either have escaped your notice, or which you have chosen to ignore. . . .

30    You forgot, Lord. You forgot how and when to be God. . . .

With kindest regards, I remain

Your,

Elihue Micah Whitcomb

*(1,360 words)*

## POSTREADING EXERCISE

Now that you have read the selection, revise the sentence you wrote in the prereading exercise.

_____

_____

_____

## PROCESSING INFORMATION

*Creative writing* is an important part of literature. It helps you dig deeper into the work of art, analyze your thoughts in relation to the author's, and express your opinion based on the ideas presented in the story.

In *The Bluest Eye*, Toni Morrison raises questions for inquiring minds. For each question below, *explain Morrison's meaning*. As you explore these ideas, on separate paper use your own background knowledge as well as evidence from the selection to support your conclusions.

1. Why does Morrison refer to Soaphead Church and "worn things"? Perhaps "worn things" symbolize, or represent, something else. If so, what might they be?

2. Why does Soaphead consider the little girl's request (blue eyes) more sensible than other requests (love, health, revenge, money)? What could inspire such reasoning?

3. Why does Morrison refer to the ink's being on the shelf with the poison instead of in the tiny nightstand drawer with the pen and paper? Perhaps poison and ink have something in common. How are these two different substances alike?

## REVIEW QUESTIONS
*Circle the letter of the best answer.*

1. The little girl wanted Soaphead Church to give her a
   a. prayer to ease her troubled heart.
   b. black eye that would later turn blue.
   c. pair of blue eyes.
   d. surgical operation on her eyes.

2. Soaphead Church was
   a. a spiritualist.
   b. a psychic reader.
   c. a magician.
   d. both a and b.

3. Why does Morrison describe the dog's eyes with expressions such as "triangle eyes," "liquid eye," and "matted in the corners like green glue"?
   a. She is using figurative language to paint a picture for the reader.
   b. She is trying to confuse the reader.
   c. She wants her words to rhyme.
   d. She can think of no other way to present her ideas.

4. According to Soaphead, God had made a mistake by
   a. making man in his own image.
   b. creating evil.
   c. designing an imperfect land.
   d. not seeking his counsel.

5. To help him grant the little girl's wish, what did Soaphead use?
   a. a violent puppy
   b. a sharp knife
   c. a beefsteak
   d. a bottle of poison

6. What is the main idea of paragraph 18?
   a. Soaphead was trying to think of a way to solve the little girl's problem.
   b. Soaphead suddenly realized that old Bob could help him solve the problem.
   c. His eyes fell on old Bob sleeping on the porch.
   d. This is how to hang on to the feeling of power.

7. What organization pattern is represented in paragraph 21?
   a. cause and effect
   b. comparison
   c. contrast
   d. example

8. What is the main idea of paragraph 21?
   a. Soaphead gives the girl the instructions and the conditions for success.
   b. "Make sure he eats it."
   c. "And mark well how he behaves."
   d. If the dog behaves abnormally, the girl's wish will come true.

9. The organization pattern best represented in paragraph 26 is
   a. cause-effect.
   b. process-chronology.
   c. classification.
   d. comparison and contrast.

10. Why did the little girl choose Soaphead Church to perform the miracle?
    a. She had read one of his business cards.
    b. She knew nobody else with his powers.
    c. She liked his name.
    d. She had seen him with other ministers in church.

11. What conclusion can you draw regarding Soaphead's feelings for old Bob?
    a. He liked old Bob.
    b. He believed that old Bob was useless.
    c. He believed that old Bob was mean-spirited and evil.
    d. He loved old Bob's lively spirit.

12. Why did the little girl want to change the color of her eyes?
    a. She wanted dogs to stop chasing her.
    b. She wanted a glowing personality.
    c. She wanted the other children at school to stop teasing her about her looks.
    d. She wanted to join a gang called "Blue Eyes."

13. When the little girl looked into the mirror the day after her visit with Soaphead Church, what color eyes did she see?
    a. green
    b. brown
    c. blue
    d. none of the above

14. Which of these conclusions can you draw about the little girl?
    a. She was naïve.
    b. She had never given much thought to her looks.
    c. She felt attractive but wanted to be a model.
    d. She had prayed for inner beauty.

15. The author portrays Soaphead Church as a
    a. moral person.
    b. stupid person.
    c. God-fearing, holy man.
    d. crafty person.

16. When Soaphead Church thinks to himself, "Here was an ugly little
    girl asking for beauty," he is
    a. making an assumption.
    b. drawing a conclusion.
    c. predicting an outcome.
    d. making a valid generalization.

17. Why does the author use dialogue to present her ideas in
    paragraphs 6–13?
    a. She wants to play down the ideas.
    b. She knows of no other way to present the conversation.
    c. She wants the reader to feel the effects of the conversation
       between the two parties.
    d. She wants to narrate the entire story, but it's too long.

18. Why does Soaphead sign his real name to his letter to God?
    a. He does not want God to mistake him for someone else.
    b. He feels that God would not know him by the phony name people
       had given him.
    c. He wants God to believe in his powers.
    d. He is proud of himself and feels that this good deed will excuse
       his past sins.

19. Which of the following generalizations is a valid one to make about
    Soaphead's clients?
    a. Confused girls should seek help from any source.
    b. People who visit psychics believe that someone else and not they
       themselves control their destiny.
    c. Young girls who are dissatisfied with their looks must seek
       expert advice.
    d. All men believe in the power of human beings.

20. What is the author's purpose in this story?
    a. to entertain
    b. to expose psychics
    c. to mystify the reader
    d. to inform

**Score:** Number correct _____ (out of 20) × 5 = _____

## REFLECTING

Have you ever called the Psychic Hotline or visited a psychic? Discuss your thoughts about psychics and their usefulness to society, if any.

_____

_____

_____

_____

_____


## COLLABORATING

With a group, identify several problems that might lead people to consult psychics. Then propose another solution for each problem.

**PROBLEMS**                          **OTHER SOLUTIONS**

_____          _____

_____          _____

_____          _____

_____          _____

_____          _____


## WEB WATCH

Locate Web sites that deal with astrology and/or psychics. Read two or more articles that give differing viewpoints on the subject. Then look at several psychic sites and the services they provide. (Be sure to get your horoscope reading for the day!) Which sites have the greatest credibility?

## VOCABULARY EXERCISE

Complete the puzzle with words from the box.

| | | | |
|---|---|---|---|
| ennobled | frivolous | mortality | phlegmy |
| poignant | surge | | |

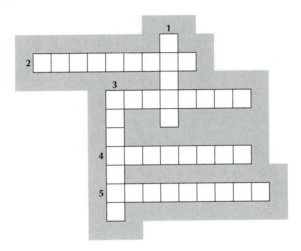

### ACROSS
2. lacking in seriousness
3. emotionally touching
4. raised to noble rank
5. state of being human

### DOWN
1. quick rush
3. containing thick mucous

# When Words Hurt

*Bebe Moore Campbell*

## VOCABULARY REVIEW

**berating (be-rat-ing):** scolding severely
**depressed (de-pressed):** low in spirits
**devastating (dev-a-stat-ing):** overwhelming
**illiterate (il-lit-e-rate):** unable to read or write
**incentive (in-cen-tive):** something causing one to act
**ingrained (in-grained):** firmly fixed
**initiate (in-i-ti-ate):** to begin
**projecting (pro-ject-ing):** putting feelings off onto another
**resolved (re-solved):** made a decision about
**transition (tran-si-tion):** a move from one activity to another
**undermine (un-der-mine):** to weaken slowly
**virtually (vir-tu-al-ly):** for all practical purposes

## PREREADING EXERCISE

Study the title, the Vocabulary Review, and the first paragraph of the selection. Then write a sentence expressing what you believe this selection is about.

_____

_____

_____

"What I remember most about my childhood is my father calling me    1
stupid," says Janice, 24, a hairstylist. "He'd ask me to read for him, and if I stumbled or missed a word, he'd say, 'You're so goddamn stupid!' I remember crying about that. His words hurt a lot."

"Sticks and stones may break my bones, but names will never hurt    2
me" goes the children's rhyme. Sadly, being called names does hurt. While headlines scream about physical abuse against children, emotional abuse, which is possibly as **devastating,** is **virtually** ignored. "Emotional abuse is an attack on the child's need to feel and give love. It's an attack on her sense of self-worth," explains Hershel K. Swinger, Ph.D., director of the Southern California Child Abuse Prevention Training Center in Los Angeles. "If I call my kid fat, that hurts her. She begins to devalue herself and sees herself negatively. Because she's been hurt by her parent, she begins to expect this hurt from others. She feels that if she cares about people they will hurt her. So she becomes **depressed** and withdrawn. Or else

she becomes very aggressive. Verbal abuse says to a child, 'You don't deserve love.' "

## UNDERSTANDING THE PROBLEM

3    Some experts suggest that parents sometimes lash out at children because they feel they lack control of their own stressful lives. Most parents don't realize the damage they're causing, or they may feel that **berating** the child will give her the **incentive** to do better. Instead, "negative comments **undermine** the child's self-confidence and ability to think for him or herself," says Dr. Leon Eisenberg, a Boston-based child psychologist.

4    In most instances, according to Swinger, mothers and fathers learn abusive behavior from their own parents. Janice admits that she picked up her father's hurtful tendencies and verbally abused her own son, who is now 7. "I started calling my son stupid, bad, and lazy when he was around 3 years old. Finally, when he was 5, he said to me, 'Don't call me stupid. I don't like it.' When he said that I remembered my own childhood, and I started crying. I **resolved** to change the way I was dealing with my son," says Janice.

## BREAKING OUT OF THE PATTERN

5    Can **ingrained** patterns of abuse be changed? Yes, with effort, affirms Swinger. Parents can begin by recognizing how and when they abuse their children by answering a few questions: Do you lash out at your children after a rough day, after you've had too much to drink, or too little sleep? Are you verbally abusive to all your children or just to one? Does your child remind you of a former mate or unkind family member? Does your son or daughter remind you of yourself?

6    By thinking seriously about what you call your youngsters, how you speak to them, and which of them you target for abuse, you may learn how you feel about yourself, Swinger adds. When she was in high school, Janice found out that her father was **illiterate.** When he called her stupid, he was **projecting** his negative feelings about himself onto her. When parents label their children fat, lazy, dumb, or ugly, they may need to come to grips with their own lack of self-esteem.

## HEALING THE HURT

7    Ending verbal abuse means being in control of what we say. To avoid hurtful remarks brought on by job fatigue, try making a **transition** from the workplace to the home. **Initiate** a quiet-time routine with your children when you get home. Have them read to you, watch television with you, or join you on a walk. Create peaceful time for all of you. To avoid lashing out at a child in anger when you feel your temper rising, speak with the misbehaving child at a later time. Avoid any contact until then. "Sometimes when I get angry, I'll count to ten and send my son to his room. If I do slip, I apologize," says Janice. "I keep trying to work on me because I want him to be the best he can be."

8    "A parent can undo abuse by listening to a child in a structured way," suggests Swinger. Give your child positive attention. Compliment

her when she does something well. "When my son was little I never told him I loved him or that he was smart. I do it now," says Janice. "And he responds to me better. He gets higher grades, and he's more cooperative."

*(740 words)*

## POSTREADING EXERCISE

Now that you have read the selection, revise the sentence you wrote in the prereading exercise.

_____

_____

_____

1. Discuss the revised sentence with a partner, giving support for your ideas. Your partner will listen, take notes, and use the notes to repeat your key ideas.

2. Now trade places with your partner.

## COMPREHENSION EXERCISE
*Circle the letter of the best answer.*

### SKIMMING FOR FACTS

1. How old was Janice's son when he told her to stop calling him stupid?
   a. three years old        b. five years old
   c. seven years old        d. nine years old

2. Mothers and fathers learn abusive behavior from their
   a. doctors.        b. parents.
   c. friends.        d. grandparents.

3. Which of the following questions is used to determine whether abusive behavior exists?
   a. Do you lash out at your children after a good day?
   b. Are you abusive toward all your children?
   c. Does your child remind you of a former teacher?
   d. Does your son or daughter remind you of yourself?

4. To avoid lashing out at a child when you get angry, you should
   a. speak with the child later.
   b. count to ten and go to your room.
   c. stare the child down in the same room.
   d. try to understand the child's reason for misbehaving.

5. Which of the following is recommended when making a transition from the workplace to the home?
   a. Play a question-answer game with your children.
   b. Have children sing old songs.

c. Create peaceful time for all of you.

d. Talk about the children's bad habits.

**RELATING THE FACTS**

6. Label ideas from paragraph 2 as C = cause, E = effect, or B = both.
   _____ a. calls her child fat
   _____ b. has been hurt by parent
   _____ c. begins to devalue herself
   _____ d. sees herself negatively
   _____ e. becomes very aggressive
   _____ f. expects hurt from others
   _____ g. feels that caring brings hurt
   _____ h. becomes depressed and withdrawn

7. Study this sentence from paragraph 2: "While headlines scream about physical abuse against children, emotional abuse, which is possibly as devastating, is virtually ignored." Which of the following relationships is expressed?
   a. comparison            b. contrast
   c. addition              d. cause-effect

8. Which statement best expresses the main idea of paragraph 5?
   a. Parents can begin to end patterns of verbal abuse by answering several questions.
   b. Questions are important in ending abuse.
   c. Children who look like grandparents are often abused.
   d. A process is used to bring verbal abuse to an end.

9. Complete the concept map of paragraph 7 below.

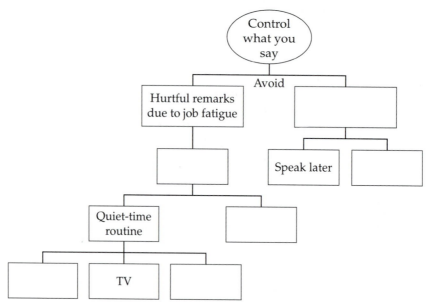

10. Which statement best expresses the main idea of paragraph 7?
    a. Parents should control what they say when tired.
    b. Ending verbal abuse means controlling what you say when tired or angry.
    c. Control is the key to stopping verbal abuse.
    d. Reading, walking, and watching TV are important.

CONNECTING WITH THE AUTHOR

11. According to paragraph 5, the author believes that
    a. abusive behavior cannot be stopped.
    b. it takes years to break any habit.
    c. ending abusive behavior is a process that requires conscious effort.
    d. abusive behavior no longer exists.

12. In paragraph 2, the author suggests that abused children may have problems with
    a. eating.
    b. drugs and alcohol.
    c. partners.
    d. all of the above.

13. Which of the following can you infer from paragraph 3?
    a. An unhappy parent is a poor parent.
    b. A parent will train a child in the right way.
    c. A nonworking parent is the best parent.
    d. A parent can be almost as wise as a child.

14. The author suggests in paragraph 3 that verbal abuse occurs most often when parents are
    a. struggling with weight problems.
    b. having marital problems.
    c. working two and three jobs to make ends meet.
    d. all of the above.

15. In paragraph 5, the author suggests that
    a. divorced parents sometimes substitute a child for the absent spouse.
    b. parents can never see themselves in their children.
    c. children of divorced parents should care for themselves.
    d. alcohol brings out the best in all of us.

16. Saying "I love you" to a child
    a. is not that important.
    b. shows negative attention.
    c. spoils the child.
    d. makes the child feel really special.

17. Why does the author provide first names of some people quoted and last names of others?
    a. to set apart expert from nonexpert testimony
    b. to respect the wishes of those quoted

c. to decrease the amount of space used

d. to separate fact from opinion

18. Which sentence from the selection states a fact?

a. "Sadly, being called names does hurt."

b. "I resolved to change the way I was dealing with my son."

c. "Most parents don't realize the damage they're causing, or they may feel that berating the child will give her the incentive to do better."

d. "When parents label their children fat, lazy, dumb, or ugly, they may need to come to grips with their own lack of self-esteem."

19. What image does the children's rhyme "Sticks and stones may break my bones but names will never hurt me" convey?

a. pain and suffering    c. abstract and concrete

b. modern weapons    d. building materials

20. Which of the following words best represents the tone of this selection?

a. angry    c. humorous

b. informative    d. instructive

### PROGRESS CHART

*Circle the correct responses for each section below. Add the circles and multiply by 5. Record the total here and on the score chart in the Appendix.*

| Skimming for Facts | Relating the Facts | Connecting with the Author | Total |
|---|---|---|---|
| 1  2  3  4  5 | 6  7  8  9  10 | 11  12  13  14  15  16  17  18  19  20 | |

## REFLECTING

Think of a situation in which you believe verbal abuse could occur. Identify the specifics of the abuse, describe possible causes, and suggest a remedy.

Abuse: _____

Causes: _____

Remedy: _____

_____

## COLLABORATING

With a group, make a concept map of the selection. You may use the following three major headings from the selection to help organize your ideas: "Understanding the Problem," "Breaking Out of the Pattern," and

"Healing the Hurt." Be sure to eliminate repeated words and show relationships among ideas.

## WEB WATCH

On the Internet, locate several research articles on child abuse. Skim the articles, looking for answers to questions like these: Where does most child abuse occur in the United States? Who is involved? When does it occur? Why does it occur? What are the circumstances?

## VOCABULARY EXERCISE

Complete the puzzle with words from the box.

| berating | depressed | devastating | illiterate |
|----------|-----------|-------------|------------|
| incentive | ingrained | initiate | projecting |
| resolved | transition | undermine | virtually |

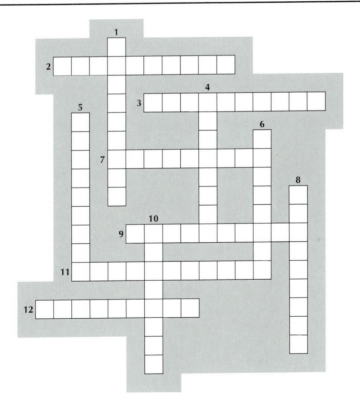

**ACROSS**

  2. If making the _____ from work to home places undue pressure on parents, maybe they should consider not working.

  3. I would imagine a(n) _____ person to be frustrated and lost trying to conduct research at a library.

  7. When children are given a(n) _____ for cleaning their room, they do it more readily.

  9. By _____ their shortcomings onto others instead of accepting personal blame, adults can sometimes resemble children.

  11. The tornado was _____, not painless, for all who saw its aftermath.

  12. Because cigarette smokers can't quit, they _____ ignore the Surgeon General's warning on cigarette packs.

**DOWN**

  1. Rather than being open and honest, Sam tried to _____ the jury's intelligence.

  4. Angry couples should _____ positive self-talk routines rather than end all conversation.

  5. Mary was _____, no longer enthusiastic, when she found out that she had been fired from her job.

  6. Instead of _____ the student for writing on the walls, the principal praised his artistry.

  8. After driving for years, you cannot forget the procedure overnight; it is _____ in your mind for years to come.

  10. After failing all tests, the student _____ to study daily instead of cramming.

Selection 8

# She Sat Still

*Robert Fulghum*

●●●●●●●●●●●●●●●●●●●●●●●●●●●●●●●●●●●●●●●●●●●●●●●●●●●●●●●●●●●●●●●●●●

**VOCABULARY REVIEW**
**anchored (an-chored):** fixed
**conservative (con-ser-va-tive):** cautious
**eloquent (el-o-quent):** fluent, expressive, forceful in speaking or writing
**inferior (in-fe-ri-or):** a person of low rank
**memorials (me-mo-ri-als):** things meant to help people remember some
   person or event
**passive resistance (pas-sive re-sist-ance):** nonviolence
**radical (rad-i-cal):** one who holds extreme beliefs
**sacrament (sac-ra-ment):** a holy act
**tributes (trib-utes):** honors, praises
**versions (ver-sions):** particular forms; differing viewpoints

●●●●●●●●●●●●●●●●●●●●●●●●●●●●●●●●●●●●●●●●●●●●●●●●●●●●●●●●●●●●●●●●●●

**PREREADING EXERCISE**

Study the title, the Vocabulary Review, and the first paragraph of the selection. Then write a sentence expressing what you think this selection is
about.

_____

_____

_____

"SIT STILL—JUST SIT STILL!" My mother's voice. Again and again.   1
Teachers in school said it, too. And I, in my turn, have said it to my
children and my students. Why do adults say this? Can't recall any child
ever really sitting still just because some adults said to. That is why several "sit stills" are followed by "SIT DOWN AND SHUT UP!" or "SHUT
UP AND SIT DOWN!" My mother once used both **versions** back to back,
and I, smart-mouth that I was, asked her just which she wanted me to do
first, shut up or sit down? My mother gave me that look. The one that
meant she knew she would go to jail if she killed me, but it just might be
worth it. At such a moment an adult will say very softly, one syllable at a
time: "Get-out-of-my-sight." Any kid with half a brain will get up and go.
Then the parent will sit very still.

Sitting still can be powerful stuff, though. It is on my mind as I   2
write this on the first day of December in 1988, the first anniversary of a
moment when someone sat still and lit the fuse to social dynamite. On
this day in 1955, a forty-two-year-old woman was on her way home from

work. Getting on a public bus, she paid her fare and sat down on the first vacant seat. It was good to sit down—her feet were tired. As the bus filled with passengers, the driver turned and told her to give up her seat and move on back in the bus. She sat still. The driver got up and shouted, "MOVE IT!" She sat still. Passengers grumbled, cursed her, pushed at her. Still she sat. So the driver got off the bus and called the police, and they came to haul her off to jail and into history.

3      Rosa Parks. Not an activist or a **radical.** Just a quiet, **conservative,** church-going woman with a nice family and a decent job as a seamstress. For all the **eloquent** phrases that have been turned about her place in the flow of history, she did not get on that bus looking for trouble or trying to make a statement. Going home was all she had in mind, like everybody else. She was **anchored** to her seat by her own dignity. Rosa Parks simply wasn't going to be an **inferior** for anybody anymore. And all she knew to do was to sit still.

4      There is a sacred simplicity in not doing something—and doing it well. All the great religious leaders have done it. The Buddha sat still under a tree. Jesus sat still in a garden. Muhammad sat still in a cave. And Gandhi and King and thousands of others have brought sitting still to perfection as a powerful tool of social change. **Passive resistance,** meditation, prayer—one and the same.

5      It works even with little kids. Instead of telling them to sit still, you yourself can sit very still and quiet. Before long they will pay a great deal of attention to you. Students in class are also thrown by silent stillness on the part of a teacher. It is sometimes taken for great wisdom.

6      And sitting still works with grown-ups. On the very same bus route Rosa Parks used to travel, anybody can sit anywhere on the buses now, and some of the drivers are black—both men and women. The street where she was pulled off the bus has been renamed: Rosa Parks Avenue.

7      A new religion could be founded on this one **sacrament.** To belong would be simple. You wouldn't have to congregate on a special day in a special place. No hymns, no dues, no creeds, no preachers, and no potluck suppers. All you have to do is sit still. Once a day, for fifteen minutes, sit down, shut up, and be still. Like your mother told you. Amazing things might happen if enough people did this on a regular basis. Every chair, park bench, and sofa would become a church.

8      Rosa Parks is in her seventies now, doing most of her sitting in a rocking chair, living in quiet retirement with her family in Detroit. The **memorials** to her sitting still are countless, but the best ones are the living **tributes** in the form of millions of people of every color getting on thousands of buses every evening, sitting down, and riding home in peace.

9      If there is indeed a heaven, then I've no doubt that Rosa Parks will go there. I imagine the moment when she signs in with the angel at the pearly gates.

"Ah, Rosa Parks, we've been expecting you. Make yourself at 10 home—take any seat in the house."

*(800 words)*

## POSTREADING EXERCISE

Now that you have read the selection, revise the sentence you wrote in the prereading exercise.

_____

_____

_____

1. Discuss the revised sentence with a partner, giving support for your ideas. Your partner will listen carefully, take notes, and repeat your key ideas.

2. Now trade places with your partner.

## COMPREHENSION EXERCISE
*Circle the letter of the best answer.*

### SKIMMING FOR FACTS

1. On what date was Rosa Parks removed from the bus?
   a. December 1, 1988
   b. December 1, 1965
   c. December 1, 1955
   d. December 3, 1955

2. The driver of the bus called the
   a. police.
   b. fire department.
   c. ambulance.
   d. mayor.

3. Rosa Parks worked as a
   a. cook.
   b. bus driver.
   c. seamstress.
   d. schoolteacher.

4. According to the author, silent stillness on the part of a teacher is taken for
   a. rare patience.
   b. pure kindness.

c. great wisdom.
d. instant progress.

5. Rosa Parks sat down on the first vacant seat on the bus because
    a. it had a padded bottom.
    b. her feet were tired.
    c. all of the other seats were taken.
    d. she wanted to upset the bus driver.

RELATING THE FACTS

6. Which of the following patterns is used in paragraph 4?
    a. classification
    b. example
    c. comparison
    d. contrast

7. Fill in the ideas to complete the map of paragraph 4.

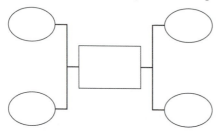

8. What is the main idea of paragraph 4?
    a. "There is a sacred simplicity in not doing something—and doing
       it well."
    b. In their own way, all great leaders have used sitting still well.
    c. Gandhi and King used passive resistance to effect social change.
    d. Although Buddha meditated, Jesus prayed, and King and Gandhi
       practiced passive resistance, it is all considered one and the same.

9. What relationship is signaled in the following sentence? "The
   memorials to her sitting still are countless, but the best ones are
   the living tributes in the form of millions of people of every color
   getting on thousands of buses every evening, sitting down, and
   riding home in peace."
    a. cause-effect
    b. example
    c. comparison
    d. contrast

10. Where is the main idea located in paragraph 7?
    a. at the beginning
    b. in the middle

c. in the end

d. at the beginning and in the end

CONNECTING WITH THE AUTHOR

11. The author suggests in paragraph 3 that Rosa Parks was
    a. terrified of being called names.
    b. satisfied with her well-planned attack on the city.
    c. tired of obeying Jim Crow segregation laws.
    d. thrilled with her place in history.

12. Which types of discrimination does the author refer to in paragraph 6?
    a. race and age
    b. race and sex
    c. race and religion
    d. age and sex

13. In paragraph 10, the author suggests that Rosa Parks will
    a. sit in the back row.
    b. face no discrimination in heaven.
    c. be an unwelcome guest.
    d. be ashamed of her new home.

14. A valid generalization from paragraph 1 is that
    a. all talented children demand attention from their parents.
    b. parents cannot get the attention of their naughty children.
    c. all active, unruly children are in search of a creative outlet.
    d. many children watch their parents closely.

15. The author begins the selection with a
    a. list of serious questions.
    b. quotation from a noted author.
    c. personal story.
    d. contrast between now and then.

16. Which thought does *not* express the author's intended meaning?
    a. From paragraph 1, "half a brain" refers to great intelligence.
    b. From paragraph 2, "lit the fuse to social dynamite" refers to the civil rights movement.
    c. From paragraph 7, "special day in a special place" refers to church on Sunday.
    d. From paragraph 9, "pearly gates" refers to the doors to heaven.

17. How would you describe the author's style?
    a. excessive punctuation
    b. short, choppy sentences
    c. incomplete sentences
    d. long paragraphs

18. Which of the following sentences from the selection states a fact?
   a. "The street where she was pulled off the bus has been renamed: Rosa Parks Avenue."
   b. "There is a sacred simplicity in not doing something—and doing it well."
   c. "A new religion could be founded on this one sacrament."
   d. "Sitting still can be powerful stuff, though."

19. The event about Rosa Parks is told in a mood of
   a. regret.                          b. pride.
   c. misery.                          d. shame.

20. The author's tone is
   a. humorous.                        b. serious.
   c. emphatic.                        d. plain.

--------------------------- PROGRESS CHART ---------------------------

*Circle the correct responses for each section below. Add the circles and multiply by 5. Record the total here and on the score chart in the Appendix.*

| Skimming for Facts | Relating the Facts | Connecting with the Author | Total |
|---|---|---|---|
| 1  2  3  4  5 | 6  7  8  9  10 | 11  12  13  14  15  16  17  18  19  20 | |

## REFLECTING

Think about a favorite saying your mother or father repeated when you were growing up. Look at it from several different angles and see if you can discover meanings you never saw before. Does it provide a lesson about life? Can you relate it to a worldly event the way the author of this selection did? Write the saying and a paragraph explaining what it means to you now. Be sure to begin with a topic sentence and then give evidence to support it.

**Saying:** _____

**Topic sentence:** _____

**Supporting details:** _____

_____

_____

_____

## COLLABORATING

With a group, make a list of lessons parents teach their children. Rank the lessons from most to least important, and give a brief explanation for each ranking. Place the information in a chart with headings such as "Parental Lessons" and "Explanation."

## WEB WATCH

Conduct an Internet search on Rosa Parks. Gather facts on this noted American, and arrange these ideas in a concept map that could be used for an oral or written report.

## VOCABULARY EXERCISE

Complete the puzzle with words from the box.

| | | | | |
|---|---|---|---|---|
| anchored | conservative | eloquent | inferior | memorials |
| passive resistance | radical | sacrament | tributes | versions |

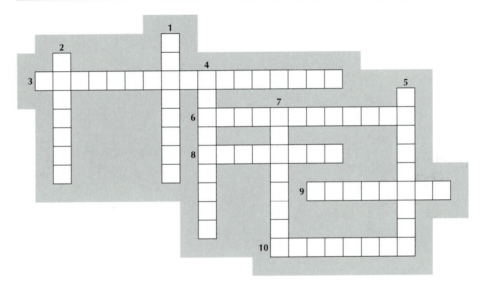

**ACROSS**

3. nonviolence
6. cautious
8. fixed
9. second-class citizen
10. thanks, honors, praises

**DOWN**

1. particular forms
2. one who holds extreme beliefs
4. a holy act
5. things meant to help people remember
7. fluent, expressive

# Tips on Reading

## *Technical Material*

Technical material covers a wide range of information that may include physical science, business, and computer science. The technical excerpt in this section comes from a current textbook article titled *Introduction to the World Wide Web*. When you read technical material, the key words to remember are *slowly* and *repeatedly*. In other words, read the contents several times—slowly—and use the following strategies:

- You may have to *read a single sentence several times* to understand its meaning. In some instances, you may have to break the sentence down to find its key idea. (You might remember this from the section on monitoring in chapter 1.) Remove all the sentence modifiers, leaving only the subject and predicate.
- *Preview the material*, paying close attention to the author's organization. This often includes a focus on steps in a process and problems and solutions.
- *Ask questions*, using the headings and subheadings in the selection, and read to find answers to these questions.
- *Study the technical vocabulary* and learn word definitions before you read.
- *Study and draw visuals* (diagrams, charts, graphs, and pictures) to strengthen your understanding.
- Be sure to use the information-processing techniques (monitoring, summarizing, outlining, mapping, paraphrasing, and annotating) from chapter 1. They will help you see relationships, understand, and remember what you read.

# Technology: Introduction to the World Wide Web

*Ernest Ackermann*

....................................................................

**VOCABULARY REVIEW**
**access (ac-cess):** to use by writing to or reading from stored data
**browse (browse):** to skim, to flip through records quickly
**click on (click on):** to position a mouse pointer on a screen object
**digital (di-gi-tal):** a type of data a computer can process
**home page (home page):** starting point for making contacts on the Web
**icon (i-con):** a picture that represents an object or program
**menu (men-u):** a detailed listing of items
**mouse (mouse):** a pointing device to select text or icons
**network (net-work):** a group of two or more linked computer systems
**select (se-lect):** to choose an object for use
**web (web):** a connection of elements; network

....................................................................

## PREREADING EXERCISE

Study the title, the Vocabulary Review, the first paragraph, and the major headings of the selection. Then ask a question that might be answered under each major heading.

| HEADING | QUESTION |
|---|---|
| _____ | 1. _____ |
| _____ | 2. _____ |
| _____ | 3. _____ |

1   Millions of people around the world use the Internet to search for and **access** information on varied topics in many areas. The World Wide Web (WWW) is a part of the Internet. It is a **network** of information that's linked together like a **web**.

## THE WORLD WIDE WEB

2   You can think of the WWW as a large store of information you can access through the Internet. Its creation goes to Tim Berners-Lee of CERN, the European Laboratory for Particle Physics in Switzerland. The idea behind the WWW is the invention of a hypertext. It provides a single means of

access into the many services, resources, and information on the Internet. You use hypertext to **browse** the Web, to find information, and, when you're ready, to add information to the WWW.

### How the WWW Works

3    You enter the WWW by using a program called a Web browser. There are several available. . . . Each browser provides a graphical interface or way of working with the Internet. You move from place to place and item to item on the Web by using a **mouse** to **select** and **click on** images, **icons,** or text. The selected items are called hyperlinks or links for short. Each link you select represents a document, an image, a video clip, or an audio clip somewhere on the Internet. The information can be in the form of programs, text, graphics, images, video, or sound. In order for this to work, you must specify the links and create documents that can be shown as part of the WWW. Items available through the WWW give hypertext access to the Internet. For this reason, all you have to know is how to select a title, phrase, word, or icon.

### What Is Available on the WWW

4    All sorts of things are available on the WWW. If something can be put into **digital** format and stored in a computer, then it's available on the WWW. You'll find items on all kinds of topics: art, science, humanities, politics, law, business education, and government information.

5    And there's lots more. You can find information about many types of products, about health issues, and about government documents. You can find tips and advice on recreational activities such as camping, cooking, gardening, and travel. You can make purchases, go shopping, or learn about something you are thinking about buying. You can tour museums, plan a trip, visit gardens throughout the world, and so on. Just a little bit of exploring will show you the wide range and types of information available.

6    To put our discussion about the WWW in context, we'll start with an example of what you're likely to see when you use Netscape Navigator to enter the WWW.

7    In going through the steps of this example, we'll start the browser, explain some of the items you'll see on your screen, and then look at one of the many available directories that give easy access to a lot of information on the WWW. We'll follow these steps:

1. **Start Netscape Navigator.**

2. **Click the directory button titled Net Search.**

3. **Explore the WWW.**

4. **Exit Netscape Navigator.**

As you work through this example, the **WWW** indicates something 8
for you to do.

1. **Start Netscape Navigator.** You start Netscape Navigator by either
   clicking on an icon labeled Netscape or choosing Netscape from a
   menu.

   Double-click on the Netscape icon. The icon may appear as the
   following:

   Netscape Communicator™

   This will start Netscape Navigator, and a window . . . will appear on
   your screen. The first document you see is called the **home page.** When
   you're browsing the Web, it's your starting point. Also, when people or
   companies want to appear on the WWW, they create a home page. In
   this sense, the home page acts as a starting or contact point for the connection between the person or company and the rest of the WWW. . . .

   If you're familiar with a Windows environment, you should feel very
   comfortable using a Web browser. The menu commands are across
   the top row:

   > **F**ile  **E**dit  **V**iew  **G**o  **B**ookmarks  **O**ptions  **D**irectory  **W**indow  **H**elp

   The commands contain the items (such as File, Edit, and Help) that
   are common to several Windows functions. Each command represents a pull-down menu. Click on it and a menu will appear.

2. **Click on the directory button Net Search.** There's lots of information 9
   on the WWW, and it's just about impossible to keep track of it all. To
   help, some hyperlinks are arranged into categories to create directories. One popular, large, and well-designed directory is named
   Yahoo. You can get to that directory (and others) by clicking on the
   directory button labeled Net Search.

   **WWW**  Use the mouse to point to the directory button Net Search
   and click the (left) mouse button.

   Clicking the directory button causes Netscape Navigator to activate a
   hyperlink to a Web page that contains hyperlinks to the Yahoo directory and a few others. . . .

3. **Explore the WWW.** All you have to do is follow hyperlinks. Starting 10
   with a directory like this one, there's plenty of exploring to do. To be

specific, click on the link Science. That will take you to a screen like the one shown below.

**WWW**   Use the mouse to point to the hyperlink Science and click on the (left) mouse button.

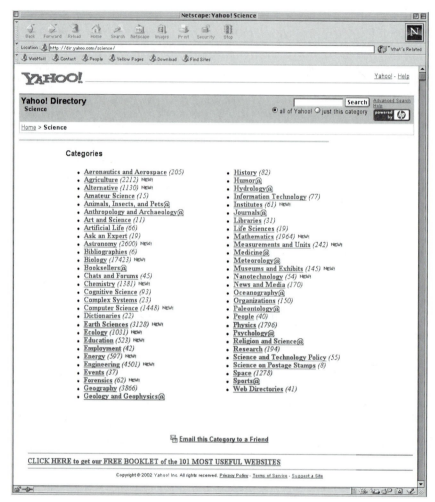

Yahoo Science

. . . There are lots of links to follow here, and you can follow these or any links to explore the WWW. You'll find you can move from page to page easily with a little practice. Remember to press the toolbar icon to go back through previous pages. Spend some time exploring these topics or others. When you're ready, go on to the next step.

**4. Exit Netscape Navigator.**

**WWW**   Click on File in the Menu Bar and then click on Exit. The window will close and you will have ended this session.

Once you've been browsing on the Web, you'll probably find lots of    11
information you'd like to save or print.

- To save a document in a file while you're using Netscape, choose File
  from the Menu bar, and then choose Save As. A dialog box will open.
  You can type in the name of the file and save it.

- To print a document while you're using Netscape, click on the Print
  icon and a dialog box will pop up on the screen. Click on the OK
  button to print, and that's all there is.

*(1260 words)*

## POSTREADING EXERCISE

Write short answers to the three questions you wrote in the prereading
exercise.

1. _____

   _____

2. _____

   _____

3. _____

   _____

## PROCESSING INFORMATION

1. Complete the exploration activity below.

2. Read the review questions.

3. Paraphrase key ideas from the selection to answer Short Answer
   questions 1–4.

4. Answer the review questions.

## EXPLORATION ACTIVITY

Visit the two Web sites listed below, if they are available, along with
another site of interest to you. For each site you visit, write down the
address (URL) and a brief description.

1. **Site 1:** http://terraserver.microsoft.com

   **Description:** _____

   _____

   _____

2. **Site 2:** http://www.pueblo.gsa.gov/

   **Description:** _____

   _____

   _____

3. **Site 3:** _____

   **Description:** _____

   _____

   _____

## REVIEW QUESTIONS

MATCHING
*Match items in column A with those in column B.*

**COLUMN A**

_____ 1. CERN
_____ 2. home page
_____ 3. hyperlinks
_____ 4. hypertext
_____ 5. graphical interface
_____ 6. menu commands
_____ 7. mouse
_____ 8. Netscape Navigator
_____ 9. Net Search
_____ 10. Tim Berners-Lee
_____ 11. Web browser
_____ 12. Web information
_____ 13. WWW
_____ 14. Yahoo

**COLUMN B**

a. person who started the WWW project
b. a laboratory in Switzerland
c. way of working with the Internet
d. used to select and click on images
e. a program to access the WWW
f. single means of access
g. arts, science, politics, etc.
h. a large store of information
i. the most popular browser
j. images, icons, or text
k. File, Edit, View, Go, Help
l. a large directory
m. directory button
n. starting or contact point

TRUE-FALSE
*Answer true or false to each statement. If false, make corrections by crossing out incorrect word(s) and putting in correct ones.*

_____ 15. The World Wide Web is a network of information that is linked together like a web.

_____ 16. Hypertext provides an opening to the information on the Internet.

_____ 17. You must be an experienced computer user to gain access to the Internet.

_____ 18. You may access the WWW by using a mouse named Web browser.

_____ 19. If something can be put into digital format and stored in a computer, then it will not be available on the WWW.

_____ 20. To get to Yahoo, you must click on the directory button labeled Yahoo.

---

**Score:** Number correct _____ (out of 20) × 5 = _____

---

**SHORT ANSWER**

*Write short answers for the following questions.*

1. What is the World Wide Web?

   _____

   _____

2. This selection identifies many types of information available on the World Wide Web. Name three.

   a. _____

   b. _____

   c. _____

3. How does the World Wide Web work?

   _____

   _____

4. What can you see on the World Wide Web?

   _____

   _____

5. What is your prediction of the future impact of the World Wide Web on education?

   _____

   _____

**REFLECTING**

Read the following paragraph and use the statistical data and other information it contains to complete the chart that follows.

   In a *USA Today* snapshot, the following data were reported on new and veteran users to show the changing face of the Internet. The five major categories included (1) males—48%/55%, (2) females—52%/45%,

(3) age 50 and older—20%/19%, (4) household income under $30,000—24%/16%, and (5) never attended college—39%/22%. (New user percentages are listed before the slash; veteran user percentages, after the slash.)

**TITLE:** _____

|  | New User | _____ |
|---|---|---|
| _____ | ____ | ____ |
| _____ | ____ | 45% |
| Age 50 and older | ____ | ____ |
| _____ | 23% | ____ |
| _____ | ____ | ____ |

## COLLABORATING

With a group, complete the following activities.

1. Compare the charts the members of your group completed in the reflecting activity above. Check them for accuracy, and then identify three trends.

   Trend A: _____

   Trend B: _____

   Trend C: _____

2. Identify and discuss recent progress in the computer world. Then group these ideas under the headings "Positive Factors" and "Negative Factors." Use these details to write two *slanted* (one-sided) paragraphs in favor of and against the future of the computer in our daily lives. Use the following worksheet to generate ideas.

### WORKSHEET

| POSITIVE FACTORS | NEGATIVE FACTORS |
|---|---|
| 1. _____ | 1. _____ |
| 2. _____ | 2. _____ |
| 3. _____ | 3. _____ |
| 4. _____ | 4. _____ |
| 5. _____ | 5. _____ |

## PARAGRAPH 1 (POSITIVE SLANT)

The future of the computer in our daily lives seems bright. _____

_____

_____

## PARAGRAPH 2 (NEGATIVE SLANT)

The future of the computer in our daily lives seems dim. _____

_____

_____

## WEB WATCH

Find a Web site where you can learn and have fun. Play educational games to improve your skills, or visit the White House, the Smithsonian, a planetarium, or another interesting site. Be sure to record URLs and write a brief description of each site for future visits.

## VOCABULARY EXERCISE

Complete the puzzle with words from the box.

| access | browse | click on | digital | home page | icon |
|--------|--------|----------|---------|-----------|------|
| menu | mouse | network | select | web | |

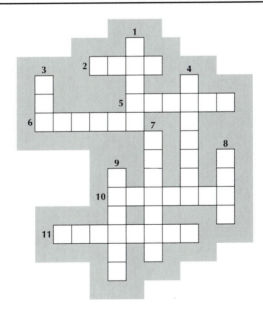

## ACROSS
2. a small picture
5. to choose, highlight text
6. to skim
10. choose a link
11. the starting point

## DOWN
1. a tool to select text
3. a group of linked elements
4. a system of connected links
7. expressed in numbers
8. a detailed list of items
9. to use

Selection 10

# Kane's Pretty Amazing Batman

*Bob Kane*

- - - - - - - - - - - - - - - - - - - - - - - - - - - - - - - - - - - - - - - - -

**VOCABULARY REVIEW**
**campy (camp-y):** outrageously amusing
**denizens (den-i-zens):** inhabitants
**feigned (feigned):** pretended
**foppish (fop-pish):** foolish
**longevity (lon-gev-i-ty):** length of time spent in service
**maniacal (ma-ni-a-cal):** insane; frantic
**persona (per-so-na):** the outer personality
**petrified (pet-ri-fied):** paralyzed with fear
**psychotic (psy-chot-ic):** having a serious mental illness
**vigilante (vi-gi-lan-te):** self-appointed crime fighter

- - - - - - - - - - - - - - - - - - - - - - - - - - - - - - - - - - - - - - - - -

## PREREADING EXERCISE

Study the title, the Vocabulary Review, and the first paragraph of the selection. Then write a sentence expressing what you believe this selection is about.

_____

_____

_____

I was born with a pencil in my hand. I'd doodle on the sidewalks in    1
New York, I'd scribble on walls. On the subway, I'd see an advertisement
with the Colgate girl smiling with that beautiful set of ivory teeth, and I'd
start blacking the teeth out. I must have been one of the all-time doodle-
holics in the early days. I just used to scribble on anything I could get my
hands on.

When I was 10, I knew I wanted to be a famous cartoonist. When my    2
dad brought home the Sunday comic pages, I used to copy them all prac-
tically as good as the cartoonists who created them. In those days, most
people didn't know what a cartoonist was. My family did, though. They
encouraged me. They certainly didn't give me any flak for wanting to
draw. My dad would bring my sketches down to the *Daily News* and
show them to the cartoonists. They'd say, "Gee, your son has talent. He
ought to stick to it."

I started selling cartoons when I was about 16. I got $5 a page for a    3
cartoon, which was a lot of money in 1936. After I graduated from high
school, I went to work for six months at Max Fleischer Studios, where

they had Popeye and Betty Boop. From there I won a scholarship and studied art for around nine months.

4     Comic books were a whole new industry, but they didn't become really popular until DC Comics' Superman hit the market in 1938. I created Batman in 1939, after I was at DC about seven months. So I didn't suffer too long.

5     Superman became a sensational runaway hit overnight. I had a talk with my editor, Vincent Sullivan, one Friday. I said, "These two guys who are doing Superman, they must be making a fortune, right?" They were making probably $1,500 a week between them, and I was making $25 a week. The editor said, "Well, do you think you could come up with a superhero?" I said, "For that kind of money, I could come up with anything over the weekend." So I went home and started superhero doodling.

6     There were three major influences on Batman. The first was Zorro. As a kid, I was a movie buff. One of my favorites was "The Mark of Zorro," with Douglas Fairbanks, Sr. Zorro had the dual identity. By day, like Bruce Wayne, he **feigned** being a bored, **foppish** count, the son of one of the richest families in Mexico. By night, he became a **vigilante.** He would disguise himself, wearing a handkerchief mask with the eyes slit out. He exited on a black horse from a cave underneath his home, and that's the inspiration for the Batcave and the Batmobile.

7     The second influence was a Leonardo da Vinci book I had seen. The book had a lot of inventions, including a flying machine. It was a man on a sled-like contraption with huge bat wings. Da Vinci had a quote that went something like, "Your bird will have no model but that of a bat." There it was—from a book 500 years old!

8     The third inspiration was a silent mystery movie called "The Bat," in which the bat was a villain. They had a searchlight in the movie with a bat in the middle, just like my Batsignal. I was always frightened by bats, but I was fascinated with them too, with the evil that they represented.

9     I wanted Bruce Wayne's costume to throw a terrible fear into the **denizens** of the underworld. If a huge bat came into your apartment, it would scare the hell out of you. I wanted to create a costume that was so awesome that the crooks would be **petrified.**

10    Batman was very crude at the beginning. He had stiff bat wings stuck behind his shoulders; he looked like a bat, actually. But I showed Vincent Sullivan my first crude sketches of Batman that Monday. He loved it and said, "Okay, let's go!"

11    I created Bruce Wayne to be a normal human being living in our society. I didn't want a second Superman. I think Batman is still the only superhero who's a normal man without superpowers. And therein I think lies the **longevity** of Batman. Every human can relate to being a Batman. Not giving Batman superpowers also gives the stories more tension because he can be killed. He'll bleed and he can die. That appeals to people because he's vulnerable.

My father died when I was 22 or 23. That left a dark mood over my    12
**persona.** Underneath it all, I'm a brooder like Batman. I really am Batman.
When I was younger, I looked just like Bruce Wayne. I got the image from
myself. Bruce Wayne—Bob Kane.

When Bruce Wayne was 10 years old, his mother and dad were mur-    13
dered coming out of the theater. This dramatic shock motivated him to
become a vigilante. Bruce Wayne isn't crazy, but he's obsessed. He
became, in his own way, as **psychotic** as the Joker, except the Joker fights
against justice and for evil. They're mirror images of each other.

Of all the villains I created, the Joker was my favorite. He's the    14
most **maniacal.** He's sick, but he's fun. His appearance is frightening and
humorous at the same time. The inspiration for the Joker was a photograph of a German actor, Conrad Veidt, from the movie "The Man Who
Laughs." The film is derived from a Victor Hugo story about rival Gypsy
gangs in France at the turn of the century. Sometimes the gangs would
raid each other's camps and slit the mouths of children from ear to ear,
so that when the children grew up, their mouths became frozen in a
ghastly grin.

It's difficult to turn a comic-book hero into a movie. The only yard-    15
stick was the TV show. We all agreed that we didn't want to do anything
**campy.** We wanted to make Batman dark and brooding, taking the story
back to its roots.

Some people expected the movie to fall on its face because of the    16
hype. We worried about that. Now the whole Batmania thing is just unbelievable to me. We had a Batmania in '66 with the TV series, but this is
even bigger. This movie is blowing through the rooftop.

And just think, I started it all with my little Batpencil when I was 18.    17
Pretty amazing, isn't it?

*(1,070 words)*

## POSTREADING EXERCISE

Now that you have read the selection, revise the sentence you wrote in
the prereading exercise.

_____

_____

_____

1. Discuss the revised sentence with a partner, giving support for your
   ideas. Your partner will listen, take notes, and use the notes to repeat
   your key ideas.

2. Now trade places with your partner.

## COMPREHENSION EXERCISE
*Circle the letter of the best answer.*

### SKIMMING FOR FACTS

1. Kane realized his lifelong career ambition when he was
   a. six years old.
   b. ten years old.
   c. twelve years old.
   d. sixteen years old.

2. How did Kane's parents react when told of his career choice?
   a. After many family fights, they finally gave in.
   b. They were always encouraging.
   c. Ashamed of his unusual talent, they hid his work.
   d. They tried to push him into other areas.

3. The Max Fleischer Studios published
   a. Porky Pig and Buggs Bunny.
   b. Popeye and Betty Boop.
   c. Superman and Batman.
   d. Veronica and Archie.

4. What were the major influences on Batman?
   a. Zorro, the Leonardo da Vinci book, and "The Bat"
   b. Zorro, the da Vinci book, the bat, and Superman
   c. Zorro, Superman, Spiderman, and the Joker
   d. Zorro, Superman, Superwoman, and Spiderman

5. What makes Batman different from other superheroes?
   a. He fights crime.
   b. He is a normal man without superpowers.
   c. He can fly.
   d. He is not afraid of villains.

### RELATING THE FACTS

6. Which pattern of development does paragraph 6 follow?
   a. example
   b. contrast
   c. comparison
   d. cause-effect

7. Which pattern of development does paragraph 11 follow?
   a. example
   b. contrast
   c. comparison
   d. cause-effect

8. Which pattern of development does paragraph 12 follow?
   a. example
   b. contrast
   c. comparison
   d. classification

9. Where is the main idea of paragraph 11 located?
   a. in the middle
   b. at the beginning
   c. at the end
   d. both b and c

10. Label the following sentences from paragraph 14 as (a) main idea, (b) major detail, (c) minor detail, or (d) none of the above.

   \_\_\_\_\_ Of all the villains I created, the Joker was my favorite.

   \_\_\_\_\_ He's the most maniacal.

   \_\_\_\_\_ He's sick but he's fun.

   \_\_\_\_\_ His appearance is frightening and humorous at the same time.

   \_\_\_\_\_ The inspiration for the Joker was a photograph . . .

   \_\_\_\_\_ The film is derived from a Victor Hugo story . . .

## CONNECTING WITH THE AUTHOR

11. As a youngster in school, the author probably scribbled
    a. on his desk.
    b. throughout his notebook.
    c. in textbooks.
    d. all of the above.

12. Which of the following factors contributed to Kane's success as a cartoonist?
    a. his inherited talent and lack of support from family
    b. his college degree in art history
    c. his forgetting to practice his craft
    d. his luck and willingness to accept a challenge

13. By saying, "Okay, let's go!" what does Vincent Sullivan imply?
    a. Batman would soon take the place of Superman.
    b. He sees great potential in Kane's work.
    c. They have a final product that's ready for the market.
    d. He is excited and ready to pay Kane $1,500 a week.

14. From paragraph 13, you can infer that Bruce Wayne
    a. has experienced some emotional trauma.
    b. takes matters into his own hands.

c. is on a mission.

d. all of the above.

15. In paragraph 13, why does the author say that Bruce Wayne and the Joker are mirror images of each other?

a. They are twins.

b. They do the same thing but for different reasons.

c. They both play the same role in society.

d. They have different personality traits.

16. In paragraph 16, what does the author mean when he uses the expression "to fall on its face"?

a. The movie would fall on Bruce Wayne's face.

b. The movie would make its mark in history.

c. The movie would drop on its front side.

d. The movie would not do well at the box office.

17. What does the author mean when he says he was "born with a pencil in my hand"?

a. He is using a figurative expression to show that he was certain to become an artist.

b. He is using propaganda to show that ordinary people can become artists, too.

c. He is using emphasis to show himself as an extraordinary baby.

d. He is using comparison to show the differences between adults and children.

18. Which statement from the selection is the author's opinion?

a. "It's difficult to turn a comic-book hero into a movie."

b. "There were three major influences on Batman."

c. "I created Batman in 1939, after I was at DC about seven months."

d. "Now the whole Batmania thing is just unbelievable to me."

19. What is the tone of this selection?

a. informative

b. humorous

c. mysterious

d. critical

20. Which of these descriptions best represents the author's audience?

a. a general readership

b. comic-book readers

c. aspiring comic-book artists

d. movie critics

—————————————— PROGRESS CHART ——————————————

*Circle the correct responses for each section below. Add the circles and multiply by 5. Record the total here and on the score chart in the Appendix.*

| Skimming for Facts | Relating the Facts | Connecting with the Author | Total |
|---|---|---|---|
| 1  2  3  4  5 | 6  7  8  9  10 | 11  12  13  14  15  16  17  18  19  20 | |

## REFLECTING

Imagine your career goal is to become a(n) _____. Using information from the article and elsewhere, list some steps you can take to become a success in your field.

_____

_____

_____

_____

_____

_____

## COLLABORATING

Bob Kane is visiting your school to speak with your class about becoming a cartoonist. With a group, prepare an introduction of this person who has made such a significant contribution to the entertainment industry. Be sure to include some background information from the selection as well as from other sources. Tell how his work has affected society at large.

## WEB WATCH

Locate articles on the Internet about two of your favorite authors, preferably comic book authors. Using a minimum of four points, contrast the authors by showing how they are different. Also, if you are interested in finding out more about Bob Kane, read the article at this site if it is still available: http://comic-art/bios-1/bobkane1.html.

## VOCABULARY EXERCISE

Complete the puzzle with words from the box.

| campy | denizens | feigned | foppish | longevity |
| maniacal | persona | petrified | psychotic | vigilante |

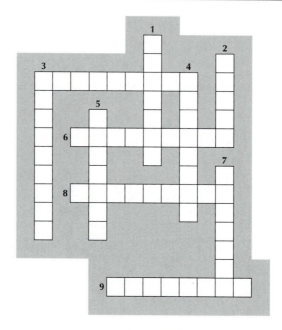

**ACROSS**
3. paralyzed with fear
6. long life
8. crime fighter
9. behaving crazily

**DOWN**
1. pretended
2. outrageously amusing
3. mentally ill
4. inhabitants
5. foolish
7. outward appearance

# Lashanda Daniels' Outstanding Essay on the Homeless

*William Plummer and S. Avery Brown*

**VOCABULARY REVIEW**
**articulate (ar-tic-u-late):** well spoken
**forfeited (for-feit-ed):** gave up, lost
**indelibly (in-del-i-bly):** permanently
**perceptive (per-cep-tive):** having keen insight or intuition
**pluck (pluck):** spirit, energy
**predicament (pre-dic-a-ment):** unpleasant situation
**relative (rel-a-tive):** comparative
**resourcefulness (re-source-ful-ness):** ability to solve problems
**splendor (splen-dor):** magnificent richness

**PREREADING EXERCISE**

Study the title, the Vocabulary Review, and the first paragraph of the selection. Then write a sentence expressing what you believe this selection is about.

_____

_____

_____

1  When it came to writing an essay on the homeless for a Boston-wide contest, seventh-grader Lashanda Daniels knew what she was talking about. Unlike the other kids, she did not need to go to the library and read a lot of news clips to write her award-winning essay. For Lashanda, living in a city shelter with her mother and four brothers for five months was research enough.

2  The truth is, it was more than that. Lashanda, 13, who now lives in the **relative splendor** of a state-subsidized, four-bedroom apartment in Roxbury, has been **indelibly** marked by the experience. She says she knew the third-floor room in the Boston Family Shelter was better than living on the street this past winter. She also knew that being in the shelter was temporary, given the **pluck** and **resourcefulness** of her mother, Carolyn.

3  Still, Lashanda could not help feeling embarrassed, even angry. "First, you hate yourself for being in this **predicament**," she wrote in the essay that earned her second place and $250. Drawing more than 600 entries, the contest was sponsored by the Boston police and a local

radio station. "Then that feeling of hate spreads toward those around you. You find yourself being jealous of those who have a home, and you feel as though everyone looks down on you."

4    The Daniels family became homeless through a chain of bad luck. It all began when Carolyn tried to find a better life for her children. Divorced more than 10 years ago, she and the family had made several visits to an aunt living in Detroit. The city struck Carolyn as a better place to live. So she saved money from her monthly assistance checks, and the family moved to Detroit in September 1987. Almost immediately, she says, she discovered "we'd made a terrible mistake. The drugs and gangs were so bad we wanted to get out right away. But we didn't have any money left."

5    According to Carolyn, her oldest son, Mory Mack, 17, was beaten up for refusing to join a gang. "But they finally got him," she says. "He began working in a drug house, and I found out later that he missed more than 60 days of school." Mory says he took the first money he made with the gang and bought himself a ticket back to Boston in March 1988. The rest of the family was not so lucky. "We had to stay until September," says Carolyn, "until I got enough money together. I was working at K Mart and a pizza restaurant, and every time I got a paycheck, I'd buy another bus ticket."

6    While saving the necessary cash, the family had to live through bottles and bricks thrown through the windows of their home by gang members. And one night, a stream of bullets. Their greeting upon returning to Boston was not much friendlier. Applying for housing assistance, Carolyn learned her family had **forfeited** such aid when they moved out of the city. She says she was told to "go back to Detroit." Shortly after, she moved her kids into the shelter. "Those five months were agony," says Carolyn. "The room seemed to shrink smaller and smaller every month. There were so many negatives in my life, but I decided I wasn't going to let them get me down."

7    Lashanda remembers the night Carolyn told them she had finally got approval for state-subsidized housing and moved them into a Roxbury apartment. "My mother was smiling. She said, 'Let's go. We don't live here anymore.' I was so happy. We drove to this big building, and I got my own room. It felt so good."

8    Lashanda's **perceptive** essay didn't surprise her teachers at James P. Timilty School one bit. "She's a bright, **articulate** girl," says Daisy Droge, the English teacher who got her to enter the contest. Adds principal Mary Grassa O'Neill: "She has seen hard times, but she has survived. I think she's going to do well. Most of us can't imagine what it's like to be homeless. But the essay showed the ordeal made her stronger."

9    Lashanda agrees. "I wanted to tell them to bear with the homeless. Don't put them down. It might not be their fault. It can feel very hopeless." While her family is still struggling, Carolyn and Mory continue to look for work to support Lashanda and her younger brothers, Eric, Derrick, and Robert. Lashanda knows it is no small blessing they live

together under one roof. "I still get very sad seeing people sleeping on the streets. I think I always will."

*(760 words)*

## POSTREADING EXERCISE

Now that you have read the selection, revise the sentence you wrote in the prereading exercise.

_____

_____

_____

1. Discuss the revised sentence with a partner, giving support for your ideas. Your partner will listen, take notes, and use the notes to repeat your key ideas.

2. Now trade places with your partner.

## COMPREHENSION EXERCISE
*Circle the letter of the best answer.*

### SKIMMING FOR FACTS

1. How many school days did Mory miss in Detroit?
   a. 60
   b. 45
   c. 13
   d. 10

2. While in Detroit, Carolyn worked two jobs at
   a. Kmart and a pizza restaurant.
   b. Kmart and KFC.
   c. Kmart and Roxbury.
   d. Kmart and Pizza Hut.

3. Which of the following is the name of Lashanda's school?
   a. James T. Timilty
   b. Lincoln Middle School
   c. Booker T. Washington
   d. Roxbury High

4. It makes Lashanda sad to see people
   a. making fun of the homeless.
   b. sleeping on the streets.
   c. moving their families out of town.
   d. putting the homeless down.

5. The writing contest was sponsored by
   a. the Boston police and a local radio station.
   b. a local radio station.

c. the Boston-wide community.

d. Help for the Homeless.

### RELATING THE FACTS

6. Which sentence best expresses the main idea of paragraph 3?
   a. Lashanda's short-lived homelessness made her feel angry and embarrassed.
   b. Homelessness is nothing to be ashamed of.
   c. Homelessness could happen to anyone.
   d. Lashanda lives in a Roxbury state-subsidized apartment.

7. Which sentence best expresses the main idea of paragraph 8?
   a. the first sentence
   b. the last sentence
   c. the fourth sentence
   d. none of the above

8. Which of these relationships is not signaled in paragraph 4?
   a. cause-effect
   b. contrast
   c. addition
   d. example

9. Sequence the chain of bad luck that led to the family's homelessness, placing the numbers 1 through 7 in the spaces provided.
   _____ a. Carolyn tries to find a better life for her children.
   _____ b. The Detroit move is a big mistake.
   _____ c. The family has no money left.
   _____ d. Mory joins a gang.
   _____ e. The family is turned down for public assistance.
   _____ f. Carolyn saves money and moves to Detroit.
   _____ g. Drugs and gangs make them want to leave Detroit right away.

10. What is the main idea of paragraph 4?
    a. The Daniels family became homeless through a chain of bad luck.
    b. The family moved to Detroit in September 1987.
    c. Drugs and gangs made the family return to Boston.
    d. Carolyn thought Detroit would be a better place to live.

### CONNECTING WITH THE AUTHOR

11. Lashanda's homelessness probably left a lasting impression on her because she
    a. hates herself and vows to get even with society.
    b. is writing to ease her pain.
    c. feels as though everyone looks down on her.
    d. still gets emotional when she sees homeless people.

12. Why is Lashanda now thinking about becoming a writer instead of a lawyer?
    a. She found out that law courses would be too hard.
    b. She wants to share her story with other mothers.
    c. She wants to help the homeless people to stay alive.
    d. She has found success in the field of writing.

13. Read paragraph 9 again. By being homeless, Lashanda seems to believe that
    a. people prejudge the homeless.
    b. people with homes understand the homeless.
    c. everyone will be homeless one day.
    d. homeless people have all the answers.

14. When terrorized by gang members, the Daniels family
    a. stayed clear of windows and took cover.
    b. feared for their lives at times.
    c. did not fight back.
    d. did all of the above.

15. What kind of relationship existed between Mory and his mother?
    a. devoted
    b. dishonest
    c. delightful
    d. demanding

16. Carolyn probably completed
    a. high school.
    b. college.
    c. law school.
    d. business college.

17. Carolyn's statement that those five months in the shelter were "agony" suggests all of the following *except*
    a. arguments and fights, substance abuse, and thefts.
    b. conflict between children and poor school performance.
    c. little privacy, crowdedness, and filth.
    d. a healthful diet, comfort, and safety.

18. Which of the following statements from the selection is a fact?
    a. "Their reception upon returning to Boston was not much friendlier."
    b. "Those five months were agony."
    c. "Most of us can't imagine what it's like to be homeless."
    d. "Mory was beaten up for refusing to join a gang."

19. Paragraph 1 begins with a contrast between
    a. Lashanda and other kids in her school.
    b. Lashanda and her brother.
    c. students with and without homes.
    d. Lashanda and the author.

20. The tone of this selection is
    a. instructive.                    b. persuasive.
    c. humorous.                       d. informative.

──────────────────── **PROGRESS CHART** ────────────────────

*Circle the correct responses for each section below. Add the circles and multiply by 5. Record the total here and on the score chart in the Appendix.*

| Skimming for Facts | Relating the Facts | Connecting with the Author | Total |
|---|---|---|---|
| 1  2  3  4  5 | 6  7  8  9  10 | 11  12  13  14  15  16  17  18  19  20 | |

## REFLECTING

Though it may be difficult, imagine yourself homeless. Describe your situation and list steps you would take to find a home.

_____

_____

_____

_____

_____

## COLLABORATING

With a group, make a diagram showing multiple causes and effects of homelessness. Complete the worksheet below, and then use these ideas in a letter to the mayor of your town proposing a solution to the problem of homelessness in your town.

**CAUSES**                          **EFFECTS**

1. _____            1. _____

2. _____            2. _____

3. _____            3. _____

4. _____            4. _____

**Solution:** _____

_____

_____

_____

_____

_____

## WEB WATCH

Pretend you are a reporter whose next assignment is to write an article about homelessness in America. Begin with a limited topic ("Helping Hands for America's Homeless Women"). Then conduct an Internet search for sites that give answers to the reporter's questions: *who, what, when, where, why,* and *how.* Write your limited topic and answers to these questions.

## VOCABULARY EXERCISE

Use the antonym (opposite meaning) clues below to complete the puzzle with words from the box.

| | | | | |
|---|---|---|---|---|
| articulate | forfeited | indelibly | perceptive | pluck |
| predicament | relative | resourcefulness | splendor | |

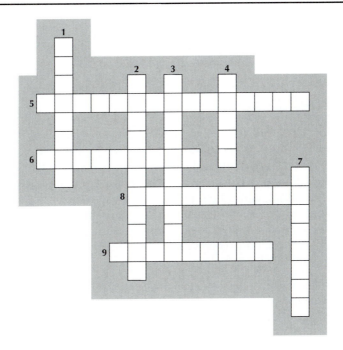

**ACROSS**
5. inability to get things done
6. held on to
8. not easily understood
9. quickly erased

**DOWN**
1. ugliness
2. fortunate situation
3. unobservant
4. lack of courage
7. disconnected

# Tips on Reading

## *Psychology*

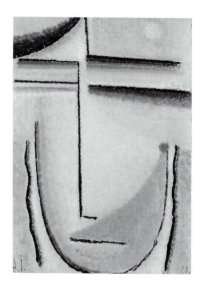

Psychology is the science of human and animal behavior. Its primary focus is on the study of the mind and emotional processes of individuals. Psychological writings are based on research. "Social Power" comes from a psychology textbook. This selection presents five types of power and a research study that shows how people react when they are given power over another. Notice how the author puts forth a point of view and supports it with evidence. As a reader, your goal is to follow the author's presentation of information. There are several steps you can take to get the most from reading in psychology:

- Use the vocabulary card system to *study the subject area terminology*.
- **Preview:** Read over the chapter outline at the beginning of each chapter. Next, skim through the entire chapter paying close attention to the major headings, subheadings, key words, and illustrations. Read the summary carefully and look at the end-of-chapter questions.
- **Question:** Turn headings into questions. Make sure the answers to your questions will yield the main idea or point the author attempts to make in each section.
- **Read:** Try to find the answers to the questions posed in Step 2. Also associate your new knowledge with what you already know. You may choose to highlight points of importance. Keep these markings to a

minimum; no more than 15 percent of the text should be marked or highlighted. Any more than this will defeat your purpose, which is to identify the major points during your review.

- **Self-Recitation:** Look away from the text and try to recall the main ideas. Say this aloud to yourself or write brief notes on the section. Check to see if you were able to remember the main ideas correctly.
- **Test:** Try to recall the main ideas in the chapter. Verify your response by reviewing your notes and definitions of key terms. Reread the summary and try to fill in details that have been omitted about each topic covered. Also practice applying what you have learned to the experiences in your life and in those of others.

## Selection 12

# Psychology: Social Power

*Dennis Coon*

**VOCABULARY REVIEW**
**adjacent (ad-ja-cent):** beside, next to
**apparatus (ap-pa-rat-us):** instruments or attachments
**astounding (a-stound-ing):** amazing
**coercive (co-er-cive):** forceful
**conformity (con-form-i-ty):** behaving like others
**disperse (dis-perse):** scatter, leave from the group
**inhumane (in-hu-mane):** uncivilized
**legitimate (le-git-i-mate):** legal
**phenomenon (phe-nom-e-non):** spectacular event
**provocative (pro-voc-a-tive):** exciting
**psychopath (psy-cho-path):** mentally unstable person
**referent (ref-e-rent):** the thing or person being referred to

## PREREADING EXERCISE

Study the title, the Vocabulary Review, the first paragraph, and the headings of the selection. Then write three questions that you believe will be answered by your reading.

1. _____

2. _____

3. _____

## WHO CAN DO WHAT TO WHOM?

Here's something to think about: Whereas strength is a quality held by  1
individuals, power is always social. It arises when people come together
and disappears when they **disperse.** To understand how people are able
to rule each other, you must learn about five types of social power.

Reward power lies in the ability to reward a person for desired be-  2
havior. Teachers try to exercise reward power over their students through
the use of grades. Employers command reward power by their control of
wages and bonuses.

Coercive power is based on the ability to punish a person for failure  3
to comply. **Coercive** power is the basis for most statute law. This type of
law is backed by fines or imprisonment to control behavior.

Legitimate power comes from acceptance of a person as an agent of a  4
fixed social order. For example, elected leaders and supervisors have

**legitimate** power. So does a teacher in the classroom. But outside the classroom that power would have to come from another source.

5      Referent power is based on respect for or identification with a person or a group. The person "refers to" the source of **referent** power for direction. Referent power is responsible for much of the **conformity** seen in groups.

6      Expert power is based on recognition that another person has knowledge or skill necessary for achieving a goal. Allowing teachers or experts to guide behavior because you believe in their ability to produce desirable results is an example. Physicians, lawyers, psychologists, and plumbers have expert power.

7      A person who has power in one situation may have very little in another. In those situations where a person has power, he or she is described as an authority. In the next section we will explore obedience. Obedience is a special type of conformity to the demands of an authority.

## OBEDIENCE: WOULD YOU ELECTROCUTE A STRANGER?

8      The question is this: If ordered to do so, would you shock a man with a known heart condition who is screaming and asking to be released? Certainly we can assume that few people would do so. Or can we? In Nazi Germany, obedient soldiers (once average citizens) helped kill over 9 million people in concentration camps. Another example of the same **phenomenon** happened during the Vietnam War. Lt. William Calley led a bloody killing of helpless women and children at a village called My Lai. Do such **inhumane** acts reveal deep character flaws? Are they the acts of heartless **psychopaths** or crazed killers? Or are they simply the result of obedience to authority? What are the limits of such obedience? These are questions that puzzled social psychologist Stanley Milgram when he began a **provocative** series of studies on obedience.

### Question: How Did Milgram Study Obedience?

9      Milgram's research is best appreciated by imagining yourself as a subject. Place yourself in the following situation.

10      *Milgram's Obedience Studies* Imagine answering a newspaper ad to take part in a learning experiment at Yale University. When you arrive, a coin is flipped. A second subject, a friendly-looking man in his 50s, is named the "learner." By chance you have become the "teacher."

11      Your task is to read a list of word pairs to be memorized by the learner. You are to punish him with an electric shock each time he makes a mistake. The learner is taken to an **adjacent** room. You watch as he is seated in an "electric chair." **Apparatus** and electrodes are attached to his wrists. You are then taken to your seat in front of a "shock generator." On this device is a row of 30 switches labeled from 15 to 450 volts. These volts are described further with labels ranging from "Slight Shock" to "Extreme Intensity Shock" and finally "Danger Severe Shock." You are told to shock the learner each time he makes a mistake. You are to begin with 15 volts and then move one switch (15 volts) higher for each additional mistake.

This experiment begins, and the learner soon makes his first mistake. 12
You flip a switch. More mistakes. Rapidly you reach the 75-volt level. The
learner moans after each shock. At 100 volts he complains he has a heart
condition. At 150 volts he says he no longer wants to continue and demands release. At 300 volts he screams and says he can no longer give
answers.

At some point during the experiment, you begin to protest to the ex- 13
perimenter. "That man has a heart condition," you say. "I'm not going to
kill that man." The experimenter says, "Please continue." Another shock
and another scream from the learner and you say, "You mean I've got to
keep going up the scale? No, sir. I'm not going to give him 450 volts!" The
experimenter says, "The experiment requires that you continue." For a
time the learner refuses to answer any more questions and screams with
each shock. Then he falls silent for the rest of the experiment.

### Question: I Can't Believe Many People Would Do This. What Happened?

Milgram also doubted that many people would obey his orders. When he 14
surveyed a group of psychiatrists before the experiment, they predicted
that less that 1 percent of those tested would obey. The **astounding** fact
is that 65 percent of those tested obeyed completely by going all the way
to the 450-volt level. And no one stopped short of 300 volts ("Severe
Shock").

### Question: Was The Learner Injured?

The time has come to confess that the "learner" was in fact an actor who 15
turned a tape recorder on and off in the shock room. No shocks were ever
carried out, but the dilemma for the "teacher" was quite real. Subjects
protested, sweated, trembled, stuttered, bit their lips, and laughed ner-
vously. Clearly they were upset by what they were doing, but most
obeyed the experimenter's orders.

*(980 words)*

## POSTREADING EXERCISE

Now that you have read the selection, answer the questions you wrote in
the prereading exercise.

1. _____

   _____

2. _____

   _____

3. _____

   _____

## PROCESSING INFORMATION

1. Read the review questions below.
2. Using the review questions as a guide, highlight the key information in the selection.
3. Write a summary of the selection.
4. Using your summary and the selection, answer the review questions.

## REVIEW QUESTIONS

*Match the numbered descriptions below with one of the types of social power listed in the word box. Write the correct letter in each space provided.*

| a. reward | b. coercive | c. legitimate | d. expert | e. referent |
|---|---|---|---|---|

_____ 1. gang member       _____ 7. supervisor
_____ 2. minister      _____ 8. judge
_____ 3. parent      _____ 9. dentist
_____ 4. police officer      _____ 10. grandparent
_____ 5. role model      _____ 11. editor
_____ 6. parole officer      _____ 12. senator

*Circle the letter before the best answer.*

13. In paragraph 1, the author contrasts
    a. power and society.
    b. power and strength.
    c. influence and quality.
    d. social power and reward.

14. How many subjects did Milgram's study use?
    a. one
    b. two
    c. three
    d. four

15. The learner in Milgram's study would be
    a. punished for making a mistake.
    b. rewarded for a correct response.
    c. respected for his ability to take pain.
    d. praised for his ability to remember word pairs.

16. The shock generator used in the experiment has
    a. 30 switches.
    b. 15 switches.
    c. 45 switches.
    d. 450 switches.

17. Each switch on the shock generator sent out
    a. 10 volts.
    b. 15 volts.
    c. 30 volts.
    d. 150 volts.

18. The shock generator was labeled
    a. moderate.
    b. dangerous.
    c. serious.
    d. slight.

19. The learner complains of a heart condition after
    a. 75 volts.
    b. 100 volts.
    c. 300 volts.
    d. 450 volts.

20. Milgram conducts his experiment
    a. in a prison.
    b. at Yale University.
    c. at Howard University.
    d. in a jail cell.

21. In the final paragraph, the author concludes that the subjects were upset by what they were doing because of
    a. their ability to feel the pain.
    b. what they did and said.
    c. the learner's death.
    d. the stress in both rooms.

22. What type of evidence does the author use to illustrate his point about obedience to authority?
    a. comparison and contrast
    b. two examples of historical reference
    c. facts about life
    d. none of the above

23. The questions that influenced Milgram's study were linked to
    a. character flaws.
    b. abnormal personalities.
    c. obedience.
    d. all of the above.

24. What is the effect of the questions in the excerpt?
    a. They help guide the reader's thoughts.
    b. They help focus and direct the reader's attention to the key points.
    c. They help to establish a purpose for reading.
    d. All of the above.

*Sequence the following events in the order in which they occur in Milgram's experiment.*

25. _____ a. The teacher reads a list of word pairs.
_____ b. The learner falls chillingly silent.
_____ c. The learner complains of a heart condition.
_____ d. The learner screams and claims he is unable to give answers.
_____ e. The learner makes mistakes.
_____ f. Taken to an adjacent room, the learner sits in an electric chair; electrodes are strapped to his wrists.
_____ g. By a flip of a coin, you become the teacher and the man the learner.
_____ h. The teacher punishes the learner with an electric shock.
_____ i. The teacher protests: "I'm not going to kill that man."
_____ j. The experimenter says, "Please continue."

**Score:** Number correct _____ (out of 25) × 4 = _____

## REFLECTING

Complete the concept map below. Extend the levels of the map by adding a brief definition and examples of authority figures for each type of social power. (An example is done for you.)

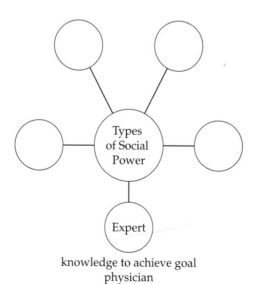

knowledge to achieve goal
physician
lawyer

## COLLABORATING

With a group, develop a ten-item true-false review test for this selection and administer it to the class. Check the answers and plot average group scores on a graph like the one below. Write a paragraph to explain the results.

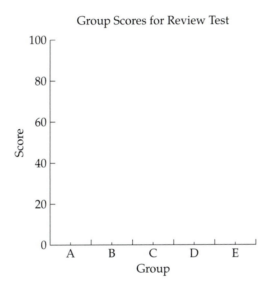

Group Scores for Review Test

## WEB WATCH

Authors often use information from a variety of sources to help prove their points. On the Internet, find two articles from a psychological journal and evaluate the authors' evidence. Look for research statistics, quotations from authorities on the subject, historical references, visual aids, and personal experience. In your judgment, which article has more credibility?

## VOCABULARY EXERCISE

Complete the puzzle with words from the box.

| | | | |
|---|---|---|---|
| adjacent | apparatus | astounding | coercive |
| conformity | disperse | inhumane | legitimate |
| phenomenon | provocative | psychopaths | referent |

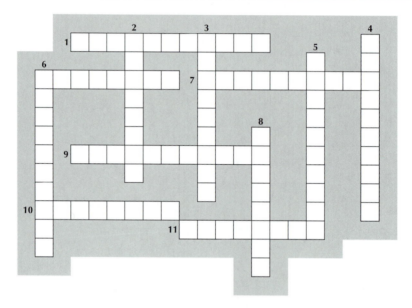

**ACROSS**
1. mentally ill people
6. beside
7. an unusual happening
9. sensual, seductive
10. uncivilized
11. scatter

**DOWN**
2. forced
3. instruments
4. conventional behavior
5. legal
6. amazing
8. person or thing referred to

Selection 13

# A Speller's Manifesto

*Jennifer Lynn Weston*

**PREREADING EXERCISE**

Study the title, the Vocabulary Review, and the first paragraph of the selection. Then write a sentence expressing what you think this selection is about.

_____

_____

1   There's a little sign tacked above my desk that says, "Being a Bad Speller Is Not a Moral Failing." I put it there as a reminder to myself more than anyone else. You see, I'm still in the process of putting my "failing" into **perspective.** I remember too clearly teachers—from elementary through graduate school—**deploring** my spelling mistakes. These teachers used a harshness of tone and **demeanor** usually reserved for criminal behavior.

2   I used to explain, apologetically, that my younger sister was given the family "spelling genes." By the time I made it to college, I was more outspoken. I'd point out that President Andrew Jackson and F. Scott Fitzgerald were spelling-impaired. Nowadays my favorite answer is that any dunce with a spell-check can get the letter-order right. What counts is whether one can group the words well enough to make the check worthwhile. This argument has won a few debates, but plenty of folks aren't yet convinced.

3   Both genetic and environmental factors account for my spelling woes. I try to spell words the way they sound. And I was born among a people who speak English, a well-known nonphonetic language. Having done some research on who's to blame for this, I find the problems started

early. The English alphabet has been understaffed since the Anglo-Saxon period: 26 letters represent 40 letter sounds.

4       After the Norman conquests, French writers got hold of the language and added extra Gs. Thus we have spellings like *thought, enough,* and *neighbor.* English was one of the earliest languages to be mechanically printed. And changes in writing have always lagged behind changes in speaking.

5       As if that weren't enough, there's the English-speaker's historical willingness to adopt foreign terms, complete with their different rules of spelling. This has greatly added to the language's power of expression. It has also left us with such phonetic demons as *psyche* and *rendezvous.*

6       Most of my spelling errors can be traced to three **idiosyncrasies** of English. The problem of "double letters—or not" is tricky since a word with a missing letter for an extra one doesn't always look wrong. Is it *iritate* or *irritate? dimension* or *dimmension? shimer* or *shimmer?* Interchangeable consonants are also difficult. Examples of these are *S* and *C* (*response/responce*) and *S* and *Z* (*advertize/advertise*). But these are small problems. I can usually get them correct by seeing the words often enough.

7       My real fear is vowels. The "Great Vowel Shift" of the 15th century has a lot to answer for. In what other language would *fur, fer,* and *fir* all spell the same sound? Why should moving the *E* change the sound of the *G* in *angel* and *angle?* What about that "Silent *E*" that's supposed to be dropped, or not, when a suffix is added? We even have words with two sounds for vowels: *wind, lead, read, bow, wound, tear, dove.* You have to see the context to know the meaning. Don't get me started on all those exceptions to the "*I* before *E* except after *C*" rule. Why do we need to put vowels together anyway when there is such a range of possible sounds?

8       I'm not the first to protest the madness. In the late 1400s, printer-publisher William Caxton wrestled with translating a book from French into English. He was afraid that "common people" would not be able to understand it. His attempts at spelling sameness were **stymied** by the difficulty of trying to fit his expected readers' many dialects. Thirty years later, Jonathan Swift called this problem an argument against "A foolish Opinion that we ought to spell exactly as we speak . . . a thing we should never see an end of."

9       Luckily for later generations, Benjamin Franklin was of that "foolish Opinion." In a 1768 essay, he proposed, among other things, getting rid of silent letters. While most of Franklin's plan was ignored, **lexicographer** Noah Webster adopted part of it in his 1828 *American Dictionary of the English Language.* The impact of Webster's work on American spelling is clear to any reader of early literature—or of "Olde Antique Shoppe" shingles.

10      There's been more progress toward the use of sound in recent years. On highway signs, due to little space, *thru* and *nite* have become acceptable alternate spellings. *Tho* is turning up in company newsletters. I continue to hope *skool* and *enuf* may gain ground in my lifetime. I guess

we can't do much about *right*. Its phonetic spelling *rite* already has another definition. Something like this has happened to *light*. It would be better spelled *lite*, except *lite* now means "low-calorie, or weightless." And we don't have to fix everything: *tion* may be an absurd way to represent *shun*, but it is consistent.

Perhaps it's time for me and my fellow bad spellers to go on the attack. We can start by inventing a new term for ourselves, preferably with many syllables. We can develop a habit of angrily chewing out anyone who refers to us by the shameful phrase, *Bad Speller*. Our platform will be that spelling by sound makes more sense and is kinder than the unchanging **quagmire** of "correct spelling." 11

Having thus gained a voice, we can propose reforms. First, misspellings shall no longer be seen as **miscreant** behavior or as a sign of low IQ. Second, there shall be higher tolerance for letting "sound-correct" spellings creep into the language. Third, schools should be ready to accept changes in spelling as a historically proven fact. 12

Finally, Mark Twain shall be **canonized** as the Patron Saint of Phonetic Letterers. He is credited with the **retort** that should be the rallying cry of our movement: "I don't give a damn for a man that can spell a word only one way." 13

*(960 words)*

## POSTREADING EXERCISE

Now that you have read the selection, revise the sentence you wrote in the prereading exercise.

_____

_____

_____

1. Discuss the revised sentence with a partner, giving support for your ideas. Your partner will listen, take notes, and use the notes to repeat your key ideas.

2. Now trade places with your partner.

## COMPREHENSION EXERCISE
*Circle the letter of the best answer.*

### SKIMMING FOR FACTS

1. Over the years, teachers acted as if the author's poor spelling was
   a. something special.
   b. delinquent behavior.
   c. lost talent.
   d. too much salt in the broccoli.

2. According to the selection, the English alphabet consists of
   a. 21 consonants and seven vowels.
   b. 26 letters that represent 40 letter sounds.
   c. 21 consonants and five vowels.
   d. consonants, vowels, and phonemes.

3. Who spells well in the author's family?
   a. her older sister
   b. her younger sister
   c. her brother
   d. her stepsister

4. To which of the following does the author trace her spelling woes?
   a. double letters
   b. vowels
   c. interchangeable consonants
   d. all of the above

5. According to the author, who wanted to get rid of silent letters?
   a. Noah Webster
   b. Mark Twain
   c. Jonathan Swift
   d. Benjamin Franklin

RELATING THE FACTS

6. Which pattern of organization does paragraph 2 follow?
   a. chronology
   b. cause-effect
   c. example
   d. comparison-contrast

7. Which pattern of organization does paragraph 7 follow?
   a. chronology
   b. cause-effect
   c. example
   d. comparison-contrast

8. Which sentence represents the main idea of paragraph 7?
   a. the first sentence
   b. the second sentence
   c. the third sentence
   d. the fourth sentence

9. Which examples does the author use in paragraph 8 to show that others have "protested the madness"?
   a. William Caxton in the late 1400s
   b. Jonathan Swift, three centuries later
   c. Benjamin Franklin and Noah Webster
   d. all of the above

10. What sentence represents the main idea of paragraph 10?
    a. the first sentence
    b. the second sentence
    c. the third sentence
    d. the last sentence

CONNECTING WITH THE AUTHOR

11. Which of the following inferences can you make from paragraph 1?
    a. The author has been praised for poor spelling throughout her schooling.
    b. The author has allowed her poor spelling to hold her back.
    c. The author's spelling skills improved after high school.
    d. At times, the author's self-esteem has been crushed.

12. Which inference can you make about the pronunciation of "rendezvous" and "psyche" in paragraph 5?
    a. The words do not sound the way they look.
    b. The words have an unusual origin.
    c. The words are good examples of phonics.
    d. The words have a similar meaning.

13. You can conclude from the selection that the author has
    a. learned all of the rules of spelling.
    b. forgotten about spelling.
    c. joined a support group.
    d. accepted her inability to spell.

14. From paragraph 9, you can infer that Noah Webster
    a. was a cousin of Daniel Webster, another poor speller.
    b. did not like silent letters either.
    c. believed that spelling was not that important.
    d. did not have common sense.

15. From paragraph 10, the author appears to believe that
    a. it is too late to make some sensible spelling changes.
    b. spelling changes are made when it becomes necessary.
    c. some change is better than none at all.
    d. all of the above.

16. The author supports her argument with all of the following *except*
    a. quotations from noted authorities.
    b. historical references.
    c. personal references.
    d. online sources.

17. The author ends the selection with
    a. a striking quotation.
    b. a summary of the evidence.
    c. a call to action.
    d. both a and c.

18. Which sentence from the selection states a fact?
    a. "What counts is whether one can group the words well enough to make the check worthwhile."
    b. "Most of my spelling woes can be traced to three idiosyncrasies of English."
    c. "Mark Twain shall be canonized as the Patron Saint of Phonetic Letterers."
    d. "Perhaps it's time for me and my fellow bad spellers to go on the attack."

19. The author appears _____ about her lack of spelling skills.
    a. defensive, angry
    b. surprised, challenged
    c. obsessed, excited
    d. pleased, embarrassed

20. The author's purpose in writing this selection is to
    a. declare publicly her intentions about poor spelling.
    b. point out problems with spelling.
    c. encourage more sensitivity toward poor spellers.
    d. do all of the above.

―――――――――――――――――  **PROGRESS CHART**  ―――――――――――――――――

*Circle the correct responses for each section below. Add the circles and multiply by 5. Record the total here and on the score chart in the Appendix.*

| Skimming for Facts | Relating the Facts | Connecting with the Author | Total |
|---|---|---|---|
| 1  2  3  4  5 | 6  7  8  9  10 | 11  12  13  14  15  16  17  18  19  20 | |

## REFLECTING

Do you agree or disagree with Jennifer Lynn Weston in regard to spelling? Explain. Be sure to mention any spelling problems you may have.

――――――――――――――――――――――――――――――――――――――――――

――――――――――――――――――――――――――――――――――――――――――

――――――――――――――――――――――――――――――――――――――――――

――――――――――――――――――――――――――――――――――――――――――

――――――――――――――――――――――――――――――――――――――――――

――――――――――――――――――――――――――――――――――――――――――

――――――――――――――――――――――――――――――――――――――――――

## COLLABORATING

Weston identifies three general categories of "spelling demons" and gives one or more examples of each. With a group, list one of the author's examples and identify an additional example for each demon listed below. Use your dictionary if needed.

|                                    | AUTHOR'S EXAMPLE | YOUR EXAMPLE |
|------------------------------------|------------------|--------------|
| **1. Double letters—or not?**      | _____  | _____ |
| **2. Interchangeable consonants**  |                  |              |
| *S* and *C*                        | _____  | _____ |
| *S* and *Z*                        | _____  | _____ |
| **3. The great vowel shift**       |                  |              |
| same sound                         | _____  | _____ |
| moved *e* changes *g* sound        | _____  | _____ |
| dual sounds                        | _____  | _____ |
| *i* before *e* exceptions          | (none given)     | _____ |
| silent *e*                         | (none given)     | _____ |

## WEB WATCH

Explore spelling sites on the Internet, looking for one that offers a spelling quiz with answers. Take the quiz and check your answers. How well did you do?

## VOCABULARY EXERCISE

Complete the puzzle with words from the box.

| | | | |
|---|---|---|---|
| canonized | demeanor | deploring | idiosyncrasies |
| lexicographer | miscreant | perspective | quagmire |
| | retort | stymied | |

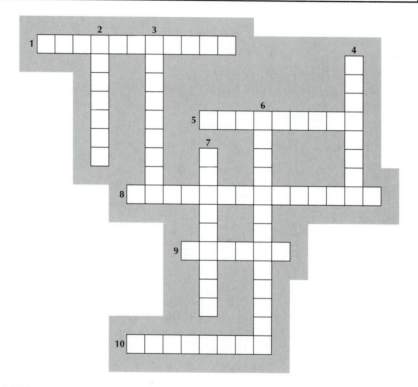

**ACROSS**
1. a view of things
5. regretting strongly
8. oddities
9. counterargument
10. conduct

**DOWN**
2. confused
3. declared a saint
4. difficult situation
6. dictionary maker
7. criminal

Selection 14

# Proper Etiquette Profits Many

*Elizabeth Large*

••••••••••••••••••••••••••••••••••••••••••••••••••••••••••••••••••••

**VOCABULARY REVIEW**
**clichés (cli-ches):** overused expressions
**faux pas (faux pas):** stupid social mistake
**filet mignon (fi-let mig-non):** choice cut of tenderloin beef
**incivility (in-ci-vil-i-ty):** discourtesy, rudeness
**multicultural (mul-ti-cul-tur-al):** having a blend of cultures
**rebellious (re-bel-lious):** opposing any control, defiant
**relevant (rel-e-vant):** relating to the matter in hand

••••••••••••••••••••••••••••••••••••••••••••••••••••••••••••••••••••

**PREREADING EXERCISE**

Study the title, the Vocabulary Review, and the first paragraph of the selection. Then write a sentence expressing what you believe this selection
is about.

_____

_____

Etiquette expert Dorothea Johnson tells the story of the businessman   1
who came to her for help after losing out on a great assignment. At a
lunch meeting with a senior officer in the company, he sat down and
promptly started eating the salad in front of him. He looked up to see his
boss, who hadn't picked up his fork yet, staring at him. "I knew right
then they weren't going to send me out," he said. If only he had taken a
dining tutorial offered by Johnson's Protocol School before his lunch, he
would have known to wait until his host started eating.

In this time of take-out food and dress-down Fridays, etiquette is   2
making a surprising comeback. There is a growing sense bad manners are
strong proof of—or perhaps the first step toward—societal breakdown.
Last year, a *U.S. News & World Report* survey found that 78 percent of
Americans feel that **incivility** has gotten worse in the last 10 years. Most
of the people surveyed believed incivility has contributed to violence,
divided the nation, and worn away values.

Bookstore shelves are filled with best-sellers on modern problems.   3
Among these are subjects such as **multicultural faux pas,** gay etiquette,
and E-mail manners. This is not to mention all-time favorites such as the
75th anniversary edition of *Emily Post's Etiquette* and an endless number
of *Miss Manners'* books.

4    Business has never been better for etiquette classes. Companies are spending hundreds of thousands of dollars for seminars and workshops. Names for this training range from "Business Basics for Professional Polish" to "Customs and Rules for Doing Business Around the World."

5    Colleges and universities have jumped on the bandwagon to give their graduates an edge in the job market. The University of Virginia, for instance, offers Corporate Etiquette Dinners to seniors who want to learn the ins and outs of power dining. Joanne Mahanes, the career counselor who planned the dinners, explains: "Recruiters have not offered jobs to applicants who salt their food before tasting (it shows hasty decision making) or who order **filet mignon.** (They think such a person would go wild on an expense account.)"

6    But why now? Why does manners suddenly matter again to so many people? We don't know how to hold a wine glass. We aren't sure when to send handwritten thank-you notes. And we need someone to tell us what gift would be right for the host or hostess at a dinner party.

7    (At a seated dinner, hold a white glass by the stem and a red wine glass by the bottom of the bowl. A handwritten thank-you note is always proper. Don't bring cut flowers because the host will have to stop preparing dinner or greeting guests to find a vase. A bottle of wine or a plant are possible choices.)

8    No one is quite sure why good manners are **relevant** again—or at least why etiquette experts are making a lot of money on classes, tutorials, and books. But here are some contributing factors.

9    We may know the right fork to use but still be unsure about the etiquette of modern technology. For that we are buying books like *Miss Manners' Basic Training: Communication.* The rules range from *Don't write e-mail in capitals* (it's the same as shouting) to *Don't pull your pager out and check it during religious services.*

10    Today's parents are aware that while good manners will help their children get along in life, they aren't the ones to teach them. "Two generations now haven't been taught manners," says columnist and author Letitia Baldrige. The **rebellious** '60s and '70s, the greedy '80s may be **clichés,** but clearly etiquette wasn't a top priority in the last few decades. Even if parents feel qualified to teach manners, they may not have time due to single-parent households or both parents working. If family mealtimes are a thing of the past, when are children going to learn not to butter all their bread at once? Or, more important, when will they learn how to hold polite dinner table conversation?

11    Mary Mitchell, who writes the newspaper column *Ms. Demeanor,* sums up three studies by Harvard, the Stanford Research Institute, and the Carnegie Foundation. These studies suggest that success in a job depends 85 percent on "people skills" and only 15 percent on trade knowledge and skills. It's no wonder companies competing in the business world have started in-house training programs for their top officers. They

are hiring etiquette consultants to teach such basics as the proper way to shake hands, how to make introductions, and where to put one's briefcase or handbag.

(Shake "web-to-web" and realize that it's the one acceptable touching between sexes in business. When making introductions, mention the most important person's name first. When visiting someone else's office, put your briefcase or purse on the floor beside you, not on a table or desk.) 12

Top companies hire Mary Crane, director of training for Jaffe Associates. She teaches *client development skills*, not manners. *Client development skills* could include anything from how to place a napkin in your lap to how to present a business card to, or accept one from, a Japanese businessman. Crane gets as much as $1,500 for a one-hour presentation. "Their willingness to pay shows that companies are fairly serious about this," she says. 13

Doing business all over the world has created a whole new set of etiquette problems. Business people are finding they need to know how to deal with a finger bowl. But they also need to know that a thumbs-up signal has the same meaning in Afghanistan as the American middle-finger gesture. Companies are finding it more and more necessary to hire experts on dealing with the social risks of a global economy. 14

Closer to home, we are becoming such a multicultural society that people need to know how to avoid embarrassment in social situations with people from different countries. Norine Dresser, in fact, writes a regular column for the *Los Angeles Times* on multicultural manners. 15

The important thing to remember, though, is that good manners are more than rules of behavior. They can make life easier. "It's not about being formal," says Peggy Post, author of *Emily Post's Etiquette*. "It's not haves and have-nots. It's a method by which we can all get along." 16

*(1,050 words)*

## POSTREADING EXERCISE

Now that you have read the selection, revise the sentence you wrote in the prereading exercise.

_____

_____

_____

1. Discuss the revised sentence with a partner, giving support for your ideas. Your partner will listen, take notes, and use the notes to repeat your key ideas.

2. Now trade places with your partner.

## COMPREHENSION EXERCISE

*Circle the letter of the best answer.*

### SKIMMING FOR FACTS

1. According to the selection, the businessman lost out on the assignment because he
   a. did not know how to do the job.
   b. ate all of his salad.
   c. used the wrong utensil to eat his salad.
   d. began eating before his boss.

2. Which one of the following sources is *not* mentioned as a way to learn about etiquette?

   a. presentations          g. dinners
   b. workshops              h. counselors
   c. classes               i. seminars
   d. newspapers            j. experts
   e. peers                 k. consultants
   f. books                 l. tutorials

3. Recruiters have *not* offered jobs to candidates who salt their food before tasting because this would show
   a. poor health.
   b. good taste.
   c. hasty decision making.
   d. high stress.

4. How much does Mary Crane charge for her training services?
   a. $100 per hour
   b. $500 per hour
   c. $1,500 per hour
   d. $2,500 per hour

5. Put a check mark in front of each statement that suggests proper etiquette.
   _____ a. At a meal, wait until your host starts eating.
   _____ b. Butter all of your bread at once.
   _____ c. Hold a white wine glass by the stem.
   _____ d. Hold a red wine glass by the bottom of the bowl.
   _____ e. Bring cut flowers to the host at a dinner party.
   _____ f. Write e-mail in capitals.
   _____ g. Check your pager during church services.
   _____ h. Shake web-to-web.
   _____ i. When visiting someone's office, place your purse or briefcase on the person's desk, not on the floor.
   _____ j. A handwritten thank-you note is always proper.

**RELATING THE FACTS**

6. Which sentence best expresses the main idea of paragraph 3?
   a. sentence 1
   b. sentence 2
   c. sentence 3
   d. none of the above

7. Which sentence best expresses the main idea of paragraph 10?
   a. Parents have not taught their children manners, and businesses are having to do it.
   b. "Two generations now haven't been taught manners."
   c. Parents know good manners are important, but clearly they are not the ones to teach them to their children.
   d. Etiquette was not a priority in the 1960s and 1970s.

8. Which sentence best expresses the main idea of paragraph 14?
   a. sentence 1
   b. sentence 2
   c. sentence 3
   d. sentence 4

9. Place a check mark beside each sentence that gives a reason for good manners to become relevant again in today's society.
   _____ a. We are unsure about the etiquette of modern technology.
   _____ b. People have lost their way in this world.
   _____ c. Children spend too much time fighting with each other.
   _____ d. Parents cannot teach their children manners.
   _____ e. Job success depends on reading skills.
   _____ f. Doing business all over the world calls for new knowledge.
   _____ g. Children embarrass their parents at company dinners.
   _____ h. We live in a multicultural society.
   _____ i. Foreigners want their habits to remain secret.
   _____ j. They make life easier and help us all get along.

10. How would you classify e-mail and pagers?
    a. communications equipment
    b. computer information networks
    c. telecommunications equipment
    d. electrical equipment

**CONNECTING WITH THE AUTHOR**

11. Why is teaching "client development skills" rather than "manners" a better title for company training?
    a. The whole person is treated.
    b. All matters related to proper behavior are being taught, not just manners.

c. Manners is just one part of etiquette.

d. Clients expect employers to teach personal development.

12. Giving an Afghan businessman the thumbs-up signal
    a. assures him of your satisfaction.
    b. insults him.
    c. gives him great satisfaction.
    d. earns his respect but not his business.

13. The author seems to suggest that
    a. there is much interest in family life today.
    b. hugging is an acceptable business practice.
    c. there are no rules for dinner-table conversation.
    d. poor etiquette carries a high price.

14. To introduce the U.S. President to your instructor, mention
    a. the instructor's name first.
    b. the president's name first.
    c. your name first.
    d. both names at the same time.

15. From the selection, you can infer that businesses today
    a. cannot help employees learn proper manners.
    b. have little or no interest in manners.
    c. see a strong relationship between profits and manners.
    d. will not hire a person known to have poor manners.

16. The author assumes that the reader is
    a. in need of help with proper manners.
    b. familiar with all rules of etiquette.
    c. a smart businessman.
    d. a savage person.

17. The author begins the selection with a
    a. riddle.
    b. comparison.
    c. short story.
    d. common voice.

18. Paragraph 4 consists of
    a. facts only.
    b. one opinion and two facts.
    c. opinions only.
    d. one fact and two opinions.

19. What does the author mean when she says that colleges and
    universities have "jumped on the bandwagon"?
    a. These schools are being taken for a ride.
    b. These schools train students to enjoy music.
    c. These schools now provide etiquette training for students.
    d. These schools carry their bands in wagons.

20. From paragraph 10, the clichés "rebellious '60s and '70s" and "greedy '80s" suggest
   a. less control and authority.
   b. unruly childhood behavior.
   c. increased yearning for days gone by.
   d. war and poverty.

**PROGRESS CHART**

*Circle the correct responses for each section below. Add the circles and multiply by 5. Record the total here and on the score chart in the Appendix.*

| Skimming for Facts | Relating the Facts | Connecting with the Author | Total |
|---|---|---|---|
| 1  2  3  4  5 | 6  7  8  9  10 | 11  12  13  14  15  16  17  18  19  20 | |

## REFLECTING

*Think of a time when you or a friend committed a manners faux pas. What was the faux pas, and what were the results?*

_____

_____

_____

## COLLABORATING

With a group, develop a ten-item true-false quiz on manners from the contents of the selection. Use your quiz to test your classmates' knowledge of manners. Summarize your findings, and share them with the class.

## WEB WATCH

On the Internet, conduct a search on the topic of manners. Take a manners quiz, play a game, or read an interesting article. Did you benefit from this experience? Explain.

## VOCABULARY EXERCISE

Complete the puzzle with words from the box.

| | | | |
|---|---|---|---|
| clichés | faux pas | filet mignon | incivility |
| multicultural | rebellious | relevant | |

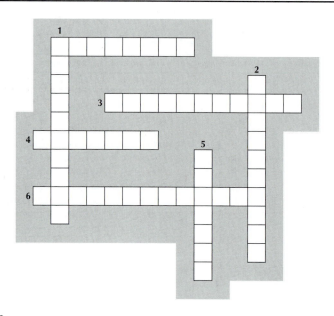

### ACROSS
1. Parents believe that manners are _____ again in our society.

3. The dinner menu offers a choice of roast beef or _____.

4. Such familiar _____ as "Have a good day" and "See you later" were worn out a long time ago.

6. A(n) _____ society may be seen as the strength of America.

### DOWN
1. The _____ daughter ran away from home.

2. _____ is often seen as a symptom of the decay of society.

5. A manners _____ can be embarrassing.

# Tips on Reading

## *Sociology*

Sociology is the study of group behavior. Its major focus involves people working together in social situations. One key topic in sociology is social institutions, such as marriage, family, education, and religion. In a civilized society, all institutions have expectations for behavior that govern individual and group conduct.

Much of the content in a sociology textbook, like other science texts, is based on research studies. "Lee's Styles of Loving" describes several different types of love. To understand this and other readings in sociology, pay close attention to the following guidelines:

- *Preview the material*, looking closely at patterns of organization, headings, examples, tables, charts and graphs, and end-of-chapter questions.
- *Study the subject area terminology*, using the vocabulary card system to learn new words.
- As you read, look for questions that are being investigated.
- *Try to recognize the scientific method* that social scientists use in their research. This method begins with an educated guess or theoretical model about group behavior. Three commonly used models in this field are conflict, functionalism, and symbolic interactionism. *Conflict*

deals with group struggles over power (e.g., the rich and poor). *Funct-ionalism* looks at different elements in society and their relationship to each other (e.g., drugs and the economy). *Symbolic interactionism* looks at and records actions of individuals operating in society (e.g., Dr. Martin Luther King, Jr.'s actions).

• *Be aware of bias,* the author's feelings about or slant on the subject. Bias may be revealed in the explanation of the results of experiments and in the generalizations made. As a critical reader, read to see if these conclusions are based on factual evidence.

Selection 15

# Sociology: Lee's Styles of Loving

*Nijole Benokraitis*

······································

**VOCABULARY REVIEW**
**altruistic (al-tru-is-tic):** having an unselfish concern for others
**conjugal (con-ju-gal):** between husband and wife
**ecstatic (ec-stat-ic):** having a feeling of overpowering joy
**epitomizes (e-pit-o-mizes):** provides a typical example of
**insatiable (in-sa-ti-a-ble):** impossible to satisfy
**masochism (mas-och-ism):** pleasure from humiliation
**palpitating (pal-pi-tat-ing):** beating rapidly
**rapport (rap-port):** sympathetic relationship; harmony
**reciprocity (rec-i-proc-i-ty):** a mutual exchange
**theory (the-o-ry):** an educated guess

······································

**PREREADING EXERCISE**

Study the title, the Vocabulary Review, the first paragraph, and the major headings of the selection. Then ask four questions that you think might be answered in this selection.

1. _____

2. _____

3. _____

4. _____

One of the most well-known and studied approaches to love was  1
developed by sociologist John A. Lee. Lee's approach is not a **theory.** It
was built on his collection of more than 4,000 statements about love from
hundreds of works of fiction and nonfiction. Included was the literature
of ancient Greece and the Bible through the work of modern writers. Lee
asked people in Great Britain and Canada 30 questions based on this
research. He grouped their responses into six basic styles of loving: eros,
mania, ludus, storge, agape, and pragma. All styles overlap and vary in
strength in real life.

## EROS

Eros (root of the word *erotic*) is the love of beauty. It is identified by  2
powerful physical attraction. It **epitomizes** "love at first sight." It is the
kind of love often seen in romance novels. The lovers are immediately
love-struck. They experience **palpitating** hearts, lightheadedness, and
intense emotional desire.

3      Erotic lovers want to know everything about the loved one. They want to know, for example, what she or he dreamed about last night and what happened on the way to work today. Erotic lovers often like to wear matching T-shirts, matching bracelets, and matching colors. They like to order the same foods when dining out. They want to be identified with each other as totally as possible.

## MANIA

4      Manic lovers are jealous, possessive, obsessive, and intensely dependent. They experience anxiety, sleeplessness, loss of appetite, and headaches. They are consumed by thoughts of their lover. They have an **insatiable** need for attention and signs of affection.

5      Often senseless, manic lovers may even consider suicide because of real or imagined rejection. Because of their high level of anxiety, manic lovers often have sexual problems. Mania is probably linked with low self-esteem and a poor self-concept. As a result, manic people are often not attractive to those who have a strong self-concept and high self-esteem.

## LUDUS

6      Ludus is carefree and casual love. It is often "fun and games." Its delight comes more from playing the game than from winning the prize. Physical appearance is less important to ludic lovers than self-sufficiency and a nondemanding partner. Ludic lovers try to control their feelings and may have several lovers at one time. They are not possessive or jealous. This is largely because they don't want lovers to become dependent on them. Ludic lovers have sex for fun, not emotional **rapport.** During sex, they are usually selfish and may even be abusive because they dislike commitment. They consider it "scary."

## STORGE

7      Storge (pronounced "stor-gay") is a slow-burning, peaceful, and tender love. It "just comes naturally" with the passage of time and the enjoyment of shared activities. Storge-type unions lack the **ecstatic** highs and lows of despair that are common among other styles. Sex occurs late, and the goals are usually marriage, home, and children. Even if they break up, storgic lovers are likely to remain good friends.

8      The storgic lover finds regular home activities relaxing and comfortable. Because there is shared trust, short separations are not seen as a problem. Anniversaries, birthdays, and Valentine's Day are not important to storgic lovers. Special times such as these may be forgotten or shaded by other matters. Storgic love may also be called **conjugal** love. Affection develops over the years, as in many lasting marriages. Passion may be replaced by spirituality, respect, and comfort in the enjoyment of each other's company.

## AGAPE

Agape (pronounced "ah-gah-pay") is the perfect Christian type of love. 9
It is **altruistic,** self-sacrificing, and directed toward all mankind. It is a
self-giving love in which partners help each other develop to their full
potential. They do this without considering the costs to themselves.
Agape is always kind and patient. It is never jealous or hard to please. It
does not seek **reciprocity.** Lee points out, however, that he has never yet
met a pure example of agape.

Intense agape can border on **masochism.** For example, an agapic per- 10
son might wait forever for a lover to be sent home from prison or from
a mental hospital. Another might put up with an alcoholic or drug-
addicted spouse. Still another might be willing to live with a partner who
engages in unlawful or sinful activities.

## PRAGMA

According to Lee, pragma is rational. It is based on practical concerns 11
such as compatibility and perceived benefits. In truth, it can be described
as "love with a shopping list." A pragmatic person seeks compatibility in
such things as background, education, religion, and vocational and professional interests. If one love does not work out, the pragmatic person
moves on, quite wisely, to search for someone else. Computer-matching
services usually are based on pragmatic views.

Pragmatic lovers are realistic about their own assets. They decide on 12
their "market value" and set off to get the best possible "deal." If the
assets of either partner change, a pragmatic lover may feel that his or her
contract has been broken and may search for another partner. Pragmatic
lovers look out for their partners. For example, they encourage them to
ask for a promotion or to finish college. They are also practical in divorce.
A couple might stay together until the youngest child finishes high school
or until both partners find better jobs.

Researchers have developed dozens of scales to measure the models 13
of love and close relations that Lee proposed. [The table below] presents
some items from the Love Attitudes Scale that was first developed by the
Lasswells and modified by later researchers.

## THE LOVE ATTITUDES SCALE

If you're dating, you can use this scale to examine your own and your
partner's feelings. If you've never been in love or have no partner now,
answer in terms of what you think your responses might be. Keep in
mind that there are no wrong answers to these statements. They're
designed simply to improve your understanding. For each item, mark a
"1" for strongly agree, "2" for somewhat agree, "3" for neutral, "4" for
somewhat disagree, and "5" for strongly disagree.

## EROS

_____ 1. My partner and I were attracted to each other immediately after we first met.

_____ 2. Our lovemaking is very intense and satisfying.

_____ 3. My partner fits my standards of physical beauty/handsomeness.

## LUDUS

_____ 4. What my partner doesn't know about me won't hurt him/her.

_____ 5. I sometimes have to keep my partner from finding out about other partners.

_____ 6. I could get over my partner pretty easily and quickly.

## PRAGMA

_____ 7. In choosing my partner, I believed it was best to love someone with a similar background.

_____ 8. An important factor in choosing my partner was whether or not he/she would be a good parent.

_____ 9. One consideration in choosing my partner was how he/she would reflect on my career.

## AGAPE

_____ 10. I would rather suffer myself than let my partner suffer.

_____ 11. My partner can use whatever I own as she/he chooses.

_____ 12. I would endure all things for the sake of my partner.

## STORGE

_____ 13. I expect to always be friends with the people I date.

_____ 14. The best kind of love grows out of a long friendship.

_____ 15. Love is a deep friendship, not a mysterious, passionate emotion.

Scoring: Average your totals for each section. The lowest total represents your style.

*(1170 Words)*

## POSTREADING EXERCISE

Write answers to the four questions you wrote in the prereading exercise.

1. _____

_____

2. _____

_____

3. _____

_____

4. _____

_____

## PROCESSING INFORMATION

1. Read the review questions that follow the concept map below.
2. Highlight key ideas in the selection.
3. Complete the concept map below with a definition of each style of loving and its chief characteristics.
4. Answer the review questions.

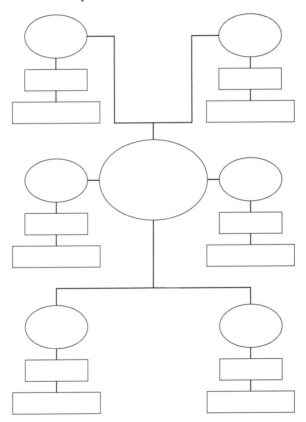

## REVIEW QUESTIONS
*Circle the letter of the best answer.*

1. Which love type exhibits jealous tendencies?
   - a. mania
   - b. ludus
   - c. storge
   - d. pragma

2. Which love type would never ask for anything in return?
   a. storge          b. eros
   c. mania           d. agape

3. Which love type has the most flexible relationship?
   a. mania           b. pragma
   c. ludus           d. agape

4. Which love type would endure much pain and suffering?
   a. storge          b. pragma
   c. eros            d. agape

5. Because manic lovers probably have low self-concepts, they are attractive to people who are
   a. bossy.
   b. able leaders.
   c. strong-willed and bold.
   d. much like themselves.

6. Why do erotic lovers want to be identified with each other as totally as possible?
   a. Outsiders will know that they belong to someone else.
   b. They can show the world that they are in harmony.
   c. They are sending a message of togetherness to others.
   d. All of the above.

7. Which love type would find it difficult to support a child?
   a. storge          b. pragma
   c. ludus           d. agape

8. If a storgic lover saw his ex-wife having lunch alone in a restaurant, which action would he most likely take?
   a. join her
   b. start a fight
   c. pretend not to see her
   d. none of the above

9. A pragmatic lover would be quite upset if her partner
   a. quit work.
   b. suffered a big loss in the stock market.
   c. did not ask for a deserved raise.
   d. did all of the above.

10. What do all love styles have in common?
   a. a passion for another person
   b. commitment to a relationship
   c. intimacy
   d. none of the above

---

Score: Number correct _____ (out of 10) × 10 = _____

## SHORT ANSWER
*Write a brief description of each of Lee's six love styles.*

1. Agape: _____

   _____

2. Eros: _____

   _____

3. Ludus: _____

   _____

4. Mania: _____

   _____

5. Pragma: _____

   _____

6. Storge: _____

   _____

*Complete the Love Attitudes Scale and answer the questions below according to your scores on the scale.*

7. Which is your preferred love style? _____

8. Which is your second preferred style? _____

9. Which is your least preferred love style? _____

10. Do you agree or disagree with these findings? _____

11. What conclusions can you draw on the basis of these results?

    _____

    _____

## REFLECTING

Mnemonics are words, rhymes, and jingles to help you remember. To make a "word mnemonic" to help you remember the six love styles, write the first letter of each of the six styles of love, arrange the six letters to form a word, and then rearrange the letters to form another word.

### Letters
1. _____     2. _____
3. _____     4. _____
5. _____     6. _____

   **Word 1:** _____

   **Word 2:** _____

## COLLABORATING

With a group, use a data collection sheet similar to the one below to collect information from your classmates. Sort and classify the information, and make comparisons between love type and other characteristics (age, height, etc.) to see if you can make some interesting discoveries. Next, draw a circle graph or bar graph to illustrate the comparisons. Then write a paragraph discussing your findings.

### Data Collection Sheet

|  |  | CHARACTERISTICS | | |
| --- | --- | --- | --- | --- |
| STUDENT | LOVE STYLE | AGE | SEX | ———— |
| 1 | ———— | ———— | ———— | ———— |
| 2 | ———— | ———— | ———— | ———— |
| 3 | ———— | ———— | ———— | ———— |
| 4 | ———— | ———— | ———— | ———— |
| 5 | ———— | ———— | ———— | ———— |
| 6 | ———— | ———— | ———— | ———— |
| 7 | ———— | ———— | ———— | ———— |
| 8 | ———— | ———— | ———— | ———— |
| 9 | ———— | ———— | ———— | ———— |
| 10 | ———— | ———— | ———— | ———— |

In surveying classmates who took the Love Attitude Scale, our group made several discoveries:

First, ———————————————————————————————————

————————————————————————————————————————

Second, ——————————————————————————————————

————————————————————————————————————————

Third, ———————————————————————————————————

————————————————————————————————————————

In conclusion, ————————————————————————————

## WEB WATCH

Check out the following Internet sites and learn something about yourself. If these sites are no longer available, locate other sites related to careers in sociology and determine the varied career paths available.

http://askDr.Love
http://lovecalculator.com
http://www.abcdating.co.uk/offers.htm

## VOCABULARY EXERCISE

Complete the puzzle with words from the box.

| | | | | |
|---|---|---|---|---|
| altruism | conjugal | ecstatic | epitomizes | insatiable |
| masochism | palpitating | rapport | reciprocity | theory |

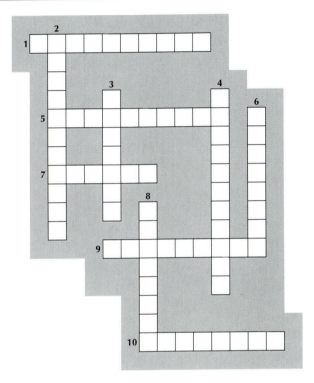

**ACROSS**

1. represents
5. not able to satisfy
7. a guess or idea
9. enjoying pain and punishment
10. of or between spouses

**DOWN**

2. beating rapidly
3. a close relationship
4. give and take
6. concern for others
8. extremely happy

# POSTTEST

PREREADING EXERCISE

Study the title, the Vocabulary Review, and the first paragraph of the selection. Then write three questions that you believe will be answered by your reading.

1. _____

2. _____

3. _____

## Married . . . with Problems

*Joannie M. Schrof*

**VOCABULARY REVIEW**
**cashmere (cash-mere):** soft woolen material
**coercion (co-er-cion):** pressure, force
**dubious (du-bi-ous):** doubtful
**embattled (em-bat-tled):** fighting
**empathy (em-pa-thy):** feelings for another
**eons (e-ons):** years; a long time
**excruciating (ex-cru-ci-at-ing):** severe, intense
**fixate (fix-ate):** focus attention; stop
**formidable (for-mi-da-ble):** strong, worthy
**impasse (im-passe):** deadlock; an inability to move further
**intractable (in-trac-ta-ble):** hard to treat
**ire (ire):** anger or irritation
**salvage (sal-vage):** to save

Last January, after 33 years together, a husband and wife in a small     1
town found their marriage crumbling. He had recently retired from the
farming business. And as the months wore on, he became depressed. He
responded to his wife only with grunts. She, meanwhile, had taken her
first job ever, in a bank. She awoke each morning excited about the day
ahead. By Christmas, his low spirits and her excitement clashed so much
that he refused to eat meals with her. She refused to sleep with him. It
took their children's refusal to visit for the wife to ask their pastor for the
name of a good counselor. After the first session, they found themselves
laughing together for the first time in **eons**—about the therapist. "We
joked that we would have made better counselors ourselves," recalls the
wife. In the end, she kept her husband and got rid of the therapist.

2      There are roughly twice as many people seeking couples therapy today as there were 20 years ago. In fact, couples now make up the fastest-growing group who come knocking on therapists' doors. Although exact statistics are hard to come by, the number of professionals licensed to practice marital therapy gives some indication of the trend. In 1972, 1,000 counselors were licensed marital therapists. A decade later, there were 9,000. Today, the number of marital therapists is fast approaching 500,000, and psychology journals regularly report on the difficulty of keeping up with demand.

3      The odds that all this therapy will keep partners together, however, are less than compelling. Couples therapy has a **dubious** success rate. In fact, research shows it is far less effective than individual therapy. In a recent review of couples-therapy research in the *Journal of Marital and Family Therapy*, psychologists James Bray and Ernest Jouriles revealed two stunning facts. Regardless of the technique used, no more than half the couples who sought therapy reported significant increases in their happiness together. And of the half who were helped, 30 percent were likely to have serious trouble again before long. Measuring the success of any type of therapy is a tricky business because different researchers use different definitions of success. However, the above figures are much lower than those commonly cited for individual treatment. Eighty percent of clients undergoing any form of therapy report significant progress after six months.

#### MAKING PROGRESS

4      In the past, most couples therapists accepted such low success rates as an inevitable fact of their work. Recently, however, researchers have begun to identify flaws in traditional couples-therapy techniques. As a result, many counselors are changing their approaches to treating couples. And at least one experimental method holds promise of increasing the chances that a couple trying to save their marriage will succeed.

5      It only makes sense that two people—especially two **embattled** people—would be harder to treat than one. "Couples therapy only becomes truly possible after the therapist learns how to keep a couple's fighting from destroying the therapy," notes psychologist Daniel Wile, author of *Couples Therapy*. Too many therapists, he says, never get that far. They act merely as "referees" for the latest fight. Some therapists even claim that by the time couples are upset enough to go to therapy, it may be too late to **salvage** the relationship.

6      But the biggest shortcoming of most therapy methods, research suggests, is that they **fixate** on changing behavior. Couples who come to therapy have usually reached an **impasse**. She can't get him to go to church with her and the kids; he can't get her to make time for just the two of them. Although most therapists try a wide range of techniques with any given couple, the most-studied method of helping partners settle disputes is known as "behavior marital therapy" (BMT). The husband, for example, agrees to change his behavior (he'll go to church once a month).

The wife agrees to one night out a month. And both agree to stop yelling at each other.

It sounds good, and in some cases it works. The problem is that change—as anyone who has tried to alter the ways of another knows—doesn't come easily. In a 1997 Yale University survey of marital therapists, 29 percent cited the unwillingness of couples to change their behavior as the main reason for therapy's failure. Even the founder of BMT, psychologist Neil Jacobsen, says that after years of practicing his own method with only a 50 percent success rate, he, too, concluded that some of his clients would never change.    7

In 1991, Jacobson teamed up with UCLA psychologist Andrew Christensen to find some other way to reach couples locked in **intractable** conflict. Their first step was to study the methods of therapists less concerned with resolving conflict and more focused on **empathy.** BMT, Jacobson and Christensen concluded, can often backfire. "We finally realized that the very pressure to change acts as a **formidable** barrier to that change," says Jacobsen. "In the face of perceived **coercion,** most people throw up their defenses and withdraw." But when that pressure disappears, he says, a new climate is created. As a result, partners sometimes change even more than their spouses had hoped.    8

The two researchers developed a new couples-therapy technique called "Integrative Couples Therapy"—often referred to as "acceptance" therapy. The goal, not surprisingly, is for spouses to quit trying to change the annoying things about each other. Instead they should find ways to accept, if not cherish, those qualities in their partner that are unlikely to change (obviously, verbal or physical abuse is never acceptable). "If a therapist can help spouses quit viewing one another's behavior as evil and begin to see it as necessary and natural," says Christensen, "then the same problems can continue to occur, but without such an emotional sting." Her temper may still flare, but he won't be as hurt by it.    9

## PROMISING RESULTS

Though acceptance therapy is not yet widely practiced, it shows promise of reaching many couples not helped by BMT or other traditional methods. A pilot study of 20 couples considering divorce found that after six months of acceptance therapy, 90 percent reported incredible increases in satisfaction. And a year later, none had split up. The National Institute of Mental Health is now funding clinical trials for acceptance therapy involving 180 couples. Results of that study are five years off, but therapists are already bringing some of the ideas into their practices. "What we're most excited about," says Jacobson, "is that this method is successful with many of the couples least helped by behavioral therapy. These couples include older people in more traditional marriages."    10

One such couple, now living in Southern California, went to Christensen after the wife blurted out to her individual therapist: "He's destroying me!" Three decades of life under the thumb of a man who constantly criticized her and their five children, she said, had left her    11 with repeated bouts of **excruciating** stomach pain. Today, after 1½ years of acceptance therapy, the couple are about to celebrate their 37th wedding anniversary. They say they're happier than ever. "I still tell her it's ridiculous to spend $500 on a coat that's really just a scarf," the husband says. But his **ire** is gone. The wife, proud owner of a new $500 **cashmere** stole, says she has learned that his criticism doesn't threaten their love for each other. "You have to make the same realization with your spouse as you do with your children," says the husband. "They are unique, separate from you. And as much as you wish they might be different, they are who they are." Couples therapists face the same challenge: The best thing they can do for their clients may be to quit trying to change them.

*(1,290 words)*

## POSTREADING EXERCISE

Now that you have read the selection, answer the questions you wrote in the prereading exercise.

1. _____

_____

2. _____

_____

3. _____

_____

## COMPREHENSION EXERCISE
*Circle the letter of the best answer.*

### SKIMMING FOR FACTS

1. The biggest shortcoming of most therapy methods is
   a. changing behavior.
   b. determining who is right.
   c. refereeing office fights.
   d. identifying the problem.

2. The new therapy technique is called
   a. Integrative Couples Therapy.
   b. Couples Therapy.
   c. Empathy Counseling.
   d. Forgiveness Counseling and Therapy.

3. In 1982, there were _____ licensed marital therapists.
   a. 1,000
   b. 2,000
   c. 5,000
   d. 9,000

4. The most-studied method of solving problems between partners is known as
   a. behavior marital therapy.
   b. acceptance therapy.
   c. couples therapy.
   d. none of the above.

5. After six months of acceptance therapy, couples considering divorce reported
   a. increased satisfaction.
   b. decreased satisfaction.
   c. excellent progress.
   d. no change.

**RELATING THE FACTS**

6. The main idea of paragraph 2 is found in the
   a. first sentence.
   b. second sentence.
   c. third sentence.
   d. last sentence.

7. The main idea of paragraph 7 is found in the
   a. first sentence.
   b. second sentence.
   c. third sentence.
   d. last sentence.

8. How would you categorize the last three sentences in paragraph 2?
   a. topic sentences
   b. major details
   c. minor details
   d. the key idea

9. Which pattern of organization does the author use in paragraph 1?
   a. chronology
   b. classification
   c. comparison-contrast
   d. example

10. Which pattern of organization does the author use in paragraph 6?
    a. chronology
    b. classification

c.  comparison-contrast

d.  example

11.  What can you infer about the husband and wife in paragraph 1?
     a.  They wanted only one child.
     b.  The husband adjusted easily to retirement.
     c.  The husband felt useless and productive.
     d.  The husband resented his wife's new sense of freedom.

12.  What can you infer from paragraph 4?
     a.  Couples therapists would consider a 90 percent success rate average.
     b.  If couples therapists were to strive for perfection, they would be disappointed every time.
     c.  Couples therapy is one profession that cannot be improved.
     d.  Older couples usually solve their own problems.

13.  From paragraph 8, you can infer that Jacobson and Christensen probably
     a.  used a scientific approach to study ways of reaching couples with serious problems.
     b.  focused on creating an environment for change.
     c.  brought unexpected satisfaction to many of their clients.
     d.  did all of the above.

14.  From paragraph 11, it appears that
     a.  the California woman wanted a trial separation.
     b.  unhappy relationships can lead to mental and physical illnesses.
     c.  financial disagreements do not affect marital relations.
     d.  children and spouses have different purchasing habits.

15.  From paragraph 2, you can conclude
     a.  that marriages are becoming more difficult to maintain.
     b.  that licensing agencies have increased their personnel.
     c.  that licensed therapists must have a degree in one of the social sciences.
     d.  All of the above.

16.  What valid generalization can you make from paragraph 10?
     a.  It is impossible to teach an old dog new tricks.
     b.  Most traditional couples will prefer the couples therapy approach.
     c.  All couples can benefit from acceptance therapy.
     d.  Both a and b.

17.  Which of the following devices does the author use to capture the reader's attention at the beginning of the selection?
     a.  a quotation
     b.  an anecdote (short story)

c. a comparison
d. a question

18. Which statement from the selection can be verified?
    a. "Her temper may still flare, but he won't be as hurt by it."
    b. "There are roughly twice as many people seeking couples therapy today as there were 20 years ago."
    c. "It sounds good, and in some cases it works."
    d. "It only makes sense that two people—especially two embattled people—would be harder to treat than one."

19. How would you describe the tone of this selection?
    a. persuasive
    b. critical
    c. optimistic
    d. humorous

20. The author's purpose in writing this selection is to
    a. criticize and humiliate.
    b. inform and give hope.
    c. interpret and entertain.
    d. identify and solve a problem.

## VOCABULARY REVIEW

*Fill in the blanks with words from the box.*

| | | | | |
|---|---|---|---|---|
| cashmere | coercion | dubious | embattled | empathy |
| eons | excruciating | fixate | formidable | impasse |
| | intractable | ire | salvage | |

21. Sally did not try to hide her _____ from the mother whose child had broken the window.

22. A(n) _____ coat is warm and soft.

23. Extracting a tooth without a painkiller causes _____ pain.

24. Perhaps we can _____ the chair; its arm is scorched slightly.

25. To _____ on a computer screen for hours at a time may tire your eyes.

26. The jury reached a(n) _____; they did not render a decision in the case.

27. His _____ for the hungry children standing at his door caused him to invite them in for breakfast.

28. After losing the game in double overtime to a "Cinderella team," the _____ football players exited the field in disgrace.

29. It was _____ ago when the pilgrims came over on the Mayflower.

30. The witness' last remark was so _____ that I don't believe any of her testimony now.

31. Couples locked in _____ conflict pose a threat to the success rate of most marriage counselors.

32. Because of the cult leader's _____, his followers filed into the cell one by one.

33. "Big Pete" and "The Roc" are _____ foes; nobody wants to wrestle them.

Name: _____ , Course/Section: _____ , Date: _____

# POSTTEST SCORE AND COMPREHENSION ERROR REVIEW CHART

## POSTTEST SCORE
*Record the number of correct answers and perform operations in the box.*

Central Idea _____ (out of 1) × 9 = _____

Vocabulary _____ (out of 13) × 7 = _____

Comprehension _____ (out of 20) × 5 = _____

Total               = _____ divided by 2 = _____

**Posttest score: _____ (out of 100)**

## COMPREHENSION ERROR REVIEW

*To identify strengths and weaknesses, circle the number of any incorrect answer in numbers 1–20 of the posttest.*

   *The numbers circled indicate your weaknesses. Read across the line to identify chapter sections and topics that require your attention.*

| Item # | Chapter Section and Reading Skill |
|---|---|
| | ***Skimming for Facts*** |
| 1 | (3b.2) Major Detail (3b.3) Minor Detail |
| 2 | (3b.2) Major Detail (3b.3) Minor Detail |
| 3 | (3b.2) Major Detail (3b.3) Minor Detail |
| 4 | (3b.2) Major Detail (3b.3) Minor Detail |
| 5 | (3b.2) Major Detail (3b.3) Minor Detail |
| | ***Relating the Facts*** |
| 6 | (3a.4) Stated Main Idea (3a.5) Implied Main Idea |
| 7 | (3b.1) Signal Words (3b.4) Paragraph Patterns |
| 8 | (3a.1) General and Specific Ideas (3a.2) Topic (3a.3) Key Idea (3a.4) Stated Main Ideas (3b.2) Major Detail (3b.3) Minor Detail |
| 9 | (3b.1) Signal Words (3b.4) Paragraph Patterns |
| 10 | (3b.1) Signal Words (3b.4) Paragraph Patterns |
| | ***Connecting with the Author*** |
| 11 | (4a.1) Inferences |
| 12 | (4a.1) Inferences |
| 13 | (4a.1) Inferences |

| 14 | (4a.1) Inferences |
| 15 | (4a.2) Conclusions (4a.3) Making Predictions |
| 16 | (4a.4) Generalizations |
| 17 | (4b.2) Style (4b.3) Figurative Language |
| 18 | (4b.1) Fact-Opinion |
| 19 | (4b.2) Tone (4b.2) Mood |
| 20 | (4b.2) Audience (4b.2) Purpose |

## GOAL STATEMENT

*Considering the error review above, write a paragraph comparing your pretest and posttest. Describe the improvements you have made in reading this semester. End with a statement of the goals you would like to achieve in your future reading development.*

# APPENDIX A:
## Phonics Review

........................................................................................

Understanding basic phonics, the sounds of letters, can help you to pronounce and spell words better. The following is a brief description of the three major aspects of phonics: vowels, consonants, and syllabication.

**Vowels** are present in all words, or syllables. They are select letters of the alphabet (*a, e, i, o, u,* and sometimes *y* and *w*). To understand vowels and their sounds, you must be able to identify their (1) type (silent, long, short, and irregular) and (2) position (beginning, middle, or end of the word).

Note: *y* and *w* may function as vowels when they appear at the end or in the middle of a word or syllable (*pyrex, duty, cow, own*). As vowels, *y* and *w* are used like any other vowel and follow the same rules.

**Silent vowels** make no sound. When there are two vowels in a word or syllable, usually the first vowel is sounded, and the second is often silent. This includes the *e* in the end position (*age, eat*).

### EXERCISE A1 SILENT VOWELS
*Cross out the silent vowel in each word.*

| | | | | |
|---|---|---|---|---|
| 1. peacock | 2. plane | 3. shame | 4. cite | 5. heal |
| 6. main | 7. mode | 8. train | 9. theme | 10. mute |

**Long vowels** appear in the middle or at the end of a word or syllable and make the sound of their names (*cāpe, bēam, hī, bōat, cūte*). They are noted in dictionaries by a bar above the vowel. Apply the following rules to identify long vowels:

**Rule 1.** When two vowels are together, the first vowel sound is usually long and the second is silent (*paid, meat*).

**Rule 2.** When two vowels are in a word or syllable and the second is an *e* in the end position, often the first vowel is long and the *e* is silent (*hope, scrape*).

**Rule 3.** When only one vowel is in a word or syllable and it is located in the end position, the vowel often has a long sound (*pi, cra*).

### EXERCISE A2 LONG VOWELS

*Place a bar over the long vowel in each word below, and write the number of the rule used.*

| | | | |
|---|---|---|---|
| ____ 1. she | ____ 2. braid | ____ 3. brute | ____ 4. use |
| ____ 5. cheap | ____ 6. tie | ____ 7. size | ____ 8. hi |
| ____ 9. pole | ____ 10. shade | ____ 11. by | ____ 12. steam |

**Short vowels** are identified in words or syllables having only one vowel. Short vowels are often shown in dictionaries either unlabeled or labeled with a ˘ sign above the vowel (*ĭt, ăsh, ĕgg, ŏf, cŭp*). Apply the following rules to identify short vowels:

**Rule 1.** When in the beginning position of a word or syllable, a single vowel is usually short (*ŭp, ĭn-ĕpt*).
**Rule 2.** When in the middle position of a word or syllable, a single vowel is usually short (*măt, căm-pŭs*).

### EXERCISE A3 SHORT VOWELS

*Place a ˘ over the short vowel in each word, and write the number of the rule used.*

| | | | |
|---|---|---|---|
| ____ 1. alps | ____ 2. brag | ____ 3. drip | ____ 4. blitz |
| ____ 5. chimp | ____ 6. apt | ____ 7. chomp | ____ 8. munch |
| ____ 9. gulp | ____ 10. cramp | ____ 11. un | ____ 12. script |

**Irregular vowels** make sounds that are neither long nor short and follow no particular pattern (*oo* in *cool* and *book; aw* in *jaw; au* in *haul; oi* in *toil; oy* in *toy; ou* in *house; ow* in *wow; a* in *ago; ar* in *car; er* in *perk; ir* in *birth; or* in *cord; ur* in *burn*).

### EXERCISE A4 IRREGULAR VOWELS

*Circle the word from each grouping that does* not *have an irregular vowel sound.*

| | | | |
|---|---|---|---|
| 1. a. pawn | b. park | c. droop | d. cheat |
| 2. a. spool | b. mouse | c. shirt | d. rote |
| 3. a. chart | b. mete | c. soothe | d. coil |
| 4. a. blame | b. thaw | c. proof | d. rook |
| 5. a. clout | b. clamp | c. crawl | d. sought |
| 6. a. burp | b. about | c. skunk | d. parlor |
| 7. a. pray | b. cough | c. farther | d. crown |
| 8. a. brawn | b. jolly | c. sought | d. mortar |
| 9. a. brought | b. crab | c. prowl | d. sharp |
| 10. a. ago | b. purge | c. caught | d. shrink |

## A2 CONSONANTS

**Consonants** are letters of the alphabet other than vowels. Each letter has its own distinctive sound. However, when there are two or more consonants together, the combination produces a blend or a digraph.

**Blends** are two or more consonants sounded together and representing the distinctive sound of each individual consonant (*brick, crank, clown, drink, dwell, fly, play, strike, school*).

### EXERCISE A5 CONSONANT BLENDS
*Circle the consonant blend in each word below.*

| | | | | |
|---|---|---|---|---|
| 1. grapes | 2. brush | 3. drip | 4. blitz | 5. glare |
| 6. crayon | 7. trump | 8. sweep | 9. strike | 10. dry |

**Digraphs** are two or more consonants sounded together in a mix that produces its own unique sound (*when, show, thick, chit, phone, ring*).

### EXERCISE A6 CONSONANT DIGRAPHS
*Circle the consonant digraphs in each word below.*

| | | | | |
|---|---|---|---|---|
| 1. phase | 2. wheel | 3. though | 4. shirt | 5. which |
| 6. swing | 7. photo | 8. chomp | 9. munch | 10. cloth |

## A3 SYLLABICATION

**Syllabication** means dividing words into syllables. Doing this may help you recognize the word and pronounce it more easily. The long word *carpenter*, for example, becomes three short words (*car, pen, ter*). When dividing words into syllables, follow these steps:

**Step 1.** Mark the sounded vowels in the word (*em-pire, ma-gen-ta*).

**Step 2.** Be sure that each syllable consists of at least one sounded vowel (*ad-ver-tise-ment, im-prove-ment*).

**Step 3.** Do not divide between blends and digraphs (*starch-ing, stretch-a-ble*).

These are the rules for syllabication:

**Rule 1.** Divide the word between compound words (*ship-mate, store-house*).

**Rule 2.** Divide the word between the prefix or suffix and the root word (*mis-spell, pre-view, help-ful*).

**Rule 3.** Divide the word between the two consonants when a single vowel is followed by two consonants and then another vowel (*chat-ter, wit-ness*).

**Rule 4.** Divide the word before the single consonant when a single vowel is followed by a consonant and then another vowel. This

results in a long vowel sound at the end of the first syllable
(*ho-tel, mu-sic, fi-nal*). Note: If the word does not sound familiar
using this rule, try rule 5.

**Rule 5.** Divide the word after the single consonant for a short vowel
sound (*cam-el, mod-est*).

**Rule 6.** Divide the word before the consonant if a word ends in *le*
preceded by a consonant (*a-ble, bu-gle*).

**Rule 7.** Divide the word between vowels having a separate sound
(*ne-on, ob-vi-ous*).

## EXERCISE A7 SYLLABICATION

*Group the following words under the headings of the rules used to divide them
into syllables.*

| biped | bullet | chapel | creole | disquiet | flatfoot |
| football | gamble | mantle | melon | meter | model |
| motel | nuance | truant | pilot | napkin | preview |
| produce | product | rescue | scramble | shopper | staple |
| | seaweed | peon | unlike | windfall | |

| Rule 1 | Rule 2 | Rule 3 | Rule 4 | Rule 5 | Rule 6 | Rule 7 |
|--------|--------|--------|--------|--------|--------|--------|
| ____ | ____ | ____ | ____ | ____ | ____ | ____ |
| ____ | ____ | ____ | ____ | ____ | ____ | ____ |
| ____ | ____ | ____ | ____ | ____ | ____ | ____ |
| ____ | ____ | ____ | ____ | ____ | ____ | ____ |

# APPENDIX B:
## Paragraph Practice

### EXERCISE B1 IMPLIED MAIN IDEAS
*Write the unstated main idea for each paragraph.*

1. If someone knocks on the door when a child is home alone, the child should be taught never to open the door. If there is a peephole in the door, the child may look to see who is there, but even if the visitor is a relative or another known person, the child should say nothing and should leave the door locked. If the parent has not instructed the child to unlock the door for a particular person, the door must remain closed. Parents should also leave a number for the child to call in case of an emergency. And, last, if the phone rings, a child should answer because it could be the parent calling. However, if it is not the parent calling, the child should say that the parent is not available rather than not home and should ask the caller to leave a message.

   Unstated main idea: _____

   _____

2. The average American child will witness about 200,000 acts of violence on television by the time he or she is 18 years old. This will include 40,000 murders. The message to our children is that violence is normal. It is the American way of dealing with problems, expressing anger, settling arguments, and proving oneself.

   *Nancy Brown, "Reading Relationships"*

   Unstated main idea: _____

   _____

3. Almost 20 percent of America's household income is used to pay debts, and that doesn't include house notes. Once those are figured in, most families are in hock for more than double their annual household income.

   *"America's Household Income"*

   Unstated main idea: _____

   _____

4. When Wendy walked into the noisy bar, everyone stopped talking and looked at her. Surprisingly, she never said a word. Her dress did all of the talking. The shining pink ankle-length dress twinkled from the strobe lights' touch on each of the many colorful beads. Peacock feathers draped from her waist to the floor. Strips of multicolored lace props growing out of the dress neckline completed the look.

Unstated main idea: _____

_____

5. My mother has seen all the *Dracula, Frankenstein,* and *Living Dead* movies. She knows all of the actors who ever played the role of Dracula and their co-stars as well. She also keeps up with the *Horror Films Digest* on the Internet and collects sweatshirts and anything else that has the word "Frankenstein" on it. She even bought a Frankenstein costume to give out candy to the kids on Halloween. Lately, she's been hanging posters of horror movie creatures all over the house.

Unstated main idea: _____

_____

## EXERCISE B2 IDENTIFYING IMPLIED MAIN IDEAS
*Place a check mark next to the unstated main idea for each paragraph.*

1. Even in the first days after birth, parents treat boy babies differently from girls. But converging evidence from psychology, science, and biology suggests that many gender differences are actually programmed from birth, if not from conception.

*Robert Epstein "Folk Wisdom"*

_____ a. Upbringing plays an important role in gender differences.

_____ b. Programming of gender differences begins before birth.

_____ c. Recent scientific evidence suggests that the origin of gender differences has an early beginning.

2. All over the country, and especially in larger cities, school and community gardens have been subject to attacks ranging from vegetable snatching to more vicious pranks. At a vegetable garden that Vernon Mullens helped start at a high school in San Antonio, Texas, all the tomatoes, herbs, and other plants were stolen or destroyed.

*Emily Yellin, "A Bountiful Harvest"*

_____ a. School and community gardens suffer from vandalism.

_____ b. Another stumbling block of garden organizers is vandalism.

_____ c. Tomatoes, herbs, and other plants were stolen.

3. *Wheel of Fortune* is a word game that provides challenging family fun for thirty minutes every weekday evening. Contestants compete against each other in choosing letters to complete one of several word puzzles. A second, more difficult game show is *Jeopardy*. Hosted by Alec Trebek, the game requires the three contestants to buzz in and provide the question to each answer given. In other words, the contestant's response must be in the form of a question beginning with *Who* or *What is*. A third game show which can be played by all members of the family is *Hollywood Squares*. Though sometimes a bit spicy, with Whoopi Goldberg in the center square, it is still fun to watch. Two contestants choose celebrities to answer appealing questions posed by host Tom Berjeren. Then the contestant determines whether the celebrity's answer is correct or incorrect. Winning contestants on all three shows earn prizes, trips, and money. If you are not careful playing along with these television game shows, you just might learn something.

_____ a. Television game shows provide challenging entertainment for the whole family.

_____ b. Television game shows provide 30 minutes of challenging entertainment for the family five nights per week.

_____ c. *Jeopardy, Wheel of Fortune,* and *Hollywood Squares* are three challenging yet different television game shows.

4. In giving a speech, it is always a good idea to surprise your audience. You might begin a speech on vitamins, for example, by saying, "Americans are shortening their lives with breakfast." Another way to get people's attention is to ask them a question, such as "What did you have for breakfast this morning?" Telling a story is another popular way to begin a speech because everyone enjoys a good story. It could be a true story about the topic of your speech or even a tall tale that makes a point. Last, a good quotation can also begin your speech on the right track.

*Richard Hudson, "Over the Fear of Speaking in Public"*

_____ a. You can capture your audience's attention by asking a question, telling a joke, or quoting a famous person.

_____ b. There are several time-honored ways of getting the audience's attention when giving a speech.

_____ c. Telling a tall tale is the best way to begin a speech.

5. Reading and writing problems are crucial and affect a child's self-esteem. A parent can hire a tutor, perhaps a high school or college student. This person can help a younger student build skills and confidence while also serving as a role model. One way to sneak in writing practice at home is for children to keep a diary and to write letters to grandparents or other relatives. Another way is for

children to help with grocery lists and to take telephone and other messages.

*"How to Nurture Your Child's Learning Style"*

_____ a. There are many ways a parent can assist children in learning basic skills.

_____ b. Act quickly when a child is struggling with math or other basic subjects.

_____ c. Parents must monitor the study habits of their children.

## B2  STATED MAIN IDEAS

### EXERCISE B3 STATED MAIN IDEAS

*For each paragraph below:*

*a. Write the topic in the space provided and <u>underline</u> the topic sentence.*
*b. Circle the signal words and write the type of paragraph pattern.*
*c. Put brackets around the major details.*

1. Higher-income households enjoy a greater subsidy for two reasons. First, unless the dependent is less than 12 months old, the tax credit is not refundable. Families who owe no taxes receive no child-care subsidy. Most families with incomes below $10,000 have zero tax liability, so they receive no benefit from being able to credit 30 percent instead of 20 percent of their child-care expenses. Second, the dollar amount of the tax credit increases as expenses increase. Higher-income families spend more on child-care, so they receive a larger allowance.

   *From "America's Household Income"*

   **Topic:** _____

   **Paragraph pattern:** _____

2. There are three types of digital photos, or pictures made up of electronic data. First, there are the photos made by digital cameras. These cameras look and operate much like ordinary cameras, but, instead of using film, they save pictures to a memory chip or a computer disk. Then there are the photos made by digital processing. This method of making photos is for those who are not yet ready to give up ordinary cameras. One can have a traditional roll of film processed in digitized form then sent via e-mail to a home computer or returned on a computer disk. The third type of digital photo is produced by a personal scanner. This device converts prints into digital images.

   **Topic:** _____

   **Paragraph pattern:** _____

3. Since the brain is the device that produces behavior, where we find behavioral differences we should also find neurological differences. Indeed, recent research suggests a host of differences between male and female brains. For example, although, on average, male brains are larger than female brains, the hemispheres of the brain seem to be better connected in females. This may help explain why females are more sensitive and emotional than males.

   *Robert Epstein, "Folk Wisdom"*

   **Topic:** _____

   **Paragraph pattern:** _____

4. Olive oil is a natural healer that may be used to treat ear complaints. To clear stopped-up ears, begin by putting a few drops of lukewarm olive oil in the affected ear. Next, lie for five minutes on the opposite side, then turn over so that the olive oil can flow out again. For ear-aches, first soak a cotton pad in olive oil, then add five drops of lavender oil. Place it loosely in your outer ear until the pain stops.

   **Topic:** _____

   **Paragraph pattern:** _____

5. High-income families have access to better-quality day care not only because they have more dollars to spend, but also because they receive bigger allowances from the federal government. The net effect is that too many low-income families are forced to rely on unlicensed family day care or on relatives and friends as child-care providers. A recent Carnegie study concludes that these are a lower quality, less reliable choice.

   *From "America's Household Income"*

   **Topic:** _____

   **Paragraph pattern:** _____

6. Our family enjoys getting together for special holiday dinners at least twice a year. For example, last Christmas eve we met at Grandma's house for turkey and ham. Each relative brought a side dish and dessert to help round out the meal. On Easter Sunday, we all gathered at my aunt's house. After eating a scrumptious meal, we hunted Easter eggs with the children. I believe the cooks have grown tired because the word is out that next year both dinners will be at a family-style restaurant.

   **Topic:** _____

   **Paragraph pattern:** _____

7. He gets kicked out of games; last week he was booted from a mural. A 32-foot-high painting of Dennis Rodman's face—complete with

hair that changed colors along with the whims of the flashy NBA star—was installed above a Chicago highway a few years ago. Rush-hour traffic jammed as drivers slowed to check out the rainbow-headed Bull. The Emergency Traffic Patrol began whining about accidents. It wasn't long before city officials went on the offensive, and the painting—created by men's clothier Bigsby & Kruthers—was painted over, two days after Rodman returned from a six-game suspension. "If they want to take me down, then they can," Rodman told the press. "It will save some lives, I guess." At least that's one call he can live with.

**Topic:** _____

**Paragraph pattern:** _____

8. The widely held (though politically incorrect) belief that boys are predisposed from birth to feel, learn, and perform differently from girls is strongly supported by research. For example, boys are, on average, considerably more physically aggressive than girls after age 4. They are left-handed more frequently than girls and tend to be better at math and at spinning tasks. Girls, meanwhile, may perform certain kinds of memory tasks better. They also start talking earlier than boys, and, at the playground, they're more likely to imitate boys than boys are to imitate girls. And boys tend to listen more with their right ear, while girls tend to listen with both ears equally. These findings generally hold up cross-culturally. This suggests that they are at least somewhat free of environmental influences.

*Robert Epstein, "Folk Wisdom"*

**Topic:** _____

**Paragraph pattern:** _____

9. Emmanuelle and Adrienne are two young females who have a lot in common. First, both still live with their mothers. This allows them to work for Roc-A-Fella without pay. Second, both hope that street team-ing will lead to something better. In the club, they network ferociously. They are commonly referred to as dream girls in nylon running pants. "We're strong; we're smart," says Emmanuelle. "Five years from now, there'll be someone else our age doing this, and we'll be running labels." As Jay-Z's song winds down, Adrienne and Em-manuelle keep dancing. They've already given out all their fliers, so there's nothing left but to keep on keeping on. Being on a street team may be all business, but that doesn't mean it's not about pleasure.

**Topic:** _____

**Paragraph pattern:** _____

10. Study after study confirms the dangers of overwork. It may or may not make you a dull person, but it clearly dulls your mind. For exam-

ple, recent research on firefighters by Peter Knauth, Ph.D., shows that long work shifts increase reaction time and lower alertness. And studies with emergency room physicians show that overwork increases errors and hinders judgment. Indeed, a Hollywood cameraman, coming off an 18-hour work shift, made news recently when he lost control of his car and died in a crash.

*Robert Epstein, "Folk Wisdom"*

**Topic:** _____

**Paragraph pattern:** _____


## EXERCISE B4 STATED MAIN IDEAS

*For each paragraph below:*

*a. Write the topic in the space provided and <u>underline</u> the topic sentence.*

*b. Circle the signal words and write the type of paragraph pattern.*

*c. Put brackets around the major details.*

*d. Map the key ideas of the passage.*

1. "Three basic reasons exist for halitosis, or bad breath," explains Deborah Bailey McFall, president-elect of the American Dental Hygienist's Association. The first is simple: an unclean mouth. If you don't routinely clean your teeth, gums, and tongue, you're just setting the table for an unwanted odor. The same holds true if you fail to clean your dentures or partials. Second, medical problems can upset fresh breath. For example, bad breath can be caused by a stomach disorder, a sinus infection with lots of postnasal drip, or the way your body chemistry interacts with medications. Third, your daily habits also play a role. Smoking or chewing tobacco, or drinking heavily, affects your breath.

**Topic:** _____

**Paragraph pattern:** _____

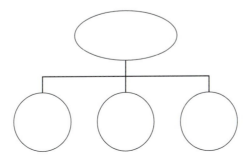

2. Each bird possesses several different kinds of feathers. The flight feather, for example, is a remarkably complex mechanism that is both strong and flexible enough to survive the harshness of changing air pressure during flight. Contour feathers make up the surface plumage of a bird and determine its outer contour. Down feathers are small, fluffy, and soft, lacking the central shafts of the other types of feathers. Ornamental feathers—such as the long, decorated tails of peacocks and pheasants—come in a great variety of shapes and sizes, some of which hardly resemble the more familiar feather shape.

**Topic:** _____

**Paragraph pattern:** _____

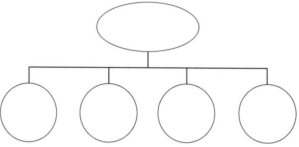

3. Although the olive tree originated in Asia, it has been cultivated for over 3,000 years in Mediterranean countries. Here much of the olive crop is used to make olive oil. In this process, olives are pitted and ground to a thick pulp. The pulp is then pressed to remove the juices. Lastly, these juices are placed in a centrifuge to separate the water from the oil.

**Topic:** _____

**Paragraph pattern:** _____

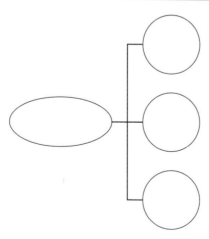

## PROGRESS CHART AND SCORE SHEET (GENERAL-INTEREST SELECTIONS)

*For each section, draw an X on the point nearest your score. Connect the points to graph your progress.*

### Comprehension Exercises

| SECTION | PERCENT | GENERAL-INTEREST SELECTIONS | | | | | | | | | |
|---------|---------|----|----|----|----|----|----|----|----|----|----|
| | | *01* | *02* | *04* | *05* | *07* | *08* | *10* | *11* | *13* | *14* |
| *Skimming* | 25 | • | • | • | • | • | • | • | • | • | • |
| *for* | 20 | • | • | • | • | • | • | • | • | • | • |
| *Facts* | 15 | • | • | • | • | • | • | • | • | • | • |
| | 10 | • | • | • | • | • | • | • | • | • | • |
| | 5 | • | • | • | • | • | • | • | • | • | • |
| | 0 | • | • | • | • | • | • | • | • | • | • |
| *Relating* | 25 | • | • | • | • | • | • | • | • | • | • |
| *the* | 20 | • | • | • | • | • | • | • | • | • | • |
| *Facts* | 15 | • | • | • | • | • | • | • | • | • | • |
| | 10 | • | • | • | • | • | • | • | • | • | • |
| | 5 | • | • | • | • | • | • | • | • | • | • |
| | 0 | • | • | • | • | • | • | • | • | • | • |
| *Connecting* | 50 | • | • | • | • | • | • | • | • | • | • |
| *with the* | 45 | • | • | • | • | • | • | • | • | • | • |
| *Author* | 40 | • | • | • | • | • | • | • | • | • | • |
| | 35 | • | • | • | • | • | • | • | • | • | • |
| | 30 | • | • | • | • | • | • | • | • | • | • |
| | 25 | • | • | • | • | • | • | • | • | • | • |
| | 20 | • | • | • | • | • | • | • | • | • | • |
| | 15 | • | • | • | • | • | • | • | • | • | • |
| | 10 | • | • | • | • | • | • | • | • | • | • |
| | 5 | • | • | • | • | • | • | • | • | • | • |
| | 0 | • | • | • | • | • | • | • | • | • | • |
| *Total* | 100 | • | • | • | • | • | • | • | • | • | • |
| | 90 | • | • | • | • | • | • | • | • | • | • |
| | 80 | • | • | • | • | • | • | • | • | • | • |
| | 70 | • | • | • | • | • | • | • | • | • | • |
| | 60 | • | • | • | • | • | • | • | • | • | • |
| | 50 | • | • | • | • | • | • | • | • | • | • |
| | 40 | • | • | • | • | • | • | • | • | • | • |
| | 30 | • | • | • | • | • | • | • | • | • | • |
| | 20 | • | • | • | • | • | • | • | • | • | • |
| | 10 | • | • | • | • | • | • | • | • | • | • |
| | 0 | • | • | • | • | • | • | • | • | • | • |

## PROGRESS CHART AND SCORE SHEET (TEXTBOOK SELECTIONS)

*For each selection, draw an X on the point nearest your score. Connect the points to graph your progress.*

### *Review Questions

| PERCENTAGE CORRECT | SELECTIONS | | | | |
|---|---|---|---|---|---|
| | *03* | *06* | *09* | *12* | *15* |
| 100 | • | • | • | • | • |
| 90 | • | • | • | • | • |
| 80 | • | • | • | • | • |
| 70 | • | • | • | • | • |
| 60 | • | • | • | • | • |
| 50 | • | • | • | • | • |
| 40 | • | • | • | • | • |
| 30 | • | • | • | • | • |
| 20 | • | • | • | • | • |
| 10 | • | • | • | • | • |

*Information-processing exercises are not included.

## READING RATE CHART

*To find your reading rate, go to the column under the selection you read. Then find the time it took you to read the selection in the left-hand column. You will find your words per minute in the area where the two lines cross.*

| | | 1 | 2 | 3 | 4 | 5 | 6 | 7 | 8 | 9 | 10 | 11 | 12 | 13 | 14 | 15 |
|---|---|---|---|---|---|---|---|---|---|---|---|---|---|---|---|---|
| **READING TIME** | | | | | | | | *WORD COUNT* | | | | | | | | |
| Min. | Sec. | 260 | 260 | 550 | 530 | 670 | 1360 | 740 | 790 | 1200 | 1070 | 760 | 980 | 960 | 1050 | 1170 |
| 1 | 00 | 260 | 260 | 550 | 530 | 670 | 1360 | 740 | 790 | 1200 | 1070 | 760 | 980 | 960 | 1050 | 1170 |
| 1 | 30 | 173 | 173 | 367 | 353 | 447 | 907 | 493 | 527 | 800 | 713 | 507 | 653 | 640 | 700 | 780 |
| 2 | 00 | 130 | 130 | 275 | 265 | 335 | 680 | 370 | 395 | 600 | 535 | 380 | 490 | 480 | 525 | 585 |
| 2 | 30 | 104 | 104 | 220 | 212 | 268 | 544 | 296 | 316 | 480 | 428 | 304 | 392 | 384 | 420 | 468 |
| 3 | 00 | | | 183 | 177 | 223 | 453 | 247 | 263 | 400 | 357 | 253 | 327 | 320 | 350 | 390 |
| 3 | 30 | | | 157 | 151 | 191 | 389 | 211 | 226 | 343 | 306 | 217 | 280 | 274 | 300 | 334 |
| 4 | 00 | | | 138 | 133 | 168 | 340 | 185 | 198 | 300 | 268 | 190 | 245 | 240 | 263 | 293 |
| 4 | 30 | | | 122 | 118 | 149 | 302 | 164 | 176 | 267 | 238 | 169 | 218 | 213 | 233 | 260 |
| 5 | 00 | | | 110 | 106 | 134 | 272 | 148 | 158 | 240 | 214 | 152 | 196 | 192 | 210 | 234 |
| 5 | 30 | | | 100 | | 122 | 247 | 135 | 144 | 218 | 195 | 138 | 178 | 175 | 191 | 213 |
| 6 | 00 | | | | | 112 | 227 | 123 | 132 | 200 | 178 | 127 | 163 | 160 | 175 | 195 |
| 6 | 30 | | | | | 103 | 209 | 114 | 122 | 185 | 165 | 117 | 151 | 148 | 162 | 180 |
| 7 | 00 | | | | | | 194 | 106 | 113 | 171 | 153 | 109 | 140 | 137 | 150 | 167 |
| 7 | 30 | | | | | | 181 | | 105 | 160 | 143 | 101 | 131 | 128 | 140 | 156 |
| 8 | 00 | | | | | | 170 | | | 150 | 134 | | 123 | 120 | 131 | 146 |
| 8 | 30 | | | | | | 160 | | | 141 | 126 | | 115 | 113 | 124 | 138 |
| 9 | 00 | | | | | | 151 | | | 133 | 119 | | 109 | 107 | 117 | 130 |
| 9 | 30 | | | | | | 143 | | | 126 | 113 | | 103 | 101 | 111 | 123 |
| 10 | 00 | | | | | | 136 | | | 120 | 107 | | | | 105 | 117 |
| 10 | 30 | | | | | | 130 | | | 114 | 102 | | | | 100 | 111 |
| 11 | 00 | | | | | | 124 | | | 109 | | | | | | 106 |
| 11 | 30 | | | | | | 118 | | | 104 | | | | | | 102 |
| 12 | 00 | | | | | | 113 | | | 100 | | | | | | |
| 12 | 30 | | | | | | 109 | | | | | | | | | |
| 13 | 00 | | | | | | 105 | | | | | | | | | |
| 13 | 30 | | | | | | 101 | | | | | | | | | |
| 14 | 00 | | | | | | | | | | | | | | | |
| 14 | 30 | | | | | | | | | | | | | | | |
| 15 | 00 | | | | | | | | | | | | | | | |

SELECTION

## READING RATE PROGRESS CHART

*Draw an X on the point nearest your reading rate for each selection. Connect the points to graph your progress.*

### General Interest and Textbook Reading Selections

| | WPM | 01 | 02 | 03 | 04 | 05 | 06 | 07 | 08 | 09 | 10 | 11 | 12 | 13 | 14 | 15 |
|---|---|---|---|---|---|---|---|---|---|---|---|---|---|---|---|---|
| S | 500 | • | • | • | • | • | • | • | • | • | • | • | • | • | • | • |
| K | | | | | | | | | | | | | | | | |
| I | 475 | • | • | • | • | • | • | • | • | • | • | • | • | • | • | • |
| M | | | | | | | | | | | | | | | | |
| - | 450 | • | • | • | • | • | • | • | • | • | • | • | • | • | • | • |
| S | | | | | | | | | | | | | | | | |
| C | 425 | • | • | • | • | • | • | • | • | • | • | • | • | • | • | • |
| A | | | | | | | | | | | | | | | | |
| N | 400 | • | • | • | • | • | • | • | • | • | • | • | • | • | • | • |
| ======== | 375 | • | • | • | • | • | • | • | • | • | • | • | • | • | • | • |
| R | 350 | • | • | • | • | • | • | • | • | • | • | • | • | • | • | • |
| A | | | | | | | | | | | | | | | | |
| P | 325 | • | • | • | • | • | • | • | • | • | • | • | • | • | • | • |
| I | | | | | | | | | | | | | | | | |
| D | 300 | • | • | • | • | • | • | • | • | • | • | • | • | • | • | • |
| | 275 | • | • | • | • | • | • | • | • | • | • | • | • | • | • | • |
| ======== | 250 | • | • | • | • | • | • | • | • | • | • | • | • | • | • | • |
| S | 225 | • | • | • | • | • | • | • | • | • | • | • | • | • | • | • |
| T | | | | | | | | | | | | | | | | |
| U | 200 | • | • | • | • | • | • | • | • | • | • | • | • | • | • | • |
| D | | | | | | | | | | | | | | | | |
| Y | 175 | • | • | • | • | • | • | • | • | • | • | • | • | • | • | • |
| | 150 | • | • | • | • | • | • | • | • | • | • | • | • | • | • | • |
| ======== | 125 | • | • | • | • | • | • | • | • | • | • | • | • | • | • | • |
| | 100 | • | • | • | • | • | • | • | • | • | • | • | • | • | • | • |
| S | | | | | | | | | | | | | | | | |
| L | 75 | • | • | • | • | • | • | • | • | • | • | • | • | • | • | • |
| O | | | | | | | | | | | | | | | | |
| W | 50 | • | • | • | • | • | • | • | • | • | • | • | • | • | • | • |
| | 25 | • | • | • | • | • | • | • | • | • | • | • | • | • | • | • |

# CREDITS

Ackerman, Ernest. "Introduction to the World Wide Web" from *Learning to Use the World Wide Web*. Copyright © 1997 Ernest Ackerman. Reprinted by permission of the author.

Ambrose, Jeanne. "Holiday Magic." *Better Homes and Gardens,* December 1999.

"America's Household Income." *Black Enterprise,* July 1987.

"Andrew Sorkin's Business." *Newsweek*, October 1994.

Applegate, Jane. "The Toxic Customer." *Success*, December 1998.

Benokraitis, Nijole. "Lee's Styles of Loving" from *Marriage and Family*. Copyright © 1996 by Nijole Benokraitis. Reprinted by permission of the author.

Brown, Nancy. From *Reading Relationships*. New York: Houghton Mifflin Company, 1999.

Burns, Diane. "Sure You Can Ask Me a Personal Question." Reprinted by permission of the author.

Campbell, Bebe Moore. "When Words Hurt." *Essence*, March 1989. Copyright © 1989 by Bebe Moore Campbell. Reprinted by permission of Essence Communications Partners and the author.

Chira, Susan. "What Makes a Good Mother." *Family Circle*, June 2, 1998. Copyright © 1998 by Susan Chira. Reprinted by permission of the author.

Coon, Dennis. From *Introduction to Psychology: Exploration and Application*. Copyright © 1992 Dennis Coon. Reprinted by permission of Brooks/Cole, a division of Thompson Learning. Thompson Learning is a division of the Thompson Corporation. All rights reserved.

Covey, Stephen R. *The Seven Habits of Highly Effective People: Restoring the Character Ethic*. Copyright © 1989, 1997 by Stephen R. Covey. Reprinted with the permission of Simon & Schuster, Inc., and Franklin Covey Co.

Edgar, Carol. "All About Garlic." *McCall's* September 1986.

Epstein, Robert. "Folk Wisdom." *Psychology Today* Vol. 30, Issue 6, November/December 1997.

Ganeri, Anita. "Yin, Yang, and The Cosmic Egg" from *Out of the Ark: Stories From the World's Religions*. Copyright © 1997 by Anita Ganeri, reprinted by permission of Harcourt, Inc.

Geiger, Constance F. "The Payoff." *Better Homes and Gardens*, December 1999. Copyright ©1999 by Constance R. Geiger. Reprinted by permission of Meredith Corporation. All rights reserved. Reprinted by permission.

Hallowell, Edward H. "Why Worry." *Psychology Today* November/December 1997.

Harrison-Lee, D. M. B.; Larson, Matt. "Eight Terrific Tips for Managing Time." *Time*, November 11, 1998. Copyright © 1998 Time, Inc. All rights reserved. Reprinted by permission.

Hawkes, Ellen. "Mondavi Family Values." *Success*, December 1998.

Heins, Kathleen. "Composing a Cure for Arthritis." *Better Homes and Gardens*, April 1999.

Hickman, Jr., Cleveland P.; Roberts, Larry S.; and Hickman, Frances M. *From Biology of Animals*, fifth edition. Copyright © 1990 Cleveland P. Hickman, Jr., Larry S. Roberts, and Frances M. Hickman. Reproduced with permission of Times Mirror/Mosby College Publishing.

"Home for the Holidays." The Face. *Success*, December 1998.

"How to Nurture Your Child's Learning Style." *Family Circle*, 1997. Copyright © 1997 Gruner+Jahr USA Publishing Magazines. Reprinted with permission. All rights reserved.

Jasper, Margie. "Your Credit Profile Rights." *Essence*, October 1987.

Kane, Bob. "Kane's Batman," *Newsweek*, November 12, 1989. Copyright © 1989 Newsweek, Inc. All rights reserved. Reprinted by permission.

Kinnon, Joy Bennett. "Homebrew Erykah Badu." *Ebony* July 1997.

Large, Elizabeth. "The Return to Civility." *The Baltimore Sun*, October 19, 1997. Copyright © 1997 The Baltimore Sun. Reprinted by permission.

Maker, Janet; Lenier, Minnette. "Reading Rate Flexibility Chart" from *College Reading*. Copyright © 1997 by the Wadsworth Group, a division of Thompson Learning. Thompson Learning is a division of the Thompson Corporation. All rights reserved. Reprinted by permission.

Millard, Bob. "Blues Roots." *Teaching Tolerance*, Spring 1999. Reprinted by permission of the author

Moberg, David. "Brothers and Sisters." *Sierra 2*, January/February 1999.

Morrison, Toni. From *The Bluest Eye*. Copyright © 1970, 1993 by Toni Morrison. Used by permission of Alfred A. Knopf, a division of Random House, Inc.

Fulghum, Robert. From *It Was on Fire When I Lay Down on It*. Copyright © 1989 by Robert Fulghum. Used by permission of Villard Books, a division of Random House.

Netscape Logo Copyright © 2002 Netscape. The Netscape Logo is provided by and is used with permission of Netscape, http://www.netscape.com.

Morrow, Lance. "The Strange Burden of a Name." *Time*, March 8, 1993. Copyright © 1993 Time, Inc. All rights reserved. Reprinted by permission.

Nivens, Beatryce. "Six Steps to a Winning Job Interview." *Essence*, October 1987.

Nokes, Nancy. "The Real Secret to Becoming a Millionaire." *First Tennessee Bank Newsletter*, 2000. Copyright © 2000 First Tennessee National Corporation. All rights reserved. Reprinted by permission.

Overton, Sharon. "The Festival of Las Posadas." *Better Homes and Gardens* December 1999.

Pandya, Mukul. "Top Drawer Desk Cleaning." *The New York Times*, September 11, 1994. Copyright © 1994 The New York Times Co. Reprinted by permission.

"Positioning Automobiles." *Opportunity World*, April 2000.

Republished with permission of The Boston Globe, from "Once-Homeless Girl Turns Her Past Into Prize Essay," by Michelle Locke, as it appeared in *The Boston Globe*, June 19, 1989. Permission conveyed through Copyright Clearance Center, Inc.

Schrof, Joannie M. "Married . . . with Problems." *U.S. News & World Report*, January 19, 1998. Copyright © 1998 U.S. News & World Report L.P. All rights reserved. Reprinted by permission.

"Start Moving to Stop Pain." *Let's Live* September 1999.

Strauss, Bruce "The Mouse." "What It Feels Like to Get Knocked Out." *Esquire*, June 2001.

Trotter, Jennie C. "Ten Ways to Beat Stress." Reprinted by permission of the author.

Weston, Jennifer Lynn. "A Speller's Manifesto." *Newsweek*, March 4, 1998. Copyright © 1998 Newsweek, Inc. All rights reserved. Reprinted by permission.

Yahoo: Science Screen Shot: http://dir.yahoo.com/Science. Copyright © 2002 Yahoo! Inc. All rights reserved. Used by permission.

Yellin, Emily. "A Bountiful Harvest." Garden Vandalism. *Teaching Tolerance* Spring 1999.

Zimmerman, Eilene. "Shelving Prejudice." *Success*, December 1998.

# INDEX